The Iranian Diaspora

The Iranian Diaspora

Challenges, Negotiations, and Transformations

EDITED BY MOHSEN MOSTAFAVI MOBASHER

University of Texas Press Austin

Requests for permission to reproduce material from this work should be sent to:
  Permissions
  University of Texas Press
  P.O. Box 7819
  Austin, TX 78713–7819
  utpress.utexas.edu/rp-form

♾ The paper used in this book meets the minimum requirements of
ANSI/NISO Z39.48–1992 (R1997) (Permanence of Paper).

Library of Congress Cataloging-in-Publication Data
Names: Mobasher, Mohsen Mostafavi, editor.
Title: The Iranian diaspora : challenges, negotiations, and transformations / edited by
  Mohsen Mostafavi Mobasher.
Description: First edition. | Austin : University of Texas Press, 2018. | Includes
  bibliographical references and index. Identifiers: LCCN 2017048951
    ISBN 978-1-4773-1664-1 (cloth : alk. paper)
    ISBN 978-1-4773-1666-5 (lib e-book)
    ISBN 978-1-4773-1667-2 (non-lib e-book)
Subjects: LCSH: Iranian diaspora. | Iranians—Migrations. | Iranians—Foreign
  countries. | Iranians—Foreign countries— Ethnic identity. | Iranians—Foreign
  countries—Social conditions.
Classification: LCC JV8741 .I73 2018 | DDC 305.891/55—dc23
LC record available at https://lccn.loc.gov/2017048951

doi:10.7560/316641

To
Afsaneh Ilkhan
For
her love and friendship

Contents

Tables and Figures

Tables

Figures

Foreword

NESTOR RODRIGUEZ

Long-distance migration has been an historical feature of human populations, but it has been only since the late twentieth century that social scientists and other scholars have made migration studies a major enterprise. Migration research advanced rapidly in the final decades of the twentieth century as researchers raised their focus on migration from internal migration in single countries, to international migration between different countries, to migration at the global level between world regions, and as the unit of analysis advanced from individuals, to families, to communities, and finally to whole ethnic or racial populations, that is, to diasporas. While migration researchers sought to understand the social organization of migration, diaspora scholars sought to understand the experiences of the spreading of peoples across different countries and world regions.

The Iranian Diaspora contributes to diaspora studies through its presentation of Iranian migrant experiences in eight countries, that is, the United States, five countries in Europe, Australia, and the United Arab Emirates. Given that many governments and populations in the West have treated Iranian immigrants as political outcasts, this volume does not simply add another national case study to the survey of diasporic experiences; to the contrary, it addresses various aspects of the problematic and restrictive conditions Iran immigrants face abroad because of their Iranian origin and identity. The chapters demonstrate how global politics affect individuals in the Iranian diaspora.

Scholars have undertaken different research methods to examine the experiences of migration and diaspora. Some researchers have concentrated on broad patterns of human movement between world regions, while others have focused on the experiences of individual migrants. Both approaches, and additional ones, are necessary to obtain a comprehensive understanding of the significance of long-distance migration today. The chapters in this volume provide descriptions that enable the reader to understand how the political character of the global context of migration affects the social experiences of individual Iranian migrants.

The political tension that developed after the takeover of the United States Embassy in Tehran by militants in 1979 strained relations between America and Iran, but also between other Western countries and Iran. Due in large part to the strengthening of US leadership in the West during the Cold War, the US branding of Iran as an enemy country created an identity of Iranian immigrants in Western countries as social pariahs. This development demonstrated the overarching US political influence in large regions of the global political system. US foreign policy affected how Iranian immigrants were viewed and treated in the United States as well as in allied countries in the West, including Australia.

In theory, the reception and subsequent social integration of immigrants follows a course determined by the specifics of individual immigrants. For example, in the United States the outcomes of applications for legal residence or asylum are determined by the specific facts of individual immigrants, such as the immigrant's relationship to a sponsoring citizen, or the immigrant's membership in a persecuted social group in the home country. Decisions by immigration agencies of the receiving government regarding immigrant admission into the country are not supposed to be made wholesale based on broad social identities such as the nationality, race, or ethnicity of the individual immigrant. Yet, the pattern of refugees accepted into the United States during the Cold War, including during the period of US intervention in Central American conflicts in the 1980s, indicated that the United States was far more likely to accept refugees from countries of the Soviet bloc, or countries with communist governments like China, then it was to accept refugees from countries with governments supported by the United States. As a consequence, as the number of refugees accepted by the United States from communist-led countries (China, Cuba, etc.) rose, the number of admitted refugees fleeing political violence and repression in Central American countries supported by the United States remained minuscule. These larger patterns demonstrated that the US geopolitical map of countries identified as friendly or hostile greatly affected the acceptability or not of refugees. In a word, a person's national origin in the context of US foreign policy became a determinant of acceptance or denial for asylum.

For Iranian immigrants in the United States, the terrorist attacks of September 11, 2001, brought back the harsh treatment and suspicion experienced after the US embassy takeover in Tehran in 1979. Although no Iranian was involved in the attacks of September 11, Iranian immigrant men were ordered to report to federal law enforcement in the United States for questioning. Many Iranian immigrant men were held for days. The men had not committed crimes, yet they were held for questioning simply for being Iranian, that is, for being Middle Easterners and Muslims from a country considered an enemy to the United States. The US suspicion of Iranian immigrants spilled over into other countries in the West where they were also regarded with suspicion.

In addition to demonstrating the influence of US foreign policy on the treatment of Iranian immigrants in the United States and in other countries, *The Iranian Diaspora* demonstrates that immigration in the United States does not follow a linear progression of settlement and social integration for all immigrant groups. And even though the United States remains the country with the greatest numbers of immigrants among all the countries, not all immigrant groups that arrive are treated the same. Major differences exist among the experiences of the first generation, and the differences can have lasting effects for the second generation, that is, the US-born children of foreign-born residents. In the history of US immigration, privileged reception was given to immigrants from Northern and Western Europe (with the exception of Irish immigrants, who faced harsh discrimination). Asian-origin immigrants were actually barred. Chinese immigration was halted in 1882 through the Chinese Exclusion Act, and in 1917 congressional legislation barred the remaining Asian populations. The reasons for Asian exclusion were that Asians were considered to be racially and culturally inferior, and, not being white, they did not qualify for US citizenship, which was considered to be the ultimate logic of immigration (new immigration laws in 1946 and 1952 ended the white requirement for naturalization). The melting-pot image commonly used to characterize US immigration, where all immigrant groups are seen as melting into the American people, is not historically correct—it takes longer for some groups to be accepted than for others. Moreover, for some immigrant groups, including Iranian immigrants, mistrust, suspicion, and mistreatment creates a barrier to social integration into US society.

Yet, one must recognize the fact that the United States remains the most generous country for immigrants. Indeed, since 1990 the United States has twice broken its record of immigrants legally admitted per decade. The long-lasting record of 8.2 million immigrants admitted between 1900 and 1909 was finally broken with the admission of 9.8 million immigrants in 1990–1999, and that record was broken in 2000–2009 when 10.3 million immigrants were admitted to the United States. This latter figure includes

120,235 Iranians admitted as legal permanent residents (another 41,855 Iranians were accepted into the country as refugees between 2000 and 2009).

The fact that 162,090 Iranians were legally accepted into the country during 2000–2009 but faced mistrust or suspicion from some federal agencies speaks to the complexity of the US federal system and democracy. US immigration remains regulated by the Immigration and Naturalization Act of 1965, which replaced national-origin quotas with family- and employer-related preferences for admitting new immigrants. That is to say, the value of immigration equality and fairness remains the law for accepting new immigrants as a consequence of the democratic election of members of Congress who continue to support the value. Yet, federal law enforcement agencies, which are bureaucracies not directly subject to democratic election, have remained distrustful of some Iranian immigrants because of the suspicion that, given their national origin, some can become a national security problem for the United States. To some extent, scientists and engineers who were born in China and now work in the United States in sensitive and classified research have come under similar suspicion. Democracy has opened a wider door to immigration since the 1965 immigration legislation, but it has not brought equal treatment to all immigrants who arrive.

The Iranian Diaspora provides valuable insights into the Iranian immigrant experience abroad. The chapters in the volume enable the reader to determine the extent to which Iranian immigration dynamics across different countries aggregate into a unity of experience—a diaspora—the extent to which Iranian immigration in different countries has produced distinctive situations for diasporic Iranians. The multicountry methodological approach of this volume comes at an opportune time given the increasing exodus to European countries of peoples from Middle Eastern regions such as Syria, Iraq, and Afghanistan engulfed in war or other conflict. From this perspective, *The Iranian Diaspora* provides a baseline or a reference point to gauge how immigration policies change (or not) across time and in response to different Middle Eastern group arrivals, in comparison with earlier receptions given to Iranian newcomers in Europe.

An optimistic standpoint would project that lessons learned across time would lead to improvements in immigration policies in order to increase the integration of new immigrant populations for the greater stability and unity of society. But developments in both the United States and some countries in Europe indicate that optimism may not carry the day. In the United States, one presidential candidate ascended to the nomination for his conservative political party, and won election, partly because of his proposals to build "a great wall" to halt Mexicans' unauthorized immigration and to restrict, if not outright ban, Muslims' entry. Similar voices have been heard in other Western countries, and in the United Kingdom growing sentiment against new immigrants from the Middle East was one reason behind a successful referendum in 2016 to withdraw the UK from membership in the European Union. Since the US elections of 2016 and the inauguration of the new president, restrictions against Iranians and other Muslim and Middle Eastern immigrants hardened in the United States as well as in other countries that follow its lead.

Austin, Texas
November 2017

Acknowledgments

The idea behind this book emerged after several long conversations during a summer trip to Iran with a few of my best Iranian friends who had also returned from Italy, France, Sweden, and Germany for a family visit in 2014. We all had left Iran as teenage students about the same time a few months before the Iranian Revolution in 1979. As we shared our personal stories of living outside Iran for almost four decades, it became apparent that, despite the relative similarities in our socioeconomic status, age, reason for emigration, cultural background, and premigration social and cultural experiences as teenagers in prerevolutionary Iran, each of us had a very unique migration experience; each was affected by a distinctive set of immigration policies, economic forces, ethnic and racial structures, and political features in our new host countries. Yet regardless of unique social, cultural, economic, and political host conditions, we had confronted the same integration challenges and had experienced striking similar social and cultural problems such as long-term separation from our families, marginality, loss of ethnic and national pride, lack of a unified ethnic community, concealing religious identity, discrimination, social isolation, and family fragmentation. It was in the spirit of comparative understanding, and in the hopes of gaining greater insight into the similarities and differences between Iranian immigrants and their communities in diaspora, that I decided to embark upon this project. After several months of networking and searching for potential contributors, I was fortunate to identify and bring together a group of scholars on Iranian diaspora to contribute to this edited volume. I am grateful to all of them, particularly to Nestor Rodriguez who wrote the forward to the volume, for their collaboration, support, hard work, and enduring my suggestions and demands for revising their chapters several times.

My deepest gratitude is extended to Caroline Brettell at Southern Methodist University as well as the other anonymous reviewer who diligently read the entire manuscript and provided the most constructive comments and suggestions. Without their valuable feedback this project would not have taken its current shape and structure. I also thank members of the Faculty Leave Award committee at the University of Houston–Downtown for awarding me a paid leave for one semester toward completion of this project. I thank Greg Getz and Kristin Anderson, my other colleagues at the University of Houston–Downtown, for reading and commenting on the introduction and the conclusion to the volume.

I am grateful to several individuals at the University of Texas Press for their support. I am particularly grateful to Jim Burr, who supported the project and saw its significance. He has been a wonderful editor to work with. I would also like to thank Sarah McGavick and Amanda Frost for coordinating and scheduling the copyediting as well as the other crucial steps involved in materializing the manuscript. And thanks should also go to Nancy Bryan for marketing the book and Jon Howard for copyediting.

Finally, my biggest thanks are due to my family members, particularly my sister, Maryam Mobasher, for their continuous support and encouragement.

The Iranian Diaspora

Introduction

MOHSEN MOSTAFAVI MOBASHER

For a long time the conventional concepts of diaspora were embodied by the overall Jewish and Armenian historical experiences of displacement. Diaspora has also been associated with physically dispersed groups of people sharing a common religious and cultural heritage, whose members desire to return to their homeland and maintain cultural distinctiveness and ethnic boundaries in their country of settlement. Although its etymology is linked to dispersal, the older definitions of diaspora are based on the Jewish and the Armenian dispersal from a "center" to at least two "peripheries" (Safran 1991; Cohen 1997). It is in these peripheries that a collective memory about an idealized homeland and the illusion of return to it is constructed and maintained. The myth of return to one's homeland in turn nourishes a sense of being a community in exile among diaspora members. For Safran (1991), in addition to dispersion and myth of return to the idealized homeland, diasporic groups believe that they will never be fully accepted by their new host societies and will remain "partly alienated and insulated" from them. This troubled relationship with the wider society is rooted in their belief that they should remain committed to the maintenance or restoration of the homeland and maintain a strong ongoing ethnocommunal tie with the homeland. Cohen (1997) agrees with Safran's criteria but adds that diasporic communities also maintain a sense of empathy and solidarity with co-ethnic members in other host countries. Cohen also identifies different kinds of diasporas, including victim, labor, imperial, and trade diasporas, and believes that diasporic groups may develop a distinctive and creative life with tolerance for pluralism in host countries.

Since the 1990s, as with so many concepts parallel to the increase in transnationalism studies, this ancient concept has been contested in terms of its definition and meaning, and the number of meanings attached to it continue to proliferate across disciplines (Tsolidis 2014; Vertovec 2009; Du-foix 2003). One of the major criticisms of the classical definitions of diaspora is that it is based for the most part on the historic experience of Jews and other religious minorities. Unlike most scholars who tend to recognize Jews as the archetypal diaspora in the traditional literature for interpreting diaspora as a concept, Reis (2004) locates the Jewish experience as part of a Classical Period that is primarily associated with ancient diaspora and ancient Greece. In addition to the Classical Period, she identifies the Modern Period (slave and colonial) and the Contemporary or Late-modern Period, both of which are consequences of a postcolonial, globalized world characterized by "fragmentation and dislocation."

Another criticism of the classical notions of diaspora is that they contribute to exclusion and marginalization of immigrants, minorities, and ethnic communities by failing to take into account the current global processes, political environments, and citizenship challenges that encompass all diasporic groups. To overcome these limitations—unlike the classical definitions of diaspora that was limited to religious minorities that were dispersed throughout the world with ties to an idealized mythical homeland—Carment and Bercuson (2008) offer a much broader definition that includes ethnic migrants; first-, second-, and even third-generation immigrants; expatriates; students; guest workers; and refugees. All are members of a diaspora. For Carment and Bercuson (2008), any group who can live in two places and play a simultaneous role in two communities is considered as diaspora. They also argue that "today's diaspora" differ from the previous generation of "ethnic migrants" because late–twentieth-century telecommunications advances and cheap travel allow for "a new type of hyper-connectivity between diasporas and their home communities." James Clifford (1994) makes the same argument and believes that the diaspora concept is widely appropriated for a variety of social, political, and technological forces such as decolonization, increased migration, and advances in global communication; multilocal attachment, belonging, residence, and border-crossing is prompted. In a later work Clifford goes one step further and adds: "In the late twentieth century, all or most communities have diasporic dimensions (moments, tactics, practices, articulations). Some are more diasporic than others" (1994: 310).

The newer usage of diaspora, such as the one provided by Carment and Bercuson (2008) and Clifford (1994), overlaps with transnationalism. In their views, living in diaspora and home community simultaneously through modern telecommunications systems turns diasporic communities concurrently into transnational communities, blurs the distinctions between various kinds of cross-border movements, emphasizes transnational mobility as opposed to return to homeland, and focuses on cultural innovation and co-existence of integration into the host society and cultural distinctiveness. Whereas "diaspora" has often been used to describe religious or national groups living outside their homelands, "transnationalism" is often used to denote persistent ties and networks formed by migrants, groups, and organizations across countries (Faist 2010). Scholars of transnational perspective contend that immigrants and their descendants remain strongly influenced by their continuing ties to their home societies. Rooted in a global perspective, the central element of this conceptual framework is that immigrants establish and maintain cultural, social, economic, and political ties in both the home and host societies. Through these ties, immigrants link their country of origin and their country of settlement (Basch, Schiller, and Blanc-Szanton 1992). Given their simultaneous participation in multiple transnational settings or social fields, transmigrants continuously convert the economic and social status gained in one society into political, social, and economic gains in another. Moreover, they can contribute both positively and negatively to global political and economic transformations, fortify or impede global religious movements, fuel social movements, and influence the internal functions of states (Levitt and Schiller 2004).

The ongoing transnational communications and ties between home and host countries described by scholars of transnational perspective suggest that dispersal of groups to other countries indicates neither a decisive break with the homeland nor a permanent uprooting of the diasporic groups. As such, to have a deeper understanding about modern diasporic communities, it is crucial to understand the powerful global forces that are shaping transnational social, economic, cultural, and political practices of diasporic groups and the formal and informal means through which diasporic groups create and maintain home-host ties. As indicated by Brettell (2006), transnationalism and diaspora are two key concepts in global theories of migration that are conceptually connected and used interchangeably. The connection as described by Levitt (2001b) is such that transnational communities function as building blocks of diasporas. Diasporas, according to Levitt (2001b), are formed out of transnational communities, and transnational communities are formed by individuals who have been displaced voluntarily or involuntarily by a variety of economic, political, and social forces and are scattered throughout the world.

Overall, the newer notions of diaspora are more inclusive than the classical definitions and view diaspora as dispersal of any group for any reason, including trade, entrepreneurial, and employment opportunities whose members maintain continuous cross-border linkages to both home and host countries. These notions also suggest that diaspora and transnationality are two sides of the same coin and capture different dimensions of the same global processes. Whereas transnationalism captures the dynamic process through which immigrants draw upon their multiple identities grounded in their home and host societies to create and maintain multiple linkages between different societies, diaspora is "a category or practice, project, claim and stance" (Brubaker 2005: 13) that reflects the ambivalent social space and expresses subjective imaginaries of home culture (whether real or mythical) that are rooted in a potential conflict between migrating or staying in the homeland or, as Clifford suggests, "between roots and routes" (1997: 251).

Regardless of its broad meaning, conditions, causes, trajectories, and experiences, diaspora is a social form involving a "triadic relationship" between (1) a collectively self-identified ethnic group that is globally scattered, (2) the host states and territories where such groups are settled, and (3) the home states and territorial contexts from where their ancestors originate (Vertovec 2009). Moreover, all diaspora—whether contemporary or classical—have been voluntary or imposed; maintained their ethnic identities as a basis for ethnic solidarity; established intricate ethnic and national organizations for support in their host countries; been involved in simultaneous economic activities in their host countries and cultural and political exchanges with their homeland and other diasporic countries of their national origin; and established ethnonational diasporic organization to combat blatant hostility and discrimination in their host countries (Sheffer 2003).

The experience of Iranian immigrants is a compelling story that reveals the strong triadic connections between a globally dispersed population, the home country, and the receiving host nation(s). More specifically, the Iranian experience shows the impact of global political forces and diplomatic tensions between home and host societies as well as the historical changes and structural transformation in both on integration, ethnic identity formation, and cultural (re)construction of the diasporic groups and the ways they respond to host discrimination and prejudice. The case of Iranian immigrants stands out in this regard and deserves scholarly attention for two reasons. First, the Iranian diaspora was a consequence of the indelible traumatic Iranian Revolution of 1978–1979 and a total postrevolutionary cultural transformation that forced thousands of professionals, industrialists, students, political activists, journalists, artists, members of religious minorities, and disenchanted and alienated intellectuals to live in exile indeterminately. Second, Iranian's ethnic identity (re)formation in diaspora, and the level of integration into their new host societies, have been deeply shaped by a combination of the Iranian Revolution and the ensuing political tensions between Iran and major Western powers as well as the persistent prejudice, discrimination, and media stereotypes, particularly in Europe and North America, of Muslims and Iranians as religious zealots and terrorists.

As Portes and Borocz (1989) remind us, political conditions under which an immigrant population leaves its country of origin and individual class of origin impact integration of immigrants. In addition to political conditions in home society, Portes and Borocz (1989) add, the context of reception—negative, neutral, or favorable—affects attitudes of immigrants toward the host society and their own patterns of settlement, adaptation, and integration. By "reception," Portes and Borocz (1989) mean the attitude of the host government, employers, the surrounding native population, and the characteristics of the preexisting ethnic community.

Since the 1978 Islamic Revolution and the subsequent American hostage crisis in Iran in 1979, Iranian immigrants in the West have been continually stigmatized, marginalized, demonized, and politicized due to global Iranophobia, Islamophobia, and Iran's framing as a pariah state, as part of an "axis of evil," and as a "terrorist state" by the United States and its allies. By "politicization" I mean a worldwide construction of a political discourse and narrative that categorically applies certain harmful and destructive political and religious images and behaviors to members of a diasporic group based on the political actions of its home state. Framing Iran as a state sponsor of terrorism, and bitter political relations between Iran and the West since 1979, not only provided a negative official and hostile pubic context of reception that demarcated Iranian immigrants' limit to inclusion and integration but also discredited and distorted their social identity, subjected them to various subtle and overt forms of prejudice, discrimination, and social injustice, and pushed them to the margins in their new host societies.

In writing these chapters and putting this volume together, our aims were: (1) to understand and describe how Iranians in diaspora (re)define and maintain their ethnonational identity and (re)construct and preserve Iranian culture; and (2) to explore the integration challenges they experience in such a negative context of reception. Hence, the subtitle of our book is *Challenges, Negotiations, and Transformations.* In order to answer these two issues, however, it is crucial to address three much larger interrelated questions regarding the triadic relationship between Iranian diaspora, Iran, and receiving societies where Iranians have settled. First and foremost: What is the current context of reception in the host countries, particularly in Europe and North America, where Iranians in this study have settled? Second: What is the status of the Iranian government in the global community, and how have the political and diplomatic relationships between Iran and Western powers since the Iranian Revolution impacted Iranians and their ethnic identity and culture in diaspora? And third: What is the nature of the relationship between Iranian immigrants and Iran, particularly the government, and how has this relationship shaped ethnic identity and the construction and transformation of Iranian culture in diaspora? The following three sections provide brief answers to each of these questions.

The Changing Face of the West, the Emergence of Islamophobia, and New Challenges for Muslim Immigrants

As indicated by many migration scholars, inflow of millions of immigrants, refugees, and political asylum seekers since the middle of the twentieth century has transformed and created new remarkable challenges for Western Europe and North America. These newcomers are predominantly from non-Western countries whose culture, language, religion, and racial background are significantly different from the native-born residents in these countries. The rise of ethnic, religious, racial, and cultural diversity and the shifting demographics in Europe and North America has not only created new anxieties and forms of resistance among the natives but also raised new questions and concerns about inclusion, citizenship, belonging, and the integration of immigrants and their children for host governments (Alba and Foner 2015; Reed-Danahay and Brettell 2008).

To cope with these anxieties and challenges, almost all the advanced industrial countries are developing relatively similar measures for controlling and managing immigration—especially unauthorized immigration and refugee flows—and for the integration of immigrants. Despite these efforts, industrialized countries are unable to fully control and regulate immigration flows (Hollifield et al. 2014). Hollifield and his colleagues believe that the divergence or gap between immigration policy outputs and outcomes is caused by a structural demand for foreign workers, policymaking gridlock, and amnesties and human rights conventions for migrants and refugees in advanced industrialized nations (Hollifield et al. 2014). In addition to managing and controlling immigration, another major challenge confronting Western Europe and the United States, Canada, and Australia is the integration of immigrants, particularly Muslims.

Despite the extension of rights to minorities and foreigners, the rise of multiculturalism, and the development of a rights-based politics in the advanced industrial democracies since World War II, some states have attempted to control their borders at the expense of denying the civil and human rights of noncitizens. In addition to more legal restrictions and provision of fewer rights to legal and illegal immigrants, exclusionary nationalist and extreme nativist backlashes against immigrants and liberal politicians who support civil and political rights for ethnic minorities and immigrants have grown in these countries. Moreover, low tolerance for cultural, religious, racial, and ethnic diversity; fear of terrorism and crime; and desire for maintenance of national culture, language, and identity have generated strong incentives for states in advanced industrial countries to develop major anti-immigration policies. The aim of these policies is to limit the access of illegal immigrants to tax-supported public services, block policies and programs that would promote socioeconomic and cultural integration, and discourage permanent settlement for immigrants (Hollifield et al. 2014). This "liberal paradox," as Hollifield and colleagues (2014) call it, has led to a redefinition of the relationship between the state and individuals and has created a dilemma or paradox in liberal democracies where, regardless of their ethnic heritage and religious orientation, all members of society are ideally accorded full social, political, and civil rights (Hollifield et al. 2014).

Nowhere is this liberal paradox as apparent as in the case of Muslim-origin immigrant groups. As Kaya (2012) rightfully asserts, relations between states and minorities, particularly Muslims, have shifted from normal democratic debate and negotiation to a matter of national, social, and cultural security. Under these conditions, he continues, ethnocultural and religious relations become "securitized" and states limit the democratic processes of political participation, negotiation, and compromise to protect itself. Moreover, securitization of minorities leads to erosion of democratic space to voice minority demands, rejection of minority political mobilization, multiculturalism bashing, outbreaks of right-wing extremism, stigmatization of migration in general (and Islam in particular), and the emergence of a form of governmentality and immigration policy based on Islamophobia (Kaya 2012). Islamophobia as a form of governmentality, Kaya (2012) adds, is a manufactured political discourse that aims to make the majorities believe that Muslims and Islam pose national, societal, and cultural threats and security challenges to Europe and North America from inside and outside. This political discourse views Islamic faith as a premodern religion that is incompatible with the West and incapable of innovation and liberal thinking. Islamophobia as a form of governmentality and a cultural-ideological outlook has impacted the perception of the Western public toward Muslims and Islam and has become the mainstream in the West. Consequently, Muslims and their descendants are not only viewed as threats to political and secular norms of European countries; they are also associated with fundamentalism, radicalism, terrorism, and violence (Casari 2010; Haddad and Smith 2002; Kaya 2012).

Europe is not the only region where Islamophobia has become the mainstream and a form of governmentality. Although immigration has been a fundamental part of the founding myth, historical consciousness, nation-building, and national identity of the United States (Hollifield et al. 2014), as is the case in Europe, migration of immigrants, refugees, and political asylees from Islamic countries to the United States have created widespread public hostility as well as resistance and anxieties among ordinary people and politicians. These concerns are reflected in popular writings, opinion polls, media, and the anti-immigrant rhetoric of right-wing politicians and political parties in the United States. President Donald Trump's 2017 executive order to ban citizens of seven Muslim-majority states from entering the United States for ninety days best reflects the attitude that Muslims are a threat to national security and was an attempt to curtail immigration of Muslims to the United States.

The intense opposition to Muslims in Europe and the United States is reflected in recent public opinion polls. In a 2017 Chatham House public opinion survey of 10,000 people from ten European countries, 55 percent of respondents agreed that all further migration from mainly Muslim countries should be banned.[1] Results of another survey conducted by Zogby Analytics in 2014 revealed that a growing number of Americans held negative views of Arab Americans and Muslims and that 42 percent of Americans believed law enforcement was justified in using profiling tactics against Muslim Americans and Arab Americans. The survey also showed that only 36 percent of Americans had a favorable attitude toward Arab Americans and Muslim Americans.[2]

The Islamophobic and the "orientalist" representations of Muslims and Arabs are not new and, as indicated by Edward Said (1978), are connected to political ambitions of the imperialist societies such as France, Great Britain, and the United States who produced it. However, the rise of Islamophobia and anti-Muslim attitudes in the West is primarily related to such political events as the 1979 Iranian hostage crisis, the 1989 Salman Rushdie affair, the first World Trade Center bombing in New York City in 1993, the September 11 attacks, the murder of Theo van Gogh in 2004, the bombings in Madrid, London, and Stockholm between 2004 and 2010, and Iran's attempt to develop its own nuclear capabilities. These events led to questioning the presence of Muslim immigrants and the construction of Islamophobic discourse in the West. They also led to international diplomatic and economic pressure as well as demonization of states, including Iran, that were alleged to have orchestrated such events.

The Iranian Revolution, the Hostage Crisis, and the Rise of Iranophobia in the West

In 1953, after the overthrow of the nationalist government of Mohammad Mosaddegh and the restoration of Mohammad Reza Shah Pahlavi to power in Iran through a military coup d'état financed by the US Central Intelligence Agency and British intelligence, the United States established strong economic, political, and cultural ties with Iran. As a result of this extensive partnership, the Mohammad Reza Shah borrowed millions of dollars from the United States and launched extensive modernization projects and cultural reforms on the model of the West until the overthrow of his dynasty in 1978 (Abrahamian 1982; Farr 1999; Keddie 2006; Mackey 1996). Iran's rapid economic expansion and massive investment in industrialization and modernization projects in the 1960s and 1970s created a huge demand for skilled workers and pushed thousands of Iranians to emigrate to Western countries in an unprecedented manner for the purpose of acquiring technical skills and advanced educational training. Concurrently, Iran's substantial oil revenues and its march toward modernization, combined with the Shah's cultural reforms transformed Iran into a modern secular society that attracted thousands of European and American military technicians, advisers, teachers, and entrepreneurs to Iran and poured Western products and pop culture into Iranian society.

The 1978 Iranian Revolution marked a turning point in the diplomatic relations between Iran and the United States as well as the other Western countries. Before the Iranian Revolution and the 1979 hostage crisis, Iran and the United States had strong economic and diplomatic ties, and Iran was viewed as a close US ally in the Middle East.

Despite their initial support for the new postrevolutionary government in Iran in 1979, most Western countries radically changed their perception of the Iranian government after militant, pro–Ayatollah Khomeini students seized the United States Embassy in Tehran and took fifty-two Americans hostage for 444 days. The hostage crisis destroyed the positive prerevolutionary image of Iran in the West and created an unprecedented xenophobic, anti-Iranian, and anti-Islamic reaction with new images of Iranians as barbaric, uncivilized, and terrorists. As indicated by Gary Sick (2001)—the principal White House aide for Iran during the Iranian Revolution and the hostage crisis—the invasion of the American embassy in Tehran marked Iran as a dangerous, unpredictable, and unreliable state in the international community. Moreover, as Edward Said notes, during the hostage crisis American media portrayed Iranians as "militant, dangerous, and anti-American" (Said 1997: 83). In his view, such titles as "an ideology of Martyrdom" and "Iran's Martyr Complex" in *Time* and *Newsweek* represented Iranians as "non-rational," "hungry for martyrdom," and "unwilling to compromise."

Immediately after the hostage crisis began, the US government, in addition to breaking all formal political and diplomatic ties with Iran, applied pressure on Iran and initiated severe economic and political actions against Iran and Iranian immigrants. These included the investigation of the visa status of Iranian students, expulsion of all Iranian diplomats, deportation of Iranian pilots and other military cadets, ratification of comprehensive economic sanctions, confiscation of Iranian assets, revocation of visas for Iranians who had already entered the country, and restrictions on visas for Iranians desiring to come to the United States.

Much like US-Iran diplomatic relations, the diplomatic relations between Iran and most other major Western countries was interrupted intermittently after the hostage crisis. Although not as deep-rooted and long lasting as with the United States, Iran has had turbulent and limited political and diplomatic relations with Canada, United Kingdom, Germany, the Netherlands, and France since the Iranian Revolution and the hostage crisis. Even countries such as Italy and Australia, which maintained continuous diplomatic relations with Iran after the revolution, imposed tough economic sanctions against Iran.

The horrific September 11, 2001, attacks on the United States intensified diplomatic tension between the Western countries and Iran. Immediately after 9/11, President George W. Bush labeled Iran a terrorist sponsor country and part of an "axis of evil" because of Iran's nuclear program. Consequently, led by the United States, the international community expanded the existing sanctions against Iran, limited diplomatic ties with Iran, and developed more restricted immigration policies for Iranian nationals.

The post–September 11 response had devastating impacts on Iran and Iranians' international image and increased the number of Westerners who viewed them unfavorably. Results of a poll in 2015 indicated that nearly nine in ten Americans held a negative view of Iran.[3] Across much of Western Europe, at least eight in ten respondents in most countries surveyed have a negative opinion of Iran.[4] The same survey also reveals that most countries in Latin America, Middle East, and North Africa also share the same prevailing negative opinions of Iran.

Although seventeen years have passed since 9/11, Iran still is viewed as a pariah state by the United States. Despite some diplomatic improvement between Iran and the United States during President Barack Obama's administration and a successful historic nuclear deal between Iran and six world powers known as the P5+1 (China, France, Germany, Russia, the United Kingdom, and the United States) that limited Iran's nuclear program, the Iranian government is viewed as a terrorist state and as a threat to Israel and peace in the Middle East by the Trump administration.

Between Islamophobia and Iranophobia in the West and Postrevolutionary Islamization of Iran: The Challenges for Iranians in Diaspora

The negative views of Europeans and Americans reported in the public opinion research results above suggest the inhospitable and harsh sociopolitical context under which the Iranian diaspora has been forming since the Iranian Revolution. These unfavorable images of Iran have had consequences for Iranian immigrants in diaspora. Moreover, the political tensions between Iran and the West, and the widespread negative anti-Iran views in the West, fueled fears of Iranian immigrants as persons of suspect nationalities; nurtured and justified discrimination and prejudice against Iranian immigrants; and legitimized institutionalization of some of the toughest immigration and refugee policies against Iranian nationals and tourists who desired to see their family members residing the West.

By imposing ongoing various sanctions on the Iranian government, Western countries unintentionally have been squeezing and penalizing Iranian immigrants by denying them the same legal, economic, and educational opportunities enjoyed by other dual nationals. For example, immediately after 9/11, the US government targeted persons of suspect nationalities and ordered males between the ages of sixteen and sixty-five from twenty-five Middle Eastern countries who entered the United States by September 10, 2002, to register with the Immigration and Naturalization Service, comply with the new federal alien registration program, and submit to being fingerprinted, photographed, and interrogated by federal agents or face deportation. The process was called the National Security Entry Exit Registration System. In Canada in 2010, in response to the Special Economic Measures Act of 2004, which restricted financial transactions and economic activities between Canada and Iran that were considered beneficial to the Iranian government, Toronto-Dominion Bank closed a number of accounts of Iranian Canadian customers to comply with the sanctions.[5] Similarly, because of the fear of the theft of sensitive nuclear technology that could assist the Iranian government in developing nuclear weapons, the Ministry of Education and Foreign Affairs of the Netherlands asked universities to monitor Iranian students. Other universities in the Netherlands stopped admitting Iranian applicants from Iran regardless of the degree they were seeking. After several protests, the Dutch government announced again that the Iranian students and the Dutch citizens of Iranian heritage were prohibited from studying at many Dutch universities and technical colleges that offered courses and fields of studies that provided knowledge of nuclear technology.[6]

Some Dutch universities with a large Iranian student population, including Delft University of Technology, even added additional specific information about Iranian students on their website titled "Additional Information for Iranian Students":

> The MSc program [master's degree] Aerospace Engineering contains elements that are sanctioned. You [Iranian students] will therefore have to submit an additional document to Delft University of Technology stating that you have obtained an exemption to the sanction. This exemption can be given by the Dutch Ministry of Education. If you cannot provide this document, you won't be able to get a visa to start your study programme.

The xenophobia against Iranian nationals in the West is best captured in a rejection letter from the State Secretary of Education, Culture, and Science, in response to an exemption letter for enrollment in a graduate program in a science degree program at a Dutch university that read:

> My consideration is that allowing you to take this course of study would present an unacceptable risk of contributing to Iran's proliferation-sensitive activities or to the development of nuclear weapon delivery systems in Iran.[7]

Moreover, in 2012 the Dutch Immigration Service suspended every residence permit application from Iranian nationals. Similarly, Iranian students with a student visa and a permanent residency status in Norway were denied residence permits and visas due to international sanctions against Iran, even though they studied subjects such as material engineering that did not pose any security threats to European interests and their allies.[8] These bans and legal inspections clearly demonstrate the international political context that fed bias against Iranians in diaspora because of the actions of the Iranian government.

Western states were not the only agents in framing the Iranian government as a pariah state in the global community. Supporters of the former regime of the Shah and other political opponents and disenchanted Iranians from various political and ideological backgrounds in diaspora conceived and constructed a horrific image of the Islamic government and a compelling traumatic master narrative of the Iranian Revolution and its aftermath. Mediated through the Iranian exile media, especially Iranian television networks in Southern California, Iranian dissidents played a major role in narrating the Iranian Revolution as a horrendous event and in portraying the Iranian regime as an enemy government mainly because of Islamization of the entire Iranian society and culture since the revolution and mistreatment of religious minorities and critics of the government. In their struggle against the Islamic government and postrevolutionary Islamization of Iran, some Iranian dissidents in diaspora have manufactured, revitalized, and promoted a non-Islamic Persian culture and national identity. Others vehemently attack Islam and Islamic beliefs and practices and openly denounce the Islamic faith and convert to other religions. Moreover, to cope with the stigma attached to Islam, Muslim, Iran, and Iranians, many Iranians in diaspora masked their national and religious identity, altered their Iranian names or adopted second (Western) versions of their names, and called themselves "Persians."

Construction and promotion of the non-Islamic Persian ethno-national identity by opponents of the Islamic Republic of Iran and critics of Islam have marginalized practicing Iranian Muslims and pushed them to the periphery of the Iranian communities in diaspora. Furthermore, it has intensified the political and ideological conflict and debates over national identity among various Iranian interest groups and created a major setback in the formation of solidarity among Iranians in exile. These political conflicts and ideological rivalries between various factions have divided the Iranian diaspora and fostered intra-ethnic hostility and wariness, particularly between opponents and supporters of the government and between secular and practicing Muslim Iranians. This intra-ethnic division was manifested when there were international talks about lifting some of the sanctions against Iran during Barack Obama's administration and after Donald Trump's presidential victory in November 2016. Whereas some opponents of the Iranian regime asked Obama and Trump to impose more sanctions and endorsed a regime change in Iran, other Iranians espoused lifting of the sanctions and advocated normalized relations with Iran and the Iranian government.

In summary, the interplay of politics, media, and the revitalization of the ancient pre-Islamic Persian ethnic/national identity, as well as the link between the political forces in Iran and the West and the deliberate construction of an anti-Islamic and antiregime narrative both in the West and Iranian media in exile in reaction to domestic and foreign policies of the Iranian government, point to the complexity of diasporic experience of Iranians in general, their integration, and their challenges in ethnic identity (re)formation and cultural (re)construction in particular. This complexity is both manifested and resolved in different forms by Iranian immigrants in different countries. Similarly, the coping mechanisms and the scope of the resolution are shaped by an interplay between the sociopolitical context in the host country as well as the demographic makeup and ethnic community resources where Iranians have settled.

The Need for a Comparative Book on Iranian Diaspora

This pioneering edited volume is the first book that presents a collection of original essays about the multifaceted and complex experience of Iranian diaspora that was mentioned above. It examines Iranians in eight different countries with a sizable Iranian population, with specific emphasis on the impact of sociopolitical forces in home and host societies on their integration challenges, identity (re)negotiation, and cultural transformation. With the exception of the United Arab Emirates, the eight essays in this collection deal with the diasporic experiences of Iranians in Western countries, including the United States, Germany, France, Great Britain, Italy, Australia, and the Netherlands. In choosing these countries I am keenly aware of the limitation of the geographic regions in this book. There is no doubt that there are many other countries in Asia, Latin America, Africa, and the Middle East with large Iranian populations. Therefore this project does not claim to be a comprehensive survey of all Iranian communities in diaspora. Given the breadth of the topic, no single study can claim to be exhaustive. This edited volume, too, is limited to countries with a sizable Iranian population where ample research was conducted.

The countries in this book were selected for two important methodological and theoretical reasons. Methodologically, most—if not all—of these governments provide relatively accurate and reliable systematic census data on the number of Iranians immigrants, refugees, and political asylees that have settled in these countries. This information not only helps us to discern patterns and waves of Iranians' immigration to these countries but also provides basic crucial information about their demographic composition and settlement patterns. Another methodological reason for selecting these countries was the availability of more literature and academic research findings carried out by social scientists from diverse academic backgrounds about various aspects of Iranian diaspora and Iranian immigrants in these countries, as well as the enthusiasm of scholars who have worked with Iranians in these countries for collaboration with this project. As indicated in their biographies, the contributors to this volume are among the leading scholars with specialization and extensive firsthand knowledge and publications on Iranian immigrants in their respective countries.

Theoretically, these countries were selected because since the Iranian Revolution they have been the most attractive destinations for Iranians. Therefore, these countries have had the most intense experience, the longest history of migration, and consequently fairly well-established Iranian networks and institutions within their realms. Moreover, since the 1979 Iranian Revolution, almost all of these countries, particularly the United States, have had some degree of political and diplomatic tension with Iran, and they have also adopted and implemented tougher immigration and refugee policies for Iranians and imposed crippling sanctions against Iran over its nuclear activities. This relative similarity provides a common comparative ground for examining and understanding the strong triadic relationships between a diasporic group, home state, and host states where they have settled. More specifically, it reveals the ways in which historical changes and structural transformations in home and host countries that transcend the local environment shape socioeconomic status and upward mobility of immigrants, ethnic relations between immigrants and members of the host society, and the overall integration and ethnic identity of immigrants.

The second theoretical reason for selecting these countries was to go beyond the predominantly US-centered focus of Iranian immigration and diaspora studies and to propose a paradigm shift in understanding the immigration experience of Iranians from a single case study in a single country—the United States—to a comparative study in multiple countries that considers Iranians in diaspora as a whole and in a global and transnational context. The historic impact of the Iranian Revolution on dispersion of Iranians all over the world and its consequences have been the subject of numerous multidisciplinary academic studies in recent years. These studies have generated a relatively large but uneven volume of scholarly articles, books, graduate projects, conference proceedings, and encyclopedia entries within the disciplines of sociology, anthropology, psychology, and literature, as well as interdisciplinary fields such as ethnic studies, media and cultural studies, and gender studies in recent years. Much of the published scholarship on Iranian diaspora, however, falls short significantly in two regards. First, they are predominantly noncomparative and are narrowly limited to a specific aspect of Iranians' experience in either one city, one country, or a single disciplinary perspective. Second, they are predominantly US-centered.

Comparative analysis, as Nancy Foner (2005) has aptly indicated, is a valuable methodological approach in the study of the immigration experience. Comparative perspective, Foner believes, not only provides a broader view and deeper understanding of migration by asking new research questions but also offers an opportunity to critically examine the taken-for-granted theoretical assumptions of our era, city, or nation and to generate more complex explanations that could not be made on the basis of one case or a single location. A comparative analysis, she further adds, allows us to see both the specific aspects and experiences of the migration that are unique to an immigrant group in one location at one point of time and the more general aspects of migration that are associated with immigration and pertain to all immigrants. In a similar vein, Alba and Foner (2015) argue that systematic comparison of immigrants in diverse societies not only enables us to recognize where integration seems to be successful and where it is not but also helps us to understand the internal dynamics of each country and the distinctive ways that societies respond to the challenges of integration and its outcomes. Furthermore, comparing immigrant experiences in different countries, Alba and Foner (2015) argue, provides an opportunity to examine social, political, and economic structures and institutions in receiving societies and the extent to which they hinder or facilitate integration of immigrants and their children in different societies.

Organization of the Book

As indicated earlier, this edited volume is organized with a multidisciplinary and comparative perspective in mind. All the contributors have extensive research experience with Iranian immigrants, are trained and practice in numerous academic disciplines in social sciences and the humanities, and utilize different methodological approaches and theoretical perspectives in their research. The multidisciplinary nature of the book provides not only a better and more comprehensive way to address the issue of Iranian diaspora but also an opportunity for the first time for a wider discourse across disciplines with interest in Iranian diaspora.

As indicated in the title of this book, it is organized around two major interrelated themes: (1) identity negotiation and cultural (re)construction and (2) integration challenges. Although these themes overlap and it is hard to group the chapters in the book based on a single theme, each theme is addressed in a different part through the selection of chapters that mainly address that specific theme, preceded by a short introduction. The chapters in Part I examine the theme of integration and ethnic identity formation of Iranians in host nations including the United States, Great Britain, Germany, the Netherlands, and the United Arab Emirates. The chapters in Part II examine the theme of cultural construction in Australia, France, and Italy. Despite the thematic variation between the two parts, in order to provide some consistency throughout the book each chapter first provides a brief migration history and demographic profile of Iranians, followed by a literature review and then a specific topic that tackles one of the two themes in a particular country.

Once again, by focusing on and comparing the migration experiences of Iranian immigrants who have settled in North America, Europe, and Australia, this edited volume sheds some light on the shared experiences of Iranians in diaspora and illustrates the fact that despite the specific demographic characteristics and population makeup of Iranian immigrants and the unique context of reception, including the racial/ethnic structure, social and economic features, and political structure in each receiving country, all Iranians in diaspora seem to be confronted with the same integration and identity challenges that mainly stem from the sociopolitical forces in Iran as well as politicization of Iran and Iranians and the unfavorable political status of the Iranian government internationally. As indicated in the survey results presented earlier, led by the United States, all the countries in this book except the United Arab Emirates have had some degree of political and diplomatic tension with Iran, had an overwhelmingly unfavorable view of Iran and Iranians, adopted and implemented direct sanctions against Iran over its nuclear activities, and implemented various degrees of restrictive immigration and refugee policies for Iranian nationals. Therefore, given the sociopolitical push factors at home and the harsh Iranophobic and Islamophobic sociopolitical context in the West, the comparative approach in this book will raise a number of theoretical issues about the political nature of immigration that are important in migration studies in general and Iranian diaspora in particular.

Notes

1. Matthew Goodwin and Thomas Raines (2017), "What Do Europeans Think About Muslim Immigration?," www.chathamhouse.org/expert/comment/what-do -europeans-think-about-muslim-immigration#sthash.SSa5gZ8G.dpuf.

2. Sabrina Siddiqui (2014), "Americans' Attitudes Toward Muslims and Arabs Are Getting Worse, Poll Finds," *Huffington Post*, www.huffingtonpost.com/2014 /07/29/arab-muslim-poll_n_5628919.html.

3. Frank Newport and Igor Himelfarb, "Americans Least Favorable Toward Iran," www.gallup.com/poll/161159/americans-least-favorable-toward-iran.aspx.

4. "Global Views of Iran Overwhelmingly Negative: Opposition Still Widespread to Tehran Obtaining Nuclear Arms," June 11, 2013, www.pewglobal.org/2013 /06/11/global-views-of-iran-overwhelmingly-negative.

5. "TD Bank Closing Customer Accounts as Part of Iran Sanctions," *Financial Post*, July 6, 2012, business.financialpost.com/news/td-bank-closing-customer -accounts-as-part-of-iran-sanctions.

6. Pooyan Tamimi Arab (2012), "Stop Sanctions against Iranian Students in The Netherlands," www.opendemocracy.net/pooyan-tamimi-arab/stop-sanctions -against-iranian-students-in-netherlands.

7. Pooyan Tamimi Arab (2012), "Stop Sanctions against Iranian Students in The Netherlands," Open Democracy: Free Thinking of the World, www.opendemocracy .net/pooyan-tamimi-arab/stop-sanctions-against-iranian-students-in-netherlands.

8. Pooyan Tamimi Arab (2014), "Norway's Shame: Educational Discrimination against Iranian Students," Open Democracy: Free Thinking of the world, www .opendemocracy.net/can-europe-make-it/pooyan-tamimi-arab/norway's-shame -educational-discrimination-against-iranian-stud.

PART I

ETHNIC IDENTITY AND CHALLENGES OF INTEGRATION

Social scientists have argued that identity, ethnicity, and ethnic identity are dynamic, fluid, contextual, situational, and socially constructed. According to Hall (1991: 47) identities are "always in the process of formation" in a perpetual encounter with the constitutive "others." Similarly, Barth (1969, 1994) indicated that ethnicity is socially ascribed and created as part of a labeling process between oneself and others, and one's ethnic identity is as much based on the view one has of oneself as it is based on the views held by others. Likewise, as convincingly noted by Nagel (1994), ethnic identities and ethnic boundaries are influenced by external political, economic, and social forces and formed through a dialectical process between internal and external forces as well as the subjective ethnic identification and labels designated by outsiders. In other words, ethnic identity emerges in a dialectical process involving internal and external opinions and processes, as well as the individual's self-identification and ethnic designations imposed by outsiders. If ethnic identity is socially produced and constructed through a labeling process and recognition by others, then what happens to members of ethnic and religious groups whose identity is devalued or misrecognized by the "Other" and the dominant groups? How do members of discredited, devalued, and stigmatized ethnic groups such as Iranians and Muslims perceive themselves and cope with their devalued ethnic identity and minimize the injuries caused by the stigma, prejudice, and discrimination associated with it? Finally, what is the impact of the stigmatized identity on integration of devalued ethnic groups such as Iranian immigrants in their new host society?

The five chapters in Part I deal primarily with the context of reception in the United States—the largest Iranian population outside of Iran—Great Britain, the Netherlands, Germany, and the United Arab Emirates as well as the integration challenges that Iranians face in these countries because of their devalued and stigmatized Iranian ethno-national identity and Islamic religious heritage. By comparing the migration experiences of Iranian immigrants in these countries, the series of essays in Part I illustrates the integration challenges that Iranian immigrants in diaspora confront. These chapters also explore various ways that Iranians adapt to cope with their "spoiled" and "stigmatized" identity in such highly racialized societies as Germany and the Netherlands.

In chapter 1, "Adult Children of Professional and Entrepreneurial Immigrants: Second-Generation Iranians in the United States," Mehdi Bozorgmehr, one of the first Iranian social scientists who studied Iranian immigrants in the United States after the 1978–1979 revolution, and Ketcham use interviews and the more recent merged five-year dataset (2010–2014) compiled by the US Census to update the demographic and socioeconomic characteristics of second-generation Iranian Americans, comparing them with those of the first-generation foreign-born Iranians. Their primary research question is whether native-born children of Iranian immigrant professionals and entrepreneurs are as successful as their parents. According the authors, Iranian Americans are one of the most highly educated ethnic groups, partly because a large number of Iranian students who left Iran after the revolution attended American universities. Reflecting their high educational levels, many Iranians hold professional specialty occupations and are very proficient in the English language. Despite the highly unreceptive American context since the embassy hostage crisis in 1979 and the post-9/11 backlash as well as the ongoing political tensions between Iran and the United States and discrimination and prejudice against Iranians, the educational and economic success of Iranians across the first and second generations has been remarkable. The author's findings reveal a continuation of economic and educational success from the first to the second generation. Bozorgmehr and Ketcham believe this success is attributed to the resources provided by educated Iranian parents, Iranian cultural values, and the Iranian community. Educated Iranian parents in the diaspora set a high bar for their children and provide the resources to facilitate their academic success. Fathers' high earnings often give mothers more flexibility in participating in the labor force, allowing them to spend more time at home with the children. This enables them to have control and influence over their childrens' daily activities, educational progress, and goals. Mothers also reinforce family and community pressures regarding the importance of securing a position in a lucrative professional field.

Chapter 2 is titled "Host Discrimination, Bounded Mobility, and Bounded

Belonging: Iranians in Germany." The author, Sahar Sadeghi, conducts ethnographic fieldwork and in-depth, open-ended interviews to explore the experiences of first- and second-generation Iranians in Germany. Her focus is on schooling, inclusion/exclusion, discrimination and marginality, national, ethnic/racial and religious identity, belonging and social membership, matters related to work and employment opportunities, and citizenship. By and large, according to Sadeghi, Iranians in Germany navigate a national context that neither recognizes immigration as part of its national identity and history nor is welcoming and friendly toward immigrants. Consistent with Ghorashi's research on Iranians in the Netherlands (see chapter 3), Sadeghi's findings suggest that, despite Iranians' high educational attainments and skilled professional experiences and language fluency, antiforeigner prejudice limits their ability to access greater opportunity structures and professional advancement, culminating in downward mobility, underemployment, and unemployment for some first-generation Iranians in Germany. Surprisingly enough, unlike the case of second-generation Iranians discussed by Mehdi Bozorgmehr in chapter 1, second-generation Iranians who were born and raised in Germany, attended German schools, are German citizens, and have much deeper sociocultural integration are also disadvantaged because of their Iranian foreign ancestry. Therefore, Sadeghi maintains, Iranian immigrants perceive Germany as a country where belonging and identity are defined by—and rooted in—German blood and ancestry, or the "Volk," *which* produces significant racial, ethnic, cultural, and religious boundaries between Germans and foreigners and promotes a social climate of antiforeigner sentiment as well as prejudice and discrimination against non-Germans. To cope with discrimination, prejudice, feelings of perpetual foreignness, and marginality, Sadeghi concludes, Iranians either downplay and conceal their racial/ethnic as well as Muslim religious identity or adhere to the "good foreigner" trope and marry native Germans. Overall, Sadeghi's research with first- and second-generation Iranians in Germany sheds light on how the German national context and history of racialized social belonging, coupled with a highly prejudicial post-9/11 climate, promote structural and institutional social disadvantages for those with non-Germany ancestry, especially Middle Easterners or Muslims, and motivate them to conceal their ethnic, national, and religious identities.

In chapter 3, "Challenges of Integration and Belonging: Iranians in the Netherlands," Halleh Ghorashi collects narratives and conducts in-depth focus-group discussions to chart the complex, multilayered, ambiguous, and paradoxical process of integration for Iranians in Dutch society. The discrepancy between Iranians' high-level class resources, particularly their remarkable educational achievements, and marginal professional and social status in Dutch society has caused an "integration paradox" for Iranian immigrants. This paradox is rooted in a combination of the dominant negative social discourse of othering; strong negative presentation of immigrants, particularly Muslims as problem immigrants or potential enemies; and recurring exclusionary remarks in daily interactions. The integration paradox, Ghorashi points out, has generated a clash between Iranian's self-image and the images perpetuated and constructed by the host society. The outcome of this clash has been tension, fear, social detachment, marginality, uncertainty, and cynicism for Iranian immigrants in the Netherlands. This sense of exclusion, coupled with Iranians' effort for inclusion in terms of language competency, high educational achievement, employment, and social engagement, is driving many Iranian immigrants in the Netherlands to move beyond the condition of "in-betweenness" and "unsettling space" and to actively construct, reconstruct, or negotiate their identities by selectively deploying their insider and outsider position and multicultural repertoires.

In chapter 4, "Integration, Cultural Production, and Challenges of Identity Construction: Iranians in Great Britain," Spellman Poots and Gholami rely on ethnographic fieldwork to look at the diversity and complexity of Iranian lives in Britain and describe the extent of integration, cultural production, and challenges they face in constructing their secular and religious identities. Based on the experience of Iranians in Great Britain, Spellman Poots and Gholami challenge and demonstrate the limitations of conventional approaches in migration studies that suggest a linear and definitive assimilation of migrants into their new host society and argue that adaptation and assimilation of Iranians in British society is an ongoing process that intersects with maintaining a unique Iranian place and is impacted by differing degrees of willingness and assertiveness in terms of the integration or preservation of various religious, secular, national, ethnic, and gendered subjectivities. It is also impacted by perceptions, interpretation, and narratives of a complex combination of historical, political, cultural, social, and religious aspects of their ancestral homeland including the Persian language and Persian literature and poetry; Shiite tenets, practices, and politics; wider religious, ethnic, and regional differences in Iran; group affiliations; and relation to Iran's social and political past and present. During the process of combining different cultural and political histories, the subjectivities of Iranian immigrants, according to Spellman Poots and Gholami, are negotiated, redefined, constructed, and maintained, giving rise to entirely new forms of Iranianness and new modalities of living, power structures, and sociocultural relations in exile. For example, a particular deployment of secularism that marginalizes and excludes Islamic identity has shaped formation of a new form of Iranian community and has redefined and reshaped Iranian/Persian identity.

Chapter 5 (the last chapter of Part I), "Transmigration, Proximity, and Sociopolitical Disconnection: Iranians in the United Arab Emirates," by Behzad Sarmadi, is an anthropological account of the lived experiences and structural circumstances of working-class Iranians in Dubai. This is the only chapter in the book about an Iranian community in a non-Western neighboring country. What is unique about Sarmadi's contribution is his alternative analytic lens to the broader study of Iranian migration; specifically, one that foregrounds *impermanence* and *proximity* rather than *permanence* and *distance*. As he aptly remarks, scholarship on Iranian migration continues to focus on the "Global North" with analytical tropes such as exile and hybridity as well as discourses and policies that continue to view Iranians as derived from Iran. His approach, by contrast, is to focus on the transnational experiences of Iranian immigrants in other destinations and host nations such as the United Arab Emirates that are born of proximity to Iran and impermanence of residency. According to Sarmadi, proximity to Iran and impermanence in the United Arab Emirates due to "ethnocratic" polity wherein citizenship is fortified and conflated with ethnicity create an inevitable shared cultural logic and structural arrangements that prevent Iranian immigrants to be formally incorporated into the social and political structures. This is particularly the case for the working-class Iranians who are socially registered as representing a more transient segment of Dubai's foreign population because they are lower-income foreigners without family. Moreover, the close proximity of Iran and the United Arab Emirates has facilitated the presence and the visibility of the Iranian government in Dubai and has impacted both the sociopolitical life of Iranian immigrants in Dubai and the production and reproduction of Iranian culture in diaspora. The sprawling presence of the Iranian state's socioeconomic apparatus in Dubai has also created shared anxiety among returning Iranian immigrants with a lifestyle that is radically at odds with moral norms in Iran. This presence, Sarmadi notes, is something that cannot be said of other destinations where Iranian immigrants live. Finally, proximity and the impermanent nature of diasporic life for Iranian immigrants in Dubai are embodied in distinctly gendered Iranian transnational migrants who rely on a moral geography that presumes proximity to Iran. This kind of transmigrant, Sarmadi writes, originates in Iran's orbit, visits Iran regularly, and is expected to eventually return to Iran. His represents not a *centrifugal* flight from Iran in search of destinations far afield in which to permanently settle and assimilate but a *centripetal* one that effectively renders the *khaleej* (the "Gulf") as a "transnational social field." This social field enables a moral project, and this life demonstrates one's willingness to endure hardship and distance from family in order to support them financially, and eventually begin a family of one's own, and return to Iran permanently.

CHAPTER 1

Adult Children of Professional and Entrepreneurial Immigrants: Second-Generation Iranians in the United States

MEHDI BOZORGMEHR AND ERIC KETCHAM

The United States is the premier destination of the Iranian global diaspora.[1] Decades have passed since the substantial immigration of Iranians to the United States in the late 1970s, resulting in a sizable second-generation population. Indeed, this is the most important new development in the Iranian American community. In the introduction to a 1998 special issue of *Iranian Studies* on "Iranians in America," the guest editor wrote: "Research on the second generation (i.e., US-born) Iranians is sorely needed to gauge the patterns of assimilation of this population. There is no work on the educational attainment and occupational achievement of second-generation Iranians."[2] In 2018, there are still only a handful of studies on these topics, based on small and localized samples, the findings of which are not generalizable to the nation as a whole. As Iranian Americans have come of age, researchers should turn their attention to the educational attainment and occupational achievement of the second generation. Given the high levels of education, professional specialty, and entrepreneurship of Iranian immigrant parents, it would be very interesting to examine the extent of social mobility among the second-generation population. The objective of this chapter is to compare the demographic and socioeconomic characteristics of the first- and second-generation Iranian American population by using the most recent data from the US Census Bureau. Before we delve into our analysis of second-generation Iranians, we first need to discuss our sources of data, the immigration of their parents to the United States, and the state of knowledge on the second generation in the United States.

Immigration Trends of Foreign-Born Iranians to the United States

Iranian immigration is relatively more recent than that of most other major immigrant groups. Iranian immigration is usually divided into two waves:

before and after the 1978–1979 Islamic Revolution. Since the push and pull factors of migration shifted dramatically between these two periods, they ushered in different types of migrants. The first wave consisted of mainly college students and some economic migrants, whereas exiles and political refugees have made up the bulk of the second wave.[3] Only 130 Iranians are known to have immigrated to the United States from the mid-nineteenth century to the beginning of the twentieth century. Indeed, Immigration and Naturalization Service (INS) did not report separate data for Iranian arrivals in the United States in the first quarter of the twentieth century. In the second quarter (1925–1950), fewer than 2,000 Iranians were admitted as immigrants. But in the second half of the twentieth century, immigration from Iran increased dramatically—215,000 Iranians were admitted as immigrants or permanent residents.[4] The number of Iranian immigrants more than doubled from around 25,000 during the 1975–1979 period to nearly 57,000 during the 1980–1984 period; the figure significantly increased again to around 84,000 during the 1990–1994 period. These numbers dropped considerably from 1990 until the year 2000 and have fluctuated ever since.

Mohammad Reza Shah's industrialization drive began in the 1960s and took off in the early to mid-1970s with rising oil revenues, which increased the demand for educated skilled workers in Iran. However, there were not enough universities in Iran to meet the needs of an increasingly large number of high-school graduates. For many students, overseas education became the only viable alternative for obtaining the necessary skills for the rapidly industrializing society. Although Iranian students went abroad to several countries in pursuit of higher education, their favored destination was the United States—about half of Iranian students abroad were in the United States in the mid-1970s. At its peak year in 1980, over 50,000 Iranian students were studying in American colleges and universities. At that time, one out of every six foreign students was from Iran, making it the single-largest exporter of college students to the United States.[5] They preferred the United States because English was the main foreign language taught in Iranian high schools, and because there were more universities in America than in any other English-speaking country, which increased their chances of admission. American universities also offered state-of-the-art technical education in fields such as engineering, which were in high demand in Iran.

In due course, Iranians often had their status adjusted to permanent residence after being admitted to the United States on nonimmigrant visas. Obtaining a US visa in Iran was relatively easy before the seizure of the American embassy in 1979, but it has become impossible afterward since there is no American embassy in that country. Iranians have had to go to a third country to receive a US visa. This problem is further compounded by the weak Iranian economy, highly unfavorable exchange rate between the American and the Iranian currency (one dollar hovered around 3,500 *tumans* in late 2017), and US restrictions on issuing visas to Iranians, especially after the terrorist attacks on September 11, 2001.

It is a misnomer to call all Iranians exiles or political refugees since many emigrated for educational reasons (e.g., college students) but chose to remain in the United States after the revolution. This may be construed as "self-imposed exile." The first wave of Iranian exiles, immediately after the revolution, consisted of members of the elite and the most educated segments of Iranian society. Newer waves of political refugees from Iran come from more modest backgrounds, but are still vastly different from impoverished refugees who arrive with only "the shirts on their backs," given that obtaining a US visa requires substantial resources.

Population Estimates

Like the census, the annual American Community Survey (ACS) uses "person weights" to estimate the size of a population from the collected sample. To obtain a population count of Iranian Americans, we used the single-year 2015 ACS. Using only the single-year data for population size avoids any potential confusion created by using a multiyear dataset (e.g., 2010–2014). Iranian Americans are preoccupied with their exact population size and often feel that the US Census undercounts them substantially. Nevertheless, the 2015 ACS estimates only 486,994 Iranians, of whom almost two-thirds (64.2 percent) are foreign-born and less than half (35.8 percent) are native-born (see table 1.2). The Iranian population in the United States has increased fourfold since 1980. The 1980 US Census counted about 122,000 Iranians, the 1990 census counted about 221,000, and the 2000 census counted 338,000 in the United States. While nearly 80 percent of the population was foreign-born in 1990, by the year 2000 only 68 percent was foreign-born. By 2015, this figure had decreased slightly to 64 percent, suggesting that Iranian immigration has slowed down and that some of the population growth is due to natural increase (births minus deaths).

In the ancestry data, the Iranian American population consists of those born in Iran, as well as those of Iranian ancestry born in the United States and other countries. Iranians do not have a substantial undocumented component, which would result in a major census undercount. However, it is still likely that the census undercounts Iranians, since the population estimate is based on self-reported ancestry data. The census does not count persons of Iranian origin, born in the United States or elsewhere, who report a different ancestry than Iranian as one of their two ancestry responses. This problem is exacerbated for the second generation members, who are more susceptible to assimilation than their parents and have multiple identities.

In addition to the Muslim majority, Iranian Americans include the full range of religious minorities from Iran such as Christian Armenians and Assyrians, Baha'is, Jews, and Zoroastrians. Second-generation members of these religious minorities may report their religion instead of an ancestry, which the census does not code because federal law largely prohibits the census from collecting data on religion in the United States. Religious categories such as Baha'i, Jewish, and Zoroastrian reported as ancestries will be omitted, but ethno-religious ancestries (i.e., Armenian and Assyrian) are counted by the census. If second-generation Armenians from Iran report Armenian as their first ancestry and American as their second, they will not be included among second-generation Iranian Americans. This problem is region-specific, as most Iranian Armenians reside in Los Angeles. Assyrians from Iran are also susceptible to a similar problem, but this is not significant due to their relatively small population size. Second-generation, Persian-speaking Baha'is, Jews, and Zoroastrians are intensely conscious of both their Iranian and religious minority identities and hence are more likely to report Iranian ancestry in the census and be counted.

Sources of Data

This chapter draws on national-level data from the United States Census Bureau's decennial census and the annual American Community Survey for the analysis of demographic and socioeconomic characteristics of foreign- and native-born Iranian Americans. The respondents are identified in the 2010–2014 ACS Public Use Microdata Sample (PUMS) dataset and are subsequently divided by nativity into foreign-born (first generation) and native-born (second generation). Immigration data for the foreign-born (first generation) are drawn from the Immigration and Naturalization Service and the Department of Homeland Security (DHS) Statistical Yearbooks, many of which are now available online.[6] The yearbooks provide tabular data on foreign nationals who were granted lawful permanent residence, were admitted into the United States on a temporary basis, applied for asylum or refugee status, or were naturalized during a given year. The INS category of "immigrants admitted," used later in this chapter, is a bit confusing since it includes both new arrivals and adjusters (those who were already in the United States but subsequently became permanent residents or Green Card holders). In the case of Iranians, although some had immigrant status upon arrival, most were admitted as nonimmigrants—students before the revolution and exiles that came as visitors afterward—and subsequently had their status adjusted to permanent residence. Following the 1978–1979 revolution, in the 1980s, refugee and asylee status became the most common means of obtaining permanent residence among Iranian immigrants.

The 2010–2014 ACS PUMS is used to explore various salient characteristics of the Iranian American population. While the Iranian population is sizable, the ACS uses a 1 percent sample of the US population each year, yielding a small Iranian subsample. The merged five-year dataset provides a larger Iranian subsample size for more meaningful data analysis and hence we use this source. Iranians are identified by place of birth as well as first and second reported ancestry. Individual-level data is used for variables regarding age, sex, employment, income and earnings, level of education, and occupation, among other topics. The native-born are compared to the foreign-born. While the native-born group is not identical to the second generation, it constitutes a close proxy or approximation, given that large-scale immigration from Iran dates back only to the late 1970s. In fact, nearly 90 percent of immigration from Iran has taken place since 1975, according to estimates from the 2010–2014 ACS PUMS data (see table 1.1). The mean age for the foreign-born sample is 51.4, compared to 21.2 for the native-born sample. As such, the native- or US-born population most likely corresponds closely to the second generation.

Our sample contains respondents who indicated "Iranian" in either the first or second response to the census ancestry question, as well as those who report being born in Iran. Ultimately a sizable sample of 23,096 respondents is generated, with 16,959 (73.4 percent) classified as foreign-born, and 6,137 (26.6 percent) designated as native- or US-born. From this initial sample, three subsamples are created. The first includes individuals aged twenty-five and older to assess educational attainment because a person could not normally complete a postgraduate-level education before the age of twenty-five. The second subsample consists of individuals aged twenty-five to sixty-four, the years typically spent in the labor force, to examine employment status. The third is individuals aged twenty-five to sixty-four and employed, to investigate additional employment-related topics such as self-employment, occupation, and personal income. These measures of educational and occupational attainment are disaggregated by gender for both generations since combining males and females may obscure important differences. Indeed, this level of analysis turns out to reveal the key intergenerational finding of this study.

The State of Knowledge on Second-Generation Iranians in the United States

We start this section by reviewing the seminal literature on the "new second generation" in general, based on the experiences of other ethnic groups (immigrants and their descendants) in the United States. We then turn our attention to major published scholarly chapters and books, as well as some unpublished empirical works, on second-generation Iranians. We try as much as possible to place the Iranian experience in the context of the broader literature on the second generation.

Immigration scholars define the second generation as persons born in the United States to at least one foreign-born parent and those who immigrated to the United States under the age of thirteen.[7] Although some sociologists of immigration make a distinction between these two groups by calling the latter the one-and-a-half (1.5) generation, these two subgroups are often subsumed under the second-generation category. As the children of contemporary (post-1965) immigrants to the United States have come of age (hence the moniker "the new second generation"), numerous studies have been conducted among major new second-generation groups in immigrant cities and metropolitan regions such as Southern California, South Florida, and New York.[8] However, none of these large-scale studies have included Iranians, even in Southern California, where they are most numerous.

According to segmented assimilation,[9] the most prevalent model in the subfield of second-generation studies, some children of immigrants are at risk for downward mobility and incorporation into the underclass due to their race, geographic location in inner cities, and the restructuring of the American economy.[10] On the other end of the spectrum, children of successful immigrants in white, middle-class neighborhoods are more likely to attain the prerequisite education to achieve professional and managerial/entrepreneurial occupations.[11] These two occupational categories are time-tested routes to "making it" in America, as opposed to manual labor in unskilled and semiskilled jobs.[12] In this chapter, we examine whether the children of Iranian immigrant professionals and entrepreneurs follow the successful trajectory predicted by the literature. In general, parental education is the strongest determinant of children's education, all else being the same. Indeed, among the immigrant stock population, parental education was found to be the strongest indicator of second-generation educational attainment.[13] For the most part, the majority of the second-generation population has been upwardly mobile; this is even more pronounced among groups whose immigrant parents come from low socioeconomic origins.[14] However, Iranian immigrants start with such high educational levels that it raises the bar for their children, making it challenging to surpass parental educational and occupational attainment. Preliminary analysis of the 2000 US Census data on some other highly educated immigrant groups in the United States (i.e., Taiwanese and Asian Indians) show similar challenges faced by their native-born counterparts.[15]

The scholarly consensus is that children of middle-class (entrepreneurial and professional) immigrants, such as Iranians, start their education with an advantage and are likely to move into professional careers.[16] While most immigrant parents recognize the importance of education, those with high human capital (i.e., education, occupation, and skills) like Iranians can more easily transfer those advantages to their children.[17] Additionally, direct and indirect pressures of family and community push the second generation toward higher education and the pursuit of prestigious professional occupations.[18]

Despite the burgeoning social-science literature on the second generation in the United States in general, there are only a handful of such works on second-generation Iranian Americans. Here, we review the key findings of relevant existing studies on educational and occupational trajectories, ethnicity and ethnic identity, as well as experiences of discrimination against second-generation Iranians.

Shavarini (2004) conducted a qualitative study of a religiously diverse sample of thirty undergraduate students in New England and New York. She focused on factors that influenced their educational achievement.[19] Her key findings were that parental education, employment, and income were strong predictors of childrens' academic achievement. While both fathers and mothers had high levels of education, fathers more often also held high-status jobs. Moreover, parents were very involved in their children's schooling and pressured them to do well. They socialized their children accordingly and expected them to pursue higher education. In turn, the second generation perceived education as a way to advance socioeconomically, garner respect, and even dispel the "terrorist" image associated with Iranians.

On the whole, Iranian parents tend to take an active role in their childrens' education because they perceive it as the most time-honored path to success and prestige. The second generation internalizes these values and becomes very motivated to excel in school and to choose professional occupations that will garner them respect in the Iranian community. Unlike most other immigrant groups from Latin America,[20] both Iranian fathers and mothers are often college-educated, a further contributor to their childrens' academic attainment. Moreover, the fathers usually have high earnings, enabling the mothers the flexibility to stay at home to supervise their childrens' upbringing as a family strategy. The combination of parental educational and financial resources allows them to be more involved in their childrens' lives, as well as to afford quality education and oversight.[21]

Although there is a dearth in research about the academic performance of Iranian students, the consensus is that Iranian American youths do well in school. Higgins (1997) conducted a study of the academic performance of Iranian youths in Northern California, as measured by their grade-point average, in order to assess their adjustment and success in American schools. For this study, thirty-two adolescents were interviewed, supplemented by separate interviews with at least one of their parents. Although parents had high expectations for their childrens' education, Higgins found little evidence of tension and stress between immigrant parents and their adolescent children since there was mutual agreement on expectations to achieve and excel. Parental anxiety, when it existed, was mostly caused by their children not performing up to desired academic standards in high school. Interestingly, and consistent with findings on other groups, the second-generation students who had the most difficulty academically had assimilated to American student cultural norms, often against the wishes of their parents. By contrast, those who had not become assimilated (i.e., knew their ethnic language and had co-ethnic peers), were more successful academically.[22]

In another study of education among Iranian American youths, Hoffman (1988) conducted fieldwork in a secondary school in Los Angeles with a large population of Iranian students. She states that the school fell short of acknowledging these students' national origin, especially in the aftermath of the conflict with Iran, by not recognizing Iranian national holidays or including the Persian language. What is worse, Iranians collectively were viewed negatively by the teachers, though the problem was not a lack of academic ambition or poor performance. The problem mostly centered on these students' perceived lack of respect for the rules and regulations of the school. Iranians resisted the implicit educational mission of the school (i.e., to inculcate a commitment to American culture) and steadfastly maintained their affiliation with Iran. They devised various modes of resistance to overcome what they perceived as the school's preoccupation with rules and regulations. The teachers, in turn, perceived these actions as bypassing the rules. As one student put it to other Iranians: "This is America—Speak

Persian!"[23] These problems escalated to the point that teachers became concerned that Iranian students' actions were provoking anti-Iranian racism by other students, predominantly Latino but also African American.

Bozorgmehr and Douglas (2011) present a first look at the demographic and socioeconomic characteristics of second-generation Iranians in the United States. They use data collected by the US Census in the 2005–2007 American Community Survey to assess the characteristics of the second generation and compared/contrasted them with those of the first-generation (Iran- or foreign-born) population. The results indicate a continuation of economic and educational success from the first- to the second-generation Iranians, hence the title "Success(ion)" of the article. Moreover, this achievement becomes more balanced across gender lines in the second generation.[24] Specifically, in terms of educational attainment and labor force participation, females have quickly closed the gap with their male counterparts.

Bozorgmehr, Miller, and Hanassab (2016) analyze the results of a qualitative study that examined educational goals and occupational aspirations of the second-generation Iranian. Based on interviews with a diverse sample of thirty-eight second-generation Iranian students at a nationally ranked university in California, they explore the role of parents and the Iranian ethnic community in the second generation's choices of educational majors and occupations. Not surprisingly, their findings suggest a strong proclivity toward high levels of educational and occupational attainment. Surprisingly, however, and regardless of major, the vast majority of the respondents aimed to obtain advanced degrees in professional fields in order to become doctors, dentists, and lawyers.[25]

In a reformulation of assimilation theory, Alba and Nee (2003) define the concept as the blurring of ethnic boundaries among groups.[26] Contrary to the predictions of the classic assimilation model, which argued that immigrants and their descendants must abandon their cultural heritage to move up the economic ladder, the consensus from current research on the second generation is that educational and occupational achievement need not come at the expense of ethnic identity and ethnic attachment. Successful integration often depends on ties to the family and ethnic community because they offer valuable support and resources, even in the absence of parental human capital.[27] Studies on Iranian American youth seem to indicate that many maintain their ethnic identities while making significant progress, supporting the general pattern.

However, there is very little research on ethnicity and ethnic identity of second-generation Iranians. One study suggests that about half of the Iranian 1.5 and second generations in the United States identified themselves as Iranian American, another one-third as Iranian, and only 10 percent as American.[28] Not surprisingly, identification with Iranian ethnicity was stronger in areas of high Iranian concentration (e.g., California). The study by Bozorgmehr, Miller, and Hanassab, mentioned above, also finds a strong attachment to being Iranian, regardless of religious background of the second-generation respondents (mostly Muslim and Jewish). Remarkably, only one out of thirty-eight respondents report an "American-only" ethnic identity.[29]

Komaie (2009) examines self-identification among 1.5- and second-generation Iranians in Southern California based on fifty-one in-depth interviews.[30] The findings suggest that tense US-Iran relations influence the way the members of the second generation self-identify. As was the case for Iranian exiles who arrived after the revolution,[31] the second generation is also likely to assert a Persian identity which deemphasized association with the Islamic Republic of Iran in the post-9/11 era, even if the terrorist attacks had nothing to do with Iran.

Similarly, Mobasher (2006) develops a typology of the contested and problematic ethnic identity issues faced by second-generation Iranian Americans.[32] While Mobasher is somewhat pessimistic about the identity retention of second-generation Iranians, Maghbouleh (2013), on the other hand, argues that certain activities, such as participation in summer camps organized by and for the Iranian youths, provide the context to reaffirm Iranian national identity.[33]

In general, intermarriage is the litmus test of assimilation. This is especially true in the second generation and beyond. Early studies on Iranians focused on dating preferences of the youths and spousal preferences of their immigrant parents. However, attitude is not a perfect predictor of behavior, especially when it comes to marriage. As this population has come of age, research is now needed on endogamy (in-marriage) and exogamy (inter-marriage) to ascertain the extent of intermarriage among second-generation Iranians as a whole and its ethno-religious subgroups. In general, Iranian Muslims, including the second generation, are more open to intermarriage than are ethno-religious minorities (e.g., Armenians and Jews) from Iran.[34] Thus, they are more likely to follow the traditional assimilationist path into mainstream American society. One study showed different attitudes toward intermarriage for young Muslim and Jewish Iranians in Los Angeles.[35] Reflecting a more Americanized attitude, Muslims were more open to inter-marriage than were Jews. Regardless of religion, young Iranian women, more than their male counterparts, were caught between the traditional values of their parents—who favored arranged marriages—and the liberal val-

Table 1.1. Period of Immigration and Citizenship Status (foreign-born only)

Period of Immigration	%
2005–2014	17.5
1995–2004	20.9
1985–1994	21.4
1975–1984	29.4
1965–1974	6.8
Before 1965	3.6

Citizenship Status	%
Citizen	75.8
Non-citizen	24.2

ues of American society. The conflict arose because parents did not grant their offspring total freedom in mate selection.[36] We cannot address ethnic identity or intermarriage among Iranian ethno-religious groups, however, as the census does not contain data on self-identification or religion.

Selected Characteristics of Foreign-Born Iranians

We first analyze characteristics that apply only to the foreign-born population and subsequently analyze characteristics that apply to both the first and second generations. Table 1.1 presents data on selected important characteristics of the foreign-born, specifically the period of immigration to the United States and citizenship status. According to the ACS, the largest segment (29.4 percent) of immigrants came in the period between 1975 and 1984 (which covers the Iranian Revolution). Significant numbers also came in the 1985–1994 (21.4 percent) and 1995–2004 (20.9 percent) periods, corroborating the INS-DHS data. Iranians in the United States have a high overall rate of citizenship. In general, the naturalization rate is high among educated and skilled immigrants who know the advantages of becoming a citizen. It is also high among political refugees, since repatriation is not a viable option as long as the regime that forced them into exile remains in power.[37] Both of these apply to Iranians, as reflected by their very high naturalization

Table 1.2. Population Estimates

	Foreign-born	Native-born	All Iranians
1980	N/A	N/A	121,505
1990	169,846	50,868	220,714
2000	231,138	107,128	338,266
2010	275,477	150,110	425,587
2015	312,598	174,396	486,994

Note: 1980 and 1990 from Census (census.gov/population/ancestry/data), 2000, 2010, and 2015 from ACS (American FactFinder).
N/A indicates not available in published form from the Census Bureau.

rate (75.8 percent). In terms of English proficiency, the figures were also very high, with 81.1 percent of the foreign-born reporting speaking English "Well or Very Well." This reflects that many were educated in the United States. Fluent bilingualism of an immigrant group is strongly correlated with positive educational and occupational outcomes in the second generation.[38]

Social and Economic Characteristics of the First and Second Generations

Tables 1.3 through 1.7 report data for the first and second generations, as well as for all Iranians. The latter category, "All Iranians," is included to provide useful data on Iranian Americans as a whole while also showing that aggregate data may mask important generational differences in some characteristics. As there is little data in the census on ethnic identity and ethnic attachment, we focus on settlement patterns and language as two indicators of ethnicity. Given the young average age of the second generation (21.2), we felt it was too early to assess intermarriage as an indicator of ethnicity or, conversely, of assimilation. Table 1.3 presents data on the settlement patterns (major states of residence). There is remarkable consistency insofar as nearly half (49.9 percent) of both foreign- and native-born Iranians in the United States reside in California, which outdistanced other states. New York/New Jersey/Connecticut and Washington, DC/Maryland/Virginia have the next largest concentrations of Iranian Americans. Each of these metropolitan areas contains between 7.9 and 11.7 percent of the foreign- and native-born Iranian populations. Texas also has a high concentration of Iranians (around 7 percent of both generations). Iranians in these states tend to favor major metropolitan areas such as Los Angeles, San Francisco, New York, and Houston. The consistency in residence patterns over the generations could be both a by-product of a cosmopolitan preference for major cities and of the youth of the second generation, as many may still reside with or close to their parents. This geographical concentration retards the assimilation of the second generation.

In general, immigrant professionals and entrepreneurs whose settlement patterns are concentrated tend to be fluent bilinguals (speaking their native language at home and English outside). Knowing full well the advantages of bilingualism, including its positive effects on the academic performance of children, these immigrant parents enforce the use of their ethnic language at home. Therefore, it is likely that the second generation also becomes fluent bilinguals. This is even more pronounced among Iranian exiles, given the salience of language in Persian culture, the desire to maintain a connection with the homeland, and the burden of preserving the Persian language against the widespread adoption of Arabic words in the Islamic Republic of Iran. Only 10.3 percent of the foreign-born reported speaking English at home, while the overwhelming majority (69.1 percent) reported speaking Persian at home; 13.0 percent report speaking Armenian, and 7.6 percent report speaking another language. Surprisingly, among the native-born, a very high percentage (42.6 percent) reported speaking Persian at home while 51.5 percent reported speaking English at home; 5.8 percent reported speaking another language at home. It is noteworthy that 11.6 percent of the second generation was not counted in the data on language use because they were less than five years of age. The prevalence of languages other than English and Persian is partially attributed to the presence of other Iranian linguistic minority groups, such as Armenian, Assyrian, Turkish, and Kurdish. Note that due to our method of using place of birth to identify Iranians

Table 1.3. State of Residence

	Foreign-born	Native-born	All Iranians
California	53.5	40.0	49.9
New York/New Jersey/Connecticut	8.2	11.7	9.1
Washington, DC/Maryland/Virginia	7.9	8.6	8.0
Texas	6.7	6.8	6.7
Florida	2.8	3.4	3.0
All Other States	20.9	29.5	23.3

in the ACS, Armenians born in Iran are included in our sample. However, since using Armenian ancestry would include many non-Iranian Armenians, we cannot identify US-born Armenian Iranians in the United States, thereby skewing the proportion reporting speaking Armenian toward the foreign-born rather than the native-born.

Bozorgmehr and Moeini Meybodi (2016) supplement ACS data with in-depth interviews using a purposive sample of Iranian American families in the northeastern United States about their behavior and attitudes toward learning and preserving Persian.[39] Findings show that parents and children have positive behavior and attitudes toward the preservation of Persian. As transnational families, parents have created a "tool kit" to ensure that Persian will persist at least through the second generation. Maintaining transnational ties, attending weekly cultural and religious events, providing Persian instruction, and controlling childrens' language use at home are among the most important mechanisms of ethnic language maintenance. In conclusion, although ACS data show high English-language proficiency among foreign-born Iranian immigrants, they also show a relatively high usage of Persian language among this ethnic group across generations.

The gender distribution is nearly equal for the foreign- and the native-born (52.1 percent and 50.3 percent male, respectively), which partly reflects family reunification. The mean age of the total Iranian American population is 43.4 years. The second-generation population is still very young, with a mean age of 21.2 years. The foreign-born is much older, with a mean age of 51.4 years. The difference in age distribution of the two groups is pronounced. Over half of the foreign-born population is between 40 and 64 years old. In contrast, two-thirds of the native-born is under 24. Despite the youthfulness of the second generation, it is still possible to assess their educational and occupational attainment by looking specifically at adults 25 and older, who comprise just under one-third.

Educational Attainment

We analyze socioeconomic characteristics for both the foreign- and native-born, by gender, to examine intergenerational (between two generations) differences in educational achievement between males and females. We also analyze intragenerational (within one generation) gender differences when they are noticeable.

Iranian Americans are one of the most highly educated ethnic groups in the United States, partly because large numbers of college students who attended universities in the United States settled down after the revolution and

Table 1.4. Educational Attainment

	Foreign-born		Native-born		All Iranians	
	Male	Female	Male	Female	Male	Female
Less than high school	7.2	21.1	2.6	2.3	6.7	10.9
High school or equiv.	30.2	39.5	31.4	26.2	30.4	37.9
Bachelor's degree	28.1	27.3	33.5	36.0	28.7	28.3
Advanced degree	34.5	21.1	32.5	35.5	34.3	22.8

Note: Sample 25 years old and older

were later joined by elite exiles. Table 1.4 presents data on educational attainment. Given their above-average credentials, we disaggregate educational attainment data into secondary, undergraduate, and postgraduate levels.

In general, studies of first-generation immigrants have found that men have higher educational attainment than women, but this pattern tends to be reversed in the second generation.[40] A large-scale survey of the second generation in Southern California shows that females tend to achieve higher educational levels than their male counterparts.[41] Using the 2000 US Census data, another study also reports higher levels of educational attainment for female native-born Taiwanese and Asian Indians than for males.[42] As Taiwanese Americans and Asian Indian Americans are two of the most highly educated ethnic groups in the United States, they are relevant reference groups for Iranian Americans.

Among Iranian American males, around two-thirds of both generations hold a bachelor's degree or higher. Although the foreign-born males have a slightly higher level of postgraduate education, this is likely a by-product of age. For females, there is a marked difference between the two generations. While almost half (48.4 percent) of foreign-born females hold a bachelor's degree or higher, 71.5 percent of native-born females have earned college and higher degrees. The educational attainment of native-born females has surpassed that of their male counterparts and has even surpassed the educational attainment of foreign-born males despite the apparent age gap. Remarkably, Iranian gender roles have dramatically changed in the United States in one generation, particularly in terms of women's educational aspirations. Though foreign-born females have relatively low educational levels among Iranians, they are still quite high among immigrant populations in the United States over time. As expected, there is relative parity in educational attainment between genders in the second generation (table 1.4).

Occupation and Earnings

Before proceeding to occupation, we first analyze the generational effect on the labor force participation (LFP) of men and women. Foreign-born females (67.3 percent) have a much lower rate of LFP than their male counterparts (87.6 percent), despite their relatively high educational levels (see table 1.5). This pattern has been well documented among Iranian immigrants.[43] A similar pattern (high educational levels but low employment rates) is also found among other Middle Eastern groups in the United States such as Arab immigrant women, though it does not persist among US-born Arabs.[44] Although often attributed to patriarchy, the low LFP rate of foreign-born Iranian women is also a family strategy to ensure that children get proper parental attention during their schooling, especially since self-employment forces many Iranian businessmen to spend long hours at work. When Iranian husbands' incomes are sufficiently high to support their families, wives need not work full-time, despite their relatively high levels of education. Native-born Iranian women almost close the gap in labor force participation with men (78.9 percent versus 86.6 percent). However, because native-born females are still young and likely unmarried, it is not yet clear whether they will continue their labor force participation or choose to stay home to supervise their children after marriage.

Table 1.5 also presents data on the class of worker, which divides the population into "wage and salary" and "self-employed" (the data on the unemployed are not reported due to their small percentage). In 2000, Iranians ranked third, after Greeks and Koreans, in self-employment rate among the twenty largest immigrant groups in the United States. The rate for Iranians was 22 percent, compared to 26 percent for Greeks and 23 percent for Koreans.[45] All else being equal, the self-employed earn more than their wage and salaried co-ethnics, hence the significance of ethnic entrepreneurship for both intra- and intergenerational social mobility.[46]

Reflecting their high educational levels, many Iranians hold professional specialty occupations in the United States. Table 1.6 reports these detailed occupations, as well as occupational fields that have been collapsed into broad categories to simplify analysis. Comparing the foreign- and native-born, the latter is becoming more concentrated in professional occupations in the high-skill sectors of the labor force. Employment as physicians, surgeons, and lawyers increase across genders among the native-born population. When we compare males and females, we see that high educational attainment is paying off in terms of occupational outcomes, particularly among females. In addition to gains as physicians, surgeons, and lawyers, there are substantial increases among native-born females as teachers and

Table 1.5. Employment Status

	Foreign-born		Native-born		All Iranians	
	Male	Female	Male	Female	Male	Female
Employment Status						
Employed	81.4	60.9	80.5	71.9	81.3	62.5
Unemployed	6.2	6.4	6.1	7.0	6.1	6.5
Not in labor force	12.5	32.7	13.3	21.0	12.6	31.0
Class of Worker						
Wage and salary	72.3	85.3	85.0	90.2	74.0	86.2
Self-employed	27.7	14.7	15.0	9.8	26.0	13.8

Note: Employment status for sample 25 to 64 years of age, class of worker for sample 25–64 years of age and employed

Table 1.6. Occupation

	Foreign-born		Native-born	
	Male	Female	Male	Female
Physicians and surgeons	4.1	3.4	7.0	5.2
Dentists	1.5	1.9	1.4	0.4
Lawyers	1.2	1.0	3.8	5.5
Engineers	8.2	1.8	3.4	0.7
Teachers and professors	5.7	8.3	5.1	11.6
Managers, including CEOs	18.7	9.9	17.2	11.1
Sales and related	16.0	13.3	13.4	10.5
Office and administrative support	4.0	13.7	5.1	10.5
Service occupations	1.5	10.1	0.8	3.9
Healthcare (other)	3.0	12.1	2.9	10.1
Business and financial operations, including accountants and auditors	4.1	6.1	7.4	9.0
All others	32.0	18.5	32.6	21.6

Note: 25–64 and employed

Table 1.7. Earnings

	Foreign-born		Native-born		All Iranians	
	Male	Female	Male	Female	Male	Female
30,000 or less	25.1	41.6	19.6	29.7	24.4	39.6
30,001–50,000	15.0	18.8	16.7	24.5	15.3	19.8
50,001–100,000	28.4	24.8	34.0	30.3	29.2	25.7
100,001 or greater	31.4	14.8	29.8	15.5	31.2	14.9
Mean	93,200	56,100	97,900	64,500	93,900	57,500
Median	64,300	37,200	65,100	45,800	64,300	38,900

Note: Sample 25–64 years of age and employed. 2014 constant dollars.

professors, managers, and in business professions compared to foreign-born females. The typical field of choice of engineering among foreign-born Iranians subsides in salience for the native-born, reflecting a shift in orientation toward settling in the United States as opposed to repatriating to Iran.

Unlike other immigrant groups who turn to self-employment because of disadvantages in the labor market (e.g., language barrier among Koreans), self-employment in Iran, especially among former middleman minorities such as Armenians and Jews, spurs Iranian entrepreneurship. Using data from the "Survey of Iranians in Los Angeles," Der-Martirosian (2008) identifies determinants of male Iranian immigrant entrepreneurship. These are previous experience of self-employment in Iran, belonging to a religious minority group in Iran (e.g., Jewish), and utilizing economic networks in Los Angeles (i.e., for employee or customer relations and transportation to work).[47] Availability of capital, and the presence of highly skilled self-employed professionals such as doctors and dentists, can further contribute to the high self-employment rate of Iranians.

With a self-employment rate of 26.0 percent, according to the 2010–2014 ACS data, Iranians are still one of the most entrepreneurial groups in the United States. As expected, the self-employment rate is higher among the foreign-born (27.7 percent for males, 14.7 percent for females) than among the native-born (15.0 percent for males, 9.8 percent for females). However, starting a business takes time, especially the professional incorporated type that is prevalent among the native-born (e.g., doctors, dentists, and lawyers). Hence, their incidence of self-employment may be higher in the future than the data suggest at this time.

Finally, table 1.7 presents data on personal earnings. We examine earnings rather than income, since income can be generated from non-LFP sources such as interest or investments. Among the foreign-born, the differences in educational attainment between men and women are borne out in their earnings. Foreign-born males ($93,200) earn nearly double their female counterparts ($56,100). Among the native-born, this gap begins to close with females ($64,500) earning relatively more in comparison to native-born males ($97,900). It should be noted that the earnings of the native-born are already surpassing the foreign-born, despite the thirty-year age gap between the two generations.

Conclusion

Much more than a generation has passed since the substantial immigration of Iranians to the United States in the late 1970s, which has yielded a sizable second-generation population (defined by convention as persons born in the United States and those who immigrated under the age of thirteen). In this chapter, we update the demographic and socioeconomic characteristics of the second-generation Iranian Americans and compare them with those of the first generation (Iran- or foreign-born population). We use the most recent merged five-year dataset (2010–2014) compiled by the United States Census in the American Community Survey. The results further corroborate a continuation of economic and educational success from first- to second-generation Iranians. Moreover, this achievement has become much more balanced across gender lines in the second generation. Specifically, in terms of educational attainment and labor force participation, females have further narrowed the gap with their male counterparts. Because the native-born generation is still relatively young, it is premature to assess the extent of intergenerational mobility among Iranians. But given this generation's initial achievements, one can only expect an upward trajectory.

The combination of high levels of education and top white-collar occupations accounts for the generally successful economic adaptation of Iranian immigrants and their adult children. This success, however, is qualified by the prejudice and discrimination Iranians continue to face in the American context. Sociologists emphasize the effect of context of reception on the adaptation of immigrants.[48] However, the terminology context of reception is less applicable to the second generation. In the case of Iranians, the American context has been highly unreceptive. The first generation was adversely affected during the Iran hostage crisis shortly after their influx, and the second generation has had to contend with the post-9/11 backlash. In the absence of these barriers, Iranians would probably have done even better. There are very few social problems (e.g., gangs, drug-dealing) associated with Iranian American youth, yet discrimination and prejudice afflict them perhaps more so than children of other advantaged immigrant groups such as Asian Indians and Taiwanese. This is mostly provoked by the anti-American pronouncements of the Iranian regime rather than by Iranian Americans themselves. Starting with the OPEC oil embargo in 1973, followed by the Iranian Revolution that broadcast anti-American slogans such as "Death to America" over the airwaves and culminated with the Iran hostage crisis in 1979–1981 when fifty-two Americans were taken hostage for 444 days in Iran, Iranian Americans have continuously been targets of backlash.[49]

Since then, every time tension has risen between Iran and the United States (e.g., over Iran's nuclear issue), Iranian Americans have experienced tensions with the host society. They are also often adversely affected when other Middle Easterners or Muslims engage in terrorist plots against the United States. Iranians were singled out by the National Security Entry-Exit Registration System (NSEERS), commonly known as Special Registration, after September 11, 2001. This governmental initiative resulted in the arrest of several hundred Iranians in Los Angeles who were deemed in violation of their visas. In response, Iranians staged one of their largest demonstrations outside the federal building in the Westwood area of Los Angeles in 2002. After January 2002, when President George W. Bush designated the Islamic Republic of Iran as part of the "axis of evil," individuals bearing Iranian passports were denied visas and were subjected to profiling at American airports, even though Iranians had nothing to do with the terrorist attacks.[50] While these government initiatives and policies are mainly aimed at Iranian nationals and immigrants, US citizens (native-born or naturalized) are still impacted by discrimination. Ironically, many Iranian Americans do not support the regime in the Islamic Republic of Iran. It is worth noting that Iranian Americans have become more organized and have established several organizations since 9/11 to defend their rights.

We have shown a preliminary continuity of educational and economic success for Iranian Americans across the first and second generations. Remarkably, this success has become more balanced across gender lines in the span of only one generation. Specifically, in terms of educational attainment and labor force participation, second-generation females have quickly closed the gap with their male counterparts. Because the second generation is still young, it is premature to assess the extent of intergenerational mobility. Yet, given the extent of their achievements, even at the beginning of their careers, one can only expect an upward trajectory for this population.

Future research will be needed to show the exact measure of their success and how they fare in comparison with other new second-generation groups in America.

Results from our analysis of the ACS on selected socioeconomic characteristics of the foreign- and native-born indicate a continuity of high levels of educational and occupational attainment across generations for men. Remarkably, in terms of educational attainment and labor force participation, native-born females have quickly closed the gender gap that existed among the foreign-born. This is mainly attributed to the more egalitarian and universal American educational system than prerevolutionary Iran, which was the premigration context. Similarly, the vast majority of the respondents in Bozorgmehr, Miller, and Hanassab's qualitative study follow a strong proclivity toward high levels of educational and occupational attainment and the aim to obtain advanced degrees in professional fields.[51] Following their parents' wishes, most hope to become doctors, dentists, and lawyers. The qualitative component of that study, therefore, clarified the mechanism behind this educational trend, identifying the considerable role of parents and the Iranian community in second-generation Iranians' choices of majors, degrees, and occupations.

Educated Iranian parents in the diaspora set a high bar for their children, but they also provide the resources to facilitate their academic success. Fathers' high earnings often give mothers more flexibility in participating in the labor force, allowing them to spend more time at home with the children. This enables them to have control and influence over their childrens' daily activities, educational progress, and goals. Mothers also reinforce family and community pressures regarding the importance of securing a position in a lucrative professional field. Community expectations are especially exerted on sons.

Generally, second-generation youth from most immigrant groups view education as a way to repay parental sacrifices associated with immigration to a new land. Moreover, middle-class immigrant parents' initial struggles to regain their premigration status can further serve as motivation for children to strive and succeed. This is especially true for skilled and educated foreign-born exiles like Iranians who, at least initially, often experience more downward mobility than do economic migrants.

Second-generation Iranians are not only the children of professionals, but of immigrant professionals. The culture and traditions they bring shape expectations and goals for their children, a strong factor in the socioeconomic outcome of the second generation. Unlike native-born Americans of native-born parents, the ethnic community's values and traditions can, at times, constrain immigrants' and even their childrens' pursuit of their own career goals. Like some other immigrant groups, second-generation Iranian females outperform their male counterparts educationally, which is no small feat considering the high educational disparity between their mothers and fathers. Unlike other immigrant groups, however, there is preliminary evidence of divergence in the occupational goals of second-generation Iranian males and females. While they both equally aspire to high educational levels, females are less likely to aim for demanding professional careers because they are pressured to become mothers and care for families. Even among those who have high occupational aspirations, future research will determine whether Iranian American women will opt out of the labor force after marriage and childbearing.

The fate of the second generation is not simply an academic issue, as the future of the Iranian American community is at stake. If second-generation Iranian subgroups identify more with their ethno-religious background (e.g., Armenian, Jewish, etc.) than with being Iranian, it could result in further fragmentation of the community. Because Iranian ethno-religious subgroups are concentrated in large metropolitan areas often with sizable non-Iranian coreligionist populations (e.g., Jews in Los Angeles and New York), Iranian subgroups are vulnerable to integration into the wider coreligionist group and the mainstream. The Iranian population is not large enough to offset such a loss; nor is Iranian immigration substantial enough to replenish this population. Naficy has argued that Iranian popular culture in exile transcends internal ethnicity and cuts across all subgroups by serving the needs of at least the Persian-speaking Iranians (Baha'is, Muslims, Jews, etc.).[52] While this may be true for first-generation immigrants, it is unlikely that Iranian popular culture will have the same effect on the second generation, because this group is far more exposed to American popular culture. It certainly will not be a factor for second-generation Armenian and Assyrian Americans of Iranian ancestry, who have little knowledge of Persian.

The children of immigrants in the United States are growing up in a digital age. Technological change may forge greater communication among Iranians in the United States, as shown by the nascent Iranian cyber community.[53] Alinejad's (2017) book suggests that traditional research on social networks may underestimate the extent of social ties that exist among the second generation through the internet.[54] This book is a case study of how Iranian American youths in Los Angeles negotiate their ethnic and racial identities, invoke their ancestral memory, and engage in transnational activity in a digitally connected world.

With the passage of several decades since the Iranian Revolution, US-born Iranians have long been attending universities and entering the labor market. It is time for research to direct attention to these second-generation Iranians and no longer be exclusively concerned with the first (immigrant) generation. This will invariably happen as more and more Iranians raise questions about their ethnicity, identity, and place in American society.

Notes

This is a revised and updated version of a paper that appeared in Mehdi Bozorgmehr and Daniel Douglas, "Success(ion): Second-Generation Iranian Americans," *Iranian Studies* 44 (1) (2011): 3–24.

1. Mehdi Bozorgmehr, "Diaspora in the Postrevolutionary Period," *Encyclopedia Iranica* 7 (1994): 380–383.

2. Mehdi Bozorgmehr, "From Iranian Studies to Studies of Iranians in the United States," *Iranian Studies* 31(1) (1998): 5–30.

3. Mehdi Bozorgmehr, "Iran," in *The New Americans: A Guide to Immigration since 1965*, ed. Mary Waters, Reed Ueda, and Helen Marrow (Cambridge, MA: Harvard University Press, 2007).

4. Mehdi Bozorgmehr and Georges Sabagh, "High Status Immigrants: A Statistical Profile of Iranians in the United States," *Iranian Studies* 21(3/4) (1988): 5–36.

5. Mehdi Bozorgmehr and Georges Sabagh, "High Status Immigrants."

6. United States Department of Justice, Immigration and Naturalization Service, *Annual Reports, 1970–1977* and *Statistical Yearbooks, 1978–1986* (Washington, DC); United States Department of Homeland Security, *Statistical Yearbooks , 1986–2004* (Washington, DC); United States Department of Homeland Security, *2007 Yearbook of Immigration Statistics* (Washington, DC), www.dhs.gov/xlibrary/assets /statistics/yearbook/2007/ois_2007_yearbook.pdf.

7. Alejandro Portes and Ruben Rumbaut, *Immigrant America: A Portrait*, 4th ed. (Berkeley: University of California Press, 2014).

8. Alejandro Portes and Ruben Rumbaut, *Legacies: The Story of the Immigrant Second Generation* (Berkeley: University of California Press, 2001); Philip Kasinitz et al., *Inheriting the City: The Children of Immigrants Come of Age* (Cambridge, MA: Russell Sage, 2008).

9. Straight-line assimilation theory posits upward mobility for the second and subsequent generations, resulting in full integration into the mainstream. The segmented assimilation model states that the children of new immigrants can assimilate into different segments of the host economy and society. Those from humble social origins risk downward mobility and assimilation into the urban underclass because of their nonwhite race, low levels of education, and concentration in inner cities. See Portes and Rumbaut, "The Forging of a New America"; Richard Alba and Victor Nee, *Remaking the American Mainstream: Assimilation and Contemporary Immigration* (Cambridge, MA: Harvard University Press, 2003).

10. Portes and Rumbaut, *Immigrant America*.

11. Alejandro Portes and Ruben Rumbaut, "The Forging of a New America: Lessons for Theory and Policy," in *Ethnicities: Children of Immigrants in America*, ed.

Ruben Rumbaut and Alejandro Portes (Berkeley: University of California Press, 2001), 301–317.

12. Portes and Rumbaut, *Immigrant America*.

13. Ruben Rumbaut, "The Coming of the Second Generation: Immigration and Ethnic Mobility in Southern California," *Annals of the American Academy of Political and Social Science* 620 (2008): 196–236.

14. Alejandro Portes and Patricia Fernandes-Kelly, "Introduction," *Annals of the American Academy of Political and Social Science* 620 (2008): 7–36.

15. Pyong Gap Min, "Major Issues Related to Asian American Experiences," in *Asian Americans: Contemporary Trends and Issues*, ed. Pyong Gap Min (Thousand Oaks, CA: SAGE, 2006), 80–107; Arthur Sakumoto and Yu Xie, "The Socioeconomic Attainments of Asian Americans," in *Asian Americans: Contemporary Trends and Issues*, ed. Pyong Gap Min (Thousand Oaks, CA: SAGE, 2006), 54–77.

16. Portes and Rumbaut, "The Forging of a New America."

17. Rumbaut, "The Coming of the Second Generation."

18. Portes and Fernandes-Kelly, "Introduction."

19. Mitra Shavarini, *Educating Immigrants: Experiences of Second-Generation Iranians* (New York: LFB Scholarly Publications, 2004).

20. Alejandro Portes and Ruben Rumbaut, *Immigrant America*, table 6.

21. Shavarini, *Educating Immigrants*.

22. Patricia Higgins, "Intergenerational Stress: Parents and Adolescents in Iranian Immigrant Families," in *Beyond Boundaries: Selected Papers on Refugees and Immigrants*, vol. 5, ed. Diane Baxter and Ruth Krulfeld (Arlington, VA, 1997); see also Patricia Higgins, "Interviewing Iranian Immigrant Parents and Adolescents," *Iranian Studies* 37(4) (2004): 695–706.

23. Diane M. Hoffman, "Cross-Cultural Adaptation and Learning: Iranians and Americans at School," in *School and Society: Learning Content Through Culture*, ed. Henry T. Touba and Concha Delgado-Gaitan, 163–180 (New York: Praeger, 1988).

24. Mehdi Bozorgmehr and Daniel Douglas, "Success(ion): Second-Generation Iranian Americans," *Iranian Studies* 44(1) (2011): 3–24.

25. Mehdi Bozorgmehr, Elizabeth Miller, and Shideh Hanassab, "Goals and Aspirations of Second-Generation Iranian Americans in the Context of Cultural Expectations," unpublished paper, 2016.

26. Richard Alba and Victor Nee, *Remaking the American Mainstream: Assimilation and Contemporary Immigration*, (Cambridge, MA: Harvard University Press, 2003).

27. Portes and Rumbaut, *Immigrant America*.

28. Ali Akbar Mahdi, "Ethnic Identity among Second-Generation Iranians in the United States," *Iranian Studies* 31(1) (1998): 77–95.

29. Bozorgmehr, Miller, and Hanassab "Goals and Aspirations."

30. Golnaz Komaie, "The Persian Veil: Ethnic and Racial Self-Identification among the Adult Children of Iranian Immigrants in Southern California," PhD diss. (University of California, Irvine, 2009).

31. Mohsen Mobasher, "Cultural Trauma and Ethnic Identity Formation among Iranian Immigrants in the United States," *American Behavioral Scientist* 50(1) (2006): 100–117.

32. Mohsen Mobasher, "Cultural Trauma."

33. Neda Maghbouleh, "The *Ta'arof* Tournament: Cultural Performances of Ethno-national Identity at a Diasporic Summer Camp," *Ethnic and Racial Studies* 36(5) (2013): 818–837.

34. Mehdi Bozorgmehr, "Internal Ethnicity: Iranians in Los Angeles," *Sociological Perspectives* 40(3) (1997): 387–408.

35. Shideh Hanassab and Romeria Tidwell, "Intramarriage and Intermarriage: Young Iranians in Los Angeles," *International Journal of Intercultural Relations* 22(4) (1998): 395–408.

36. Shideh Hanassab, "Sexuality, Dating, and Double Standards: Young Iranian Immigrants in Los Angeles," *Iranian Studies* 31(1) (1998): 65–75.

37. Portes and Rumbaut, *Immigrant America.*

38. Portes and Rumbaut, *Immigrant America.*

39. Mehdi Bozorgmehr and Maryam Moeini Meybodi, "The Persian Paradox: Language Use and Maintenance among Iranian Americans," *International Journal of the Sociology of Language* 237 (2016): 99–118.

40. Portes and Fernandes-Kelly, "Introduction."

41. Rumbaut, "The Coming of the Second Generation."

42. Min, "Major Issues Related to Asian American Experiences."

43. These studies are summarized in Bozorgmehr, "From Iranian Studies."

44. Jen'nan Ghazal Read and Sharon Oselin, "Gender and the Education-Employment Paradox in Ethnic and Religious Contexts: The Case of Arab Americans," *American Sociological Review* 73(2) (2008): 296–313.

45. See table 2 in Robert Fairlie, *Estimating the Contribution of Immigrant Business Owners to the US Economy* (Washington, DC: SBA, 2008).

46. Ivan Light and Steven Gold, *Ethnic Economies* (San Diego: Emerald Group Publishing, 2000).

47. Claudia Der-Martirosian, *Iranian Immigrants in Los Angeles: The Role of Networks and Economic Integration* (New York: LFB Scholarly Publications, 2008).

48. Portes and Rumbaut, *Immigrant America.*

49. For a discussion of the adverse effects of the hostage crisis on Iranian immigrants, see Bozorgmehr, "Iran," and Mohsen Mobasher, *Iranians in Texas: Migration, Politics, and Ethnic Identity* (Austin: University of Texas Press, 2012).

50. Anny Bakalian and Mehdi Bozorgmehr, *Backlash 9/11: Middle Eastern and Muslim Americans Respond* (Berkeley: University of California Press, 2009).

51. Bozorgmehr, Miller, and Hanassab, "Goals and Aspirations."

52. Hamid Naficy, *The Making of Exile Cultures* (Minneapolis: University of Minnesota Press, 1993).

53. Haleh Nazeri, "Imagined Cyber Communities, Iranians and the Internet," *Middle East Studies Association Bulletin* 30 (1996): 158–164.

54. Donya Alinejad, *The Internet and Formations of Iranian American-ness: Next Generation Diaspora* (New York: Palgrave Macmillan, 2017).

CHAPTER 2

Host Discrimination, Bounded Mobility, and Bounded Belonging: Iranians in Germany

SAHAR SADEGHI

Social scientific studies that have examined Iranian immigrants and their community in Germany are limited. This chapter provides an overview of the lived experiences of first- and second-generation Iranians in Hamburg, Germany, with a focus on belonging and social membership. I draw upon thirty-two in-depth interviews with first- and second-generation Iranians in Hamburg[1] in 2011 to demonstrate the extent of discrimination against Iranians and the ways in which Iranians cope with marginality and feelings of displacement in Germany. This chapter will also show how the culmination of lived experiences of marginality and displacement facilitate feelings of perpetual foreignness and generalized lack of belonging for Iranians in Germany.

Questions surrounding the ability of immigrants to adopt and integrate the cultural values and behaviors of their host nation have been at the forefront of sociological research on immigration and race/ethnic relations. The classic framework of assimilation considers structural opportunities like education and employment and expects cultural conformity to the dominant group (Gordon 1964; Park and Burgess 1921). More recent scholarship has added to the classical assimilation framework by examining how premigration characteristics and group-level processes are linked to patterns of class mobility and incorporation among immigrants and their children (Portes and Rumbaut 2001; Portes and Zhou 1993). Segmented assimilation theory underscores the contextual factors of immigration that provide different mechanisms for incorporation in the host society. These factors include: home and host country conditions, social and human capital, the extent to which immigrants can utilize those capitals, the structure and organization of ethnic communities, and host racialization and racial stratification (Portes and Rumbaut 2001; Portes and Zhou 1993). By accounting for the varying contextual factors of post-1965, non-European, nonwhite immigrants, the segmented assimilation framework has deepened our understanding of immigrant incorporation and stratification.

In recent years, American and European scholars have critiqued aspects of segmented assimilation theory (Alba 2005; Crul and Doomernik 2003; Kasnitz et al. 2008; Simon 2003; Worbs 2003; Zolberg and Woon 1999). They argue, for example, that the downward mobility hypothesis, which argues that the children of lower-income or working-class immigrants will experience declines in mobility, does not predict the paths of second-generation immigrants who despite growing up in poverty and segregation have been able to succeed (Kasnitz et al. 2008). Moreover, theories of boundary-making have been especially constructive for scholars engaged in comparative research on immigrant incorporation, especially second-generation populations, as the framework is not entrenched in the US national context and its structural features (Alba 2005; Zolberg and Woon 1999). Furthermore, emerging scholarship in Europe demonstrates that an institutional approach, which takes into account both the national context and the role of institutions, specifically differences in the education system and the ways in which transitions into the labor market are formalized, can help us further understand how second-generation immigrant populations are incorporated in a number of European societies (Crul and Doomernik 2003; Simon 2003; Worbs 2003).

While research continues to further our understanding of how the life chances of immigrants and their children have been impacted by premigration conditions, and the characteristics of immigrants such as human capital, there is a lack of scholarship about how marginality and host discrimination impact belonging and membership, especially among the second generation. Exploring the relationship between marginality, social mobility, and belonging is particularly important for migrants who are generally considered to be integrated and have high human capital, as in the case of the Iranians in Western nations.

This research speaks to past scholarship on Iranians in diaspora. Similar to the findings of Bozorgmehr (2000, 2007) and Mobasher (2012), my research on Iranians in the United States and Germany suggests that many have attained high educational credentials, which have enabled a significant portion of the Iranian community in Western nations to become middle class. Similar to research that highlights Iranians' experiences with discrimination in the United States and Europe (Chaichian 1997; Daha 2011; Hosseini-Kaladjahi 1997; Khanlou, Koh, & Mill 2008; Khosravi 1999; Maghbouleh 2013, 2017; Marvasti and McKinney 2004; McAuliffe 2007; Mobasher

2012; Safi 2010; Tehranian 2008), this study further illustrates that discrimination is more pervasive in Iranians' everyday lives than some Iranians are willing to admit. Additionally, like Marvasti and McKinney (2004), Mobasher (2012), and Maghbouleh (2013, 2017), many Iranians in Germany also employed a variety of tactics to reduce, soften, or bypass the discrimination that they experience.

Iranians in Europe

Since the mid-1990s, research on Iranians in Europe has been growing and sociologists have begun to more closely examine the Iranian community and the lives of Iranians and their children in European nations with a sizable Iranian population. There are common themes within the larger literature about Iranians in Europe, including the construction and·maintenance of racial/ethnic identity, discrimination and marginality, entrepreneurship, and immigrant networks (Darvishpour 2002; Ghorashi 1997; Hosseini-Kaladjahi 1997; Khosravi 1999; Lewin-Ahmadi 2001; Lindert et al. 2008; McAuliffe, 2007; Moallem 2003; Safi 2010). What is more, emerging research has begun to more deeply examine representations and practices of transnational and diasporic culture and identity among Iranians across the United States, Canada, and Europe (Malek 2015, 2016).

A number of studies highlight how ethnic, religious, as well as political identity influence Iranians' lived experiences in a number of European nations (Safi 2010; McAuliffe 2007). Research has shown that the development of strong ethnic identity, particularly for Iranian women activists, has been hindered by general distrust and suspicion within the larger Iranian community (Ghorashi 1997). Distance from co-ethnic associations, as well as religious organizations, has, in part, been shaped by the sociopolitical dissonance and lack of accommodation within the larger Iranian community. Interestingly, despite their openness toward their new society, the inability to re-create the types of political communities that Iranian activists left in Iran has also contributed to social distance and disconnection among Iranians in the Netherlands (Ghorashi 1997).

Moreover, by using data from the European Social Survey, Safi (2010) found that, among Chilean, Finnish, Iranian, and Polish immigrants, first- and second-generation Iranians were the only migrant group whose level of life satisfaction did not increase over time or across generations. Ultimately, experiences of discrimination were found to negatively impact Iranians' overall state of happiness (Safi 2010). Similarly, McAuliffe's (2007) research with second-generation Iranians in Great Britain shows that religious affiliation influences how discrimination and racism are perceived and understood and how identity is defined, shaped, and negotiated (McAuliffe 2007). Moreover, persistent negative media discourse about Islam generates more prejudice and racism against practicing Iranian Muslims compared to those of the Baha'i faith or nonpracticing Muslims (McAuliffe 2007).

Discrimination has also been shown to impact Iranians' opportunities for labor market participation in Sweden (Hosseini-Kaladjahi 1997; Khosravi 1999). Despite high levels of educational attainment, Iranians in Sweden face discriminatory practices and racial prejudice hindering upward mobility, as well social and cultural integration (Hosseini-Kaladjahi 1997). In addition, Iranians' aspirations for self-employment are strongly related to high unemployment rates among foreigners, as well as employment discrimination in the Swedish labor market (Khosravi 1999). Entrepreneurship has also helped provide new possibilities for social and political agency among Iranians in Germany (Moallem 2003). Given Iranians' regular encounters with discrimination, entrepreneurship has helped create opportunities for economic mobility, employment, and agency (Moallem 2003).

Scholarship has also explored the relationship between gender and migration and the impact of migration on family structure. For example, research in Sweden illustrates that Iranian women acquire language fluency and enter vocational programs at faster rates than Iranian men (Darvishpour 2002). What is more, the social and economic gains made by Iranian women have helped alter power structures and traditional gender and family roles within Iranian families (Darvishpour 2002). Relatedly, Iranian women have also been shown to be more successful in advancing their professional goals, compared to their male counterparts, which has, in turn, facilitated a more positive view of integration and Swedish society (Lewin-Ahmadi 2001). In the Netherlands, both Iranian women and men cite experiences of discrimination, despite their relatively high levels of education and cultural accommodation (Lindert et al. 2008). However, Iranian women cited more positive experiences with acculturation than Iranian men, demonstrating the gendered dimensions of migration, discrimination, and marginality (Lindert et al. 2008).

The body of work that emerges out of Europe illustrates that Iranians' ethnic and religious identities, particularly for practicing Muslims, hinders and retards integration and economic advancement and leads to marginality for both Iranian men and women. Marginality keeps Iranians from gaining occupational mobility; as a result, some turn toward entrepreneurship to escape or ameliorate downward mobility. It also creates a sense of outsider status among Iranians. However, marginality is not necessarily always mitigated by relationships with other co-ethnics due to the social distance and distrust among them. What is more, the existing scholarship also demonstrates the gendered aspects of migration. Namely, Iranian men in Europe are more likely to experience identity crises, feelings of low self-worth, and a sense of being outsiders compared to their female counterparts. This sense of detachment and disconnection, along with the discrimination that they experience in their professional lives, seemingly makes integration more difficult for Iranian men.

Unlike research about Iranians in Great Britain, the Netherlands, and Sweden, empirical scholarship on Iranians in Germany remains scarce. Given that Germany continues to be a prime country of migration for Iranians and their children, this chapter aims to add to the scant empirical scholarship on Iranians in Germany, as well as the larger Iranian diaspora. More specifically, in this chapter I consider how the racial/ethnic boundaries between foreigners and Germans, and the larger climate of antiforeigner prejudice in Germany, impact Iranians' lived experiences, particularly belonging and opportunities for upward social mobility.

Research Methodology

In order to build a more comprehensive understanding of Iranians' experiences in Germany, I conducted open-ended interviews with thirty-two first- and second-generation Iranians in Hamburg in 2011. My goal was to explore Iranians' experiences with schooling, inclusion/exclusion, discrimination and marginality, national, ethnic/racial and religious identity, belonging and social membership, matters related to work and employment opportunities, and citizenship. Most of the interviews were conducted in Persian, with a few in German. Less than a handful of the interviews were conducted at local coffee shops, while the majority took place at respondents' homes.

In addition to the interviews, I conducted ethnographic fieldwork and participant observation. During my fieldwork, I visited Iranian restaurants, grocery stores, and other small businesses including printing shops. I also met with Iranian students at the University of Hamburg to become acquainted with the Iranian Studies Program. The program became an important resource for my fieldwork, as the chair of the department posted my call for research participants throughout the department and allowed me to audit his seminars on Persian history and literature. He also invited me to several Iranian events, which made it possible to meet many Iranians, especially professionals and members of Iranian ethnic organizations. Through this larger network of Iranian academics and professionals, I met other Iranians who invited me to other cultural and sociopolitical events hosted local Iranian organizations.

Iranian Settlement in Germany

Until the Iranian Revolution of 1979, the migration of Iranians to the West was generally temporary and spurred by educational or commercial goals abroad. The majority of the early migrants were men who intended to acquire educational and occupational skills in order to advance socioeconomically in Iran.

Size of the Iranian Community

The first estimate of Iranians in the German census appears in 1963, when it was reported that 750 Iranians had been admitted that year. Seven years later, the census noted that another 730 Iranians had been admitted to Germany. Between 1961 and 1970, a total of 7,298 Iranian nationals entered Germany. The number of Iranians who migrated to Germany doubled between 1971 and 1980 and reached 14,173 (DeStatis 2011).

The 1979 Iranian Revolution and the Iran-Iraq War prompted an exodus of a larger population of Iranians that permanently settled in Germany. After the revolution, Germany became a top destination for Iranians, third to the United States, receiving a steady flow of Iranian-born migrants (Hakimzadeh 2006). According to the German census, between 1981 and 1990 67,022 Iranians were admitted to Germany—an almost fivefold increase in size from the previous decade. Between 1991 and 2000, the number of Iranians who immigrated to Germany dropped to 25,820 and even lower to 16,590 between 2001 and 2011 (DeStatis 2011). It is important to note that the census figure is significantly lower than those provided by the Organization for Economic Co-operation and Development, which estimated that between 2000 and 2013 a total of 75,237 Iranians were admitted to Germany. In addition to Iranian immigrants, Germany continues be a prime destination for Iranian asylum seekers (Hakimzadeh 2006). According to the report published by the United Nations High Commissioner for Refugees in 2015, between the years of 1995 and 2011 44,806 Iranians sought asylum in Germany (UNHCR 2015).

Based on the latest 2011 German census, there are approximately 148,750 persons with Iranian migrant background—also referred to as Iranian ancestry—in Germany (DeStatis 2011). Given that Iranians account for only 1 percent of the immigrant population in Germany, data regarding their employment status and education have yet to be collected. However, the census provides some information regarding their citizenship status, geographic distribution, and municipalities (*Länder*) with the largest Iranian populations.

Before presenting that information, it is important to note how "persons with a migrant background" are defined by the German census. According to the Statistisches Bundesamt, foreigners who immigrated to Germany after 1949, all foreigners born in Germany, and all persons born in Germany with at least one parent who immigrated into Germany or was born a foreigner[2] are classified as "persons with a migrant background" (DeStatis 2015). Essentially, this means that one is classified as a person with a migrant background—someone with foreign ancestry—for three generations; being born in Germany, or having a parent of German ancestry, does not exclude one from being classified as having a migrant background. This categorization has larger implications for how boundaries between foreigners and Germans are constructed and how descent-based definitions and criteria for membership continue to trump pluralistic or civil ones.

The Iranian population in Germany is most prominent in five municipalities[3]: 27 percent (41,240) of Iranians live in Nordrhein-Westfalen, 16 percent (23,240) in Hessen, 10 percent (15,100) in Hamburg, 10 percent (15,080) in Baden-Württemberg, and 9 percent (13,640) in Niedersachsen (DeStatis 2011). The most recent population statistics show that, of the 148,750 Iranians living in Germany, 73 percent (108,820) possess German citizenship and 27 percent (39,920) maintain Iranian citizenship. Among those who are German citizens, 61 percent (66,630) had firsthand migration experiences, while 39 percent (42,200) did not. Among those who hold Iranian citizenship, 87 percent (34,780) had firsthand migration experiences, while 14 percent (5,510) had not personally migrated.

Regardless of their citizenship status, 68 percent (101,410) of Iranians in Germany are first generation and the remaining 32 percent (47,340) are second-generation members who were born in Germany. The census also provides information about the parental migration background of the second-generation population. It shows that while 58 percent (24,630) of second-generation Iranians have a parent with a migrant (foreign) background, 42 percent (17,560) have parents who are both of migrant background. Finally, 88 percent (42,200) of second-generation Iranians are German citizens, while 12 percent (5,510) are Iranian nationals[4] (DeStatis 2011).

Characteristics of the Iranian Community in Germany

A variety of commercial, academic, sociocultural, and religious associations exist in large Iranian communities in Germany, including Hamburg. For example, the German-Iranian Chamber of Commerce, established in Hamburg in 1952, aims to promote "independent private-sector economic relations between the Federal Republic of Germany and the Islamic Republic of Iran." Furthermore, the Deutsch-Iranische Handelsbank AG, founded in Hamburg in 1971, which became the Europäisch Iranische Handelsbank AG in 1994, is a specialized bank that facilitates services and business opportunities with Iran. In addition to commercial organizations and associations, Iranians throughout Germany have also founded a number of academic and professional associations. Associations such as the Association of Iranian Scientists and Engineers in Berlin, the Association of Iranian Faculty Members and Academics in Germany in the city of Hurth in Nordrhein Westfalen (NRW), the Academy of Iranian Physicians and Dentists (AIA), the Deutsch-Iranischer Akademiker Club of Hamburg, the Deutsch-Iranische Gesellschaft of Hamburg, and the German-Iranian Association of Kaiserslautern provide support and networking opportunities for Iranian professionals. The specific objectives of these organizations are to foster and maintain intellectual and academic exchange among Iranians, as well as Iranian and German academics and professionals. For example, the AIA, founded in 1961, organized 41 postgraduate and continuing medical education courses between 2001 and 2012. These courses were certified and accredited by the German Academy of Postgraduate and Continuing Medical Education and the German Medical Council. Notably, the AIA also established its own interdisciplinary, international, and bilingual medical journal, *Djahne Peseschki*, in 1963, and renamed it *Kanun Medical Journal* in 1993.

What is more, a number of organizations explicitly aim to help Iranians in Germany as well as those in Iran. For example, Bonyade Kudak, a nonprofit organization located in NRW, provides financial, medical, and humanitarian aid to poor and needy children in Iran. The organization was founded in 2009 and works with the Iranian Child Foundation in providing financial need to children suffering from poverty. Importantly, Bonyade Kudak also supports the 2015 United Nations Millennium[5] Development Goals to "eradicate hunger, to promote universal primary education, and gender equality in education."

The Iranian community in Germany has also established a number of formal and informal associations and organizations aimed at social welfare, integration, and cultural and artistic engagement. For example, German-

Iranian Cancer Aid, a Munich-based organization founded in 2008, offers advice and assistance in the diagnosis, treatment, and aftercare of Iranian children and adults who suffer from cancer. Of note, German-Iranian Cancer Aid is the first official cancer organization in Germany with the specific aim of helping Iranians and Persian-speaking people suffering from cancer.

What is more, we see a number of organizations and associations that provide a variety of resources to Persian-speaking people in Germany. For example, German-Iranian Women's Integration was founded in 2007 in Dusseldorf to "help immigrants, especially Iranian and Afghani children and adolescents, parents, and senior citizens, integrate into German society." To this end, it provides resources and offers a range of opportunities to learn German, engage in intercultural dialogue and activities, and take courses that help parents with their childrens' educational needs. Notably, the association is also an "eligible migrant organization that has been recognized for promoting integration and migrants in the state capital of Dusseldorf." Peywand, also located in Dusseldorf, supports the Iranian community by providing individual and family counseling, language training, education, and social-work assistance through a variety of courses and programs. Lastly, Diwan, located in Cologne, is the first social/cultural association specifically established around the needs of second-generation Iranians in Germany. Diwan provides second-generation Iranian Germans the opportunity to learn about and engage in cultural events and traditions and to become further connected to, and involved with others, in the Iranian community in Germany.

Iranians have also established places of worship. For example, the Persian Christian Church of Germany and the Islamic Center of Hamburg and Berlin provide Iranian Christians and Iranian Muslims religious services in the Persian language, youth and senior programs, and assistance with various faith-related matters.

Turning toward the arts and media more generally, we also find a diverse array of Persian-language radio stations, news media websites, and print publications. For example, *Deutsche Welle, Sedaye Iran, Hamrah, Hamraz, Iran Bild, Iran Infos, Iran Today,* and *Iran Now* provide Iranians in Germany up-to-date news, music, and entertainment. In addition, IRTV Berlin, Mojaher TV, and Khatereh TV provide Persian-language television programming. In addition, there are a total of five Persian-language print publications: *Chapar,* based in Hamburg; *Fesgheli, Iranian Magazin,* and *Ranginkaman,* all based in Hessen; and *Payam,* based in Cologne.

An independent Iranian film festival has also been founded in Germany. The first annual Iranian Film Festival was held in Cologne in May 2014. The aim of the festival is to showcase films that look at "different social milieus, different locales . . . different ways of generational life and old and new gender roles." Importantly, the festival also provides an international platform for filmmakers, especially for young Iranians, and junior and debut filmmakers.

The ethnic organizations, associations, groups, and events discussed above underscore the growing networks and outlets that are available to the Iranian community in Germany. Furthermore, we see a variety of Iranian associations that aim to help immigrants and their children integrate into their new host society and to draw Iranians and Germans together through a variety of educational and sociocultural events. As Iranians come to form a larger part of German society, more ethnic institutions aimed at serving the growing needs of the Iranian community will flourish.

Germany and the Boundaries of Mobility and Membership

By and large, Iranians in Germany find themselves navigating a national context that they generally regard as unwelcoming toward immigrants. They perceive Germany to be a place that is mandated to accept asylum seekers but is not receptive toward immigrants. Iranian respondents repeatedly indicated that, unlike the United States, Germany is not an immigrant-friendly nation and that immigration is not a part of Germany's national identity or history. In their view, belonging and identity are defined by and rooted in German blood and ancestry, or the "Volk."[6] The concept of Volk not only produces significant racial, ethnic, cultural, and religious boundaries between Germans and foreigners; it also promotes a social climate of antiforeigner sentiment as well as prejudice and discrimination against non-Germans.

The following section details the experiences of Iranian respondents regarding opportunities for mobility through the attainment of vocational programs, employment, and professional advancement. The findings of my research suggest that, despite Iranians' high educational attainments and skilled professional experiences, antiforeigner prejudice and racism caps their ability to access greater opportunity structures and professional advancement.[7] For some, these disadvantages culminate into downward mobility, underemployment, and unemployment.

Bounded Mobility

A number of Iranians spoke of an uphill battle with regard to accessing the opportunities needed for upward professional and economic mobility in

Germany. Many believed that they were qualified for jobs yet rejected in favor of German candidates. This belief was shared by both first- and second-generation Iranians regardless of their length of residence in Germany and whether or not they were born in Germany. Furthermore, despite their language fluency, German school attendance, and deeper sociocultural integration, having foreign ancestry disadvantages second-generation Iranians as much as it did their parents. Many respondents in my research discussed common themes in connection with vocational programs, employment opportunities, and professional advancement. Particularly, many felt that while they possessed the necessary skills and were qualified for the position they applied for, antiforeigner prejudice and discriminatory employment practices limited their opportunities.

Siavash, for example, had lived in Germany for seven years and had been an electrical technician prior to his migration. He explained that, despite having been approved for a vocational program (Ausbildung) to be a certified electrician, the German employment bureau had refused to pay for his training. When I asked why, he replied:

> Because I was a foreigner, there was no other reason why I should not have been approved. I am sure that if I were a German, I would have gotten them to approve the training. I wanted to get a lawyer, but heard that it would make the situation even worse, maybe even jeopardize my safety. I know that if I would have gotten this approved the next ten years of my life would have been set, I would be set here in Germany.

Siavash's experiences were not rare; many respondents shared stories of unfair treatment at the Arbeitsamt (the employment bureau) in their pursuit of finding work and vocational training opportunities. For many Iranians, the employment office is a key site of discrimination. Many alleged that the bureau systematically places foreigners, even job candidates who are clearly qualified for higher positions, into low-skill work. Importantly, Siavash also felt that filing a complaint against the employment bureau could produce more problems for him, impacting his impending case for permanent residency.[8]

The difficulty of securing work—despite educational or professional qualifications—was a repeated theme in the respondents' narratives. For example, Paul, a second-generation respondent, outlined a number of barriers to upward mobility, especially for first-generation immigrants. His father's experiences, especially, had shown Paul that a German degree, German citizenship,[9] and the needed occupational skills do not necessarily translate into economic mobility for foreigners. What is more, similar to Siavash, Paul also cites the employment bureau as contributing to his father's persistent joblessness in Germany, contending that they constantly placed him into unbefitting low-skill work. Paul pointed out that his father's small business ownership was a response to discrimination and displacement in the formal labor market.

The pervasive and institutionalized nature of prejudice against foreigners in the labor market is also noted in Pari's narration. She migrated to Germany in 1974 to pursue her architectural dreams after receiving German-language training at the Goethe Institute in Tehran. She settled into student housing in a university town where she met a German man whom she married. Despite her more positive experiences in Germany, Pari had explicit encounters with workplace discrimination. When I asked her about the problems that immigrants face in Germany, she shared her discriminatory work experience and explained how, despite her German citizenship and long residence in Germany, her ancestry—not her skills or qualifications—have hampered her job promotion and occupational advancement in Germany. Pari also implied that non-Germans are afforded limited opportunities to excel; not all employment doors are open to them. In essence, Iranians are treated as if they should be grateful for the opportunities given to them and not to expect parity with Germans.

This drawback of having Iranian, or foreign, ancestry was also pronounced for Anahita, a second-generation respondent who had lived in Germany since the age of five, had German citizenship, a degree in international finance, and fluency in five languages. She often felt that she was not afforded employment opportunities because of her ancestry even though she was clearly qualified. She argued that, in a mostly German and Swiss male-dominated profession, her identity as an Iranian and as a woman was a double barrier. Moreover, she contemplated changing her name—at least on paper—so that the disadvantage of foreign ancestry in the labor market may be ameliorated. A name-change—a coping strategy and response to racial discrimination and blocked mobility in the job market—was mentioned by a number of other respondents. Although most of them believed that it was a short-term coping strategy (as Anahita argued, "I'm not this person. I can't just become Mueller overnight"), the changing of a "foreign-sounding" name to a German name is seemingly common practice among Iranians in Germany.

Kasra further substantiates the claim that foreign ancestry limits opportunities. When asked whether being a child of immigrant parents had affected his job prospects, he replied:

Yes, it has affected my chance to get a job, because the guy sitting at the desk and reading my resume and seeing my picture, says "oh, that's how he thinks." . . . I went to this place and tried to apply for a job, and they said that my hair was not blond and that they didn't want me. I laughed. I was not even upset, because my friend worked there and said they are crazy. When they looked at my resume they knew I did good work, but said that I did not fit their group. They did not say this to me directly, but told my friend.

In Kasra's experiences, when foreigners apply for a job—irrespective of their education, skills, and work experience—they will encounter personnel or management that will likely have negative assumptions about foreigners, employ stereotypical thinking, and ultimately discriminate against those with non-German ancestry. Pointedly, Kasra feels that the added requirement to include a picture in German job applications—in essence—allows employers to use phenotypic features as criteria for hiring. In other words, practices of racial/ethnic profiling assess the employability of candidates by how "foreign" they appear, which inevitably disadvantages the job prospects of non-Germans. What is more, unless a foreigner is professionally overqualified, or perceived as being different from the average "stereotypical foreigner," they will be marked with a set of negative stereotypes, which will make it hard to secure work in Germany.

Anahita, Kasra, Pari, Paul's father, and Siavash's experiences demonstrate how racial profiling, stereotyping, and antiforeigner discrimination cap Iranians' ability to acquire opportunities for jobs and vocational programs, especially in cases where they are just as, or more, qualified and skilled than German candidates. The experience of second-generation Iranians, like Anahita and Kasra, reveal that opportunities exist and foreigners are able to excel, but only to a certain degree. Given the pervasive level of discrimination and prejudice and the existing racial boundaries between Germans and foreigners, how do Iranians respond to and cope with marginality, discrimination, and blocked mobility?

Coping with Marginality

Iranians respond to exclusion, discrimination, and marginality and manage feelings of perpetual foreignness in a number of ways, including downplaying racial/ethnic as well as Muslim identity, adhering to the "good foreigner" trope, and intermarrying with Germans.

We Are "Good Foreigners"

One way that Iranians attempt to lessen the disadvantage of having foreign ancestry is by becoming the quintessential "good foreigner." To be a good foreigner means to be liberal and modern, to be open to German culture and values, and to be integrated. Interestingly, while Iranians generally remark that Germany is an anti-immigrant society, they also perceive that some Germans treat foreigners based on how foreign they appear or behave. A significant portion of first- and second-generation respondents feel that Iranians, and other foreigners, need to integrate and not close themselves off from German society; namely, they cannot solely speak Persian, cook and eat Persian food, and socialize with co-ethnics.

What is more, some argued that Iranians received better treatment compared to other foreigners, because they do not generally self-segregate and construct separate ethnic enclaves. For example, Kimia, a first-generation respondent, argued that:

> I think Iranians are viewed positively, because they are mostly integrated, they have mixed with the population, and they have found their place here. They have not formed ethnic enclaves. We have our own celebrations. We have not confined ourselves to one area; we are spread out. We speak Farsi and [are] interested in Iranian culture and affairs, yet we have integrated into German society.

Iranians, according to Kimia, receive better treatment compared to other foreigners because they integrate themselves by mixing with Germans. Iranians do not construct ethnic enclaves in Germany and do not exhibit clannish behaviors. Consequently, some Germans take notice of these differences and perceive and treat Iranians in a more positive manner. Interestingly, the lack of visible Iranian communities, as mentioned by several respondents, can also be read as another coping mechanism employed by Iranians in Germany. In other words, absence of visible ethnic communities is perceived as diluting "foreignness" and one's non-German identity in Germany—a way to draw less attention to oneself and one's community.

Of note, there were also respondents, mostly of the first generation, who believed that the reputation of Iranians as good foreigners is related to Iran's more positive image in the West during the time Mohammad Reza Shah ruled Iran. They felt that Germans who are aware of and interested in Iran's history not only differentiate between Iranians and the "undesirable" foreigners but also regard them as "better quality" immigrants. In their expe-

riences, some Germans also find Iranians to be more educated, socioculturally integrated, polite, hospitable, and open than other immigrant groups.
Yet, ultimately, it is difficult to assess how deep these so-called sympathies
run and if, in fact, they impact how Iranians are treated in German institutions in more tangible ways.

The narratives presented above demonstrate that being a foreigner involves a loss of status, pride, and maybe even dignity. Thus, the narrative of
being a good foreigner is appealing as it allows some Iranians—even if only
temporarily and symbolically—to feel better about their lives and position
in Germany and, ultimately, serves as a reminder that there are other immigrant groups who are treated worse than them. What is more, we can also
read Iranians' continued narrations of Persian civilization and the Shah's
"modern and secular" government, prior to the Iranian Revolution and the
establishment of a theocratic government, as attempts to differentiate themselves from and hierarchically place themselves above the "undesirable foreigners" who have yet to become modern, liberal,[10] and integrated. Lastly,
the we are "good foreigners" narrative is also a reflection of, and response to,
experiences of being racial "Others" in Germany.

Downplaying and Concealing Ethnic Identity

Another related strategy that Iranians employ in coping with the disadvantage of having foreign ancestry is to downplay or conceal their identity. This
entails a conscious distancing from ethnic behaviors or attributes that visibly signal that one is a foreigner or has a foreign background or attributes.
Effectively downplaying and covering characteristics and behaviors that appear foreign is a part of the process of becoming a "good foreigner." A central goal of assimilation in Germany, much like in other Western countries,
is for foreigners to become similar to members of their host society. In a
context where being a foreigner is disadvantageous, devalued, and stigmatized, it is not surprising that Iranians attempt to soften their racial/ethnic
identities and cultural repertoires.

A number of respondents felt that cultural and religious practices, especially those associated with Islam, were negative markers that place Iranians
and other Muslim immigrants outside the "good foreigner" category. For
example, Anna, a second-generation respondent, shared the following about
the significance of religious background in Germany:

> They ask you, "If you're Muslim, why are you not veiled?" I say, "Because
> I don't want to, and I must not do it, we are not from past times, we are in

current times." And then they make fun of it and say that "I hope you don't go to hell for not wearing one," or "I hope you don't happen to eat pork at some point and go to hell; you might end up in hell."

Anna believes that Germans often regard Muslims and Islam as more rigid, traditional, and authoritarian. For Anna, becoming a target of stereotypical and insulting interactions occurs even for nonpracticing Iranian Muslims. Ultimately, some public encounters compel Iranians like Anna to explain their background or beliefs and reassure Germans that they are modern and flexible foreigners.

Similarly, Lailea expounds on the boundaries between foreigners and Germans, being a good foreigner, and the ways that cultural and religious identity can be concealed or downplayed. When asked how Iranians were received in Germany, she stated:

> I don't ever see Iranians wearing headscarves; it's mostly Turks that wear them. Iranians dress well, are pretty, dance, and laugh, and Germans like that about us. "They are like Europeans, they're not that Muslim, they eat pepperoni pizza as well." The Muslim thing is important in Germany because it's different, it's strange to them. We drink our wine, smoke our cigarettes, dance, we wear makeup, they see us like them, and then we are a bit exotic. Turks sit there and say, "We won't eat pork, we won't drink, we won't dance to this, we pray and go to the mosque, we praise our own culture," and sometimes they don't even know one word of German.

What makes Iranians more tolerable than other foreigners, according to Germans? They are not as strongly rooted in custom or tradition, they will smoke an occasional cigarette, drink a glass of wine, and eat pepperoni pizza, even if they were raised in households where consuming these items was not the norm. Lailea sees Iranians as more malleable immigrants, immigrants who are more tolerable, more "culturally" fit and ready to become a part of German society. Iranians are not as rigid and are willing to occasionally break the rules, as they are not centrally guided by their cultural or religious traditions; they are modern and more secular. And this, ultimately, helps Iranians be viewed in a more positive light.

Given that "foreigner" is an ascribed status with a hypervisible identity in Germany, Iranians attempt to ameliorate their position by becoming good foreigners. This entails behaving "culturally German" and adhering to the norms, activities, and practices of German society. Moreover, many Iranians in Germany feel that intermingling with Germans, living in primarily

German neighborhoods, engaging in German sociocultural practices, and not visibly practicing a non-Christian faith—particularly Islam—are ways of gaining more acceptance in German society. Ultimately, for Iranians, "being good foreigners" and downplaying identity are approaches aimed at reducing the stigma, marginality, and inequality that come with being a foreigner in Germany.

Intermarriage

Another important coping mechanism to enhance integration and to combat discrimination and marginality is interethnic marriage with Germans. For some Iranians, being more accepted in Germany is tied to the kind of relationships they have with Germans. Specifically, first-generation Iranians who have German partners or spouses seem to more easily adapt to German society and the German lifestyle. For example, for Pooneh, marrying a German was not only an opportunity to appreciate German culture in a deeper and more intimate way but also a chance to free herself from some of the constraints that are tied to being an Iranian in Germany. The ability to acculturate and adapt to the host society and have a sense of belonging and membership is considered to be much easier with a German partner.

This assumption that a German spouse helps facilitate membership, especially with regard to economic mobility, is highlighted in Anahita's narrative. When asked about her preference with regard to dating or marriage, she stated, "There was a time where I only wanted to date a German man, because I thought I would be able to situate myself well in this society."

Anahita's experiences since migrating to Germany at the age of five have taught her that in order for foreigners to establish security and comfort they must surround themselves with German friends and networks and possibly take a German partner. Moreover, given that foreigners are disadvantaged and often face discrimination in the labor market, it is financially risky to marry them, as it could make mobility even more difficult. Consequently, this makes Iranian and foreign men, more generally, less desirable life partners for Iranian women. Notably, Anahita's narrative highlights a commonly held assumption among Iranians that cultural and ethnic integration, especially through marriage, can increase belonging, membership, and mobility in German society. My research with Iranians in Germany suggests that some Iranians respond to antiforeign prejudice by making more rational and economic-based decisions regarding romantic partnership and marriage. Ultimately, the blocked mobility and marginalization of both Iranian women and men make it more difficult to attain the economic security needed to start a comfortable family life.

Self-Employment and Entrepreneurship

The difficulties of securing appropriate permanent work, coupled with downward mobility, motivated some first-generation Iranians to pursue self-employment. Generally, entrepreneurship and engagement with ethnic institutions is not common among second-generation Iranians. It is possible that the second-generation's ability to better access opportunities through vocational certificates and education has made self-employment and small business ownership less necessary. While entrepreneurship does not necessarily provide profoundly high economic returns, it produces income and independence for Iranian business owners. It also provides a sense of agency and independence, the feeling that they have power, and that they control their economic position and destiny to some extent. It also gives some a sense of purpose, pride, and productivity.

Hormuz, a first-generation man, received his doctoral degree in Germany in the late 1960s and returned to Iran to teach at the University of Tabriz prior to the Iranian Revolution. He describes how he used his past research and work experiences to establish a small company in Germany:

> I was able to do some of the work I did, and use the experience I had in Iran with regard to chemical materials and chemical compounds. I realized that I could do the same thing in Germany. Many of the people that I knew who had been educated as PhD's were having a hard time finding jobs at the universities, so I decided to create my own company. Many others became small business owners, taxi drivers, things like that.

Hormuz migrated to Germany in 1962 to pursue his doctoral degree in chemistry. Despite his education and long residence in Germany, Hormuz was unable to find an academic job at a German university upon migrating back from Iran in the 1980s. Similar to others with PhDs and other professional degrees, Hormuz strategically used his educational background to overcome the exclusion he experienced in the academic job market.

The difficulty of transferring credentials and skills, especially those acquired in Iran, to the German labor market is also reflected in Shahin's work experiences. Shahin received his degree in accounting and worked at the Iranian National Bank for twenty years. Aside from manual labor jobs, the German employment office was unable to find him work in his field. Shahin's experiences echo those of Siavash and Paul's father, both of whom also faced differential treatment at the German employment office. He eventually worked as an accountant for some of the Iranian carpet businesses in Hamburg. After several years, he bought a few cars and started his own taxi company followed by a bakery shop. When asked why he wanted to start another business, he replied:

> I would like or I want to be my own boss. They do not really accept us in the labor market, especially with our credentials from Iran. What bank could I possibly work for with my degree? I worked for an Iranian bank for twenty years, and it went with a particular degree of status. Here, when they want to hire me, they want to give me lower status work. I did not get my degree here and they will not accept my degree.

As Shahin's case indicates, discrimination in the job market, rejection of foreign credentials by German employers, and underemployment and blocked professional mobility in the labor force due to ancestry motivate many Iranians to become self-employed. Ultimately, in a national context that is persistently prejudiced toward foreigners, entrepreneurship helps Iranians to overcome blocked mobility and to resist marginalization and discrimination in the labor market. It also shields some Iranian entrepreneurs from further economic marginality and provides social-psychological rewards. Similarly, as will be shown, co-ethnic community engagement also provides rewards, specifically a sense of belonging and community membership.

Community Engagement and Participation in Ethnic Events

Sustained participation and engagement with Iranian organizations is pronounced among some Iranians. Although there is variation with regard to what events are attended and how frequently, it is clear that participating in co-ethnic social spaces plays a significant role in how some Iranians deal with their sense of displacement and lack of belonging in Germany. For example, Ebrahim had been unemployed in Germany after he was diagnosed with anxiety and depression. Given his chronic mental condition, he was eligible for unemployment benefits. He said the following about his involvement in co-ethnic events:

> I attend events hosted by organizations in Hamburg to keep my interests and be involved in the community. I go to social events, some political events. But I am not a part of any organization, I learn things, and I listen to the various discussions whether it's social, cultural, or political.

Attending ethnic events offers opportunities for social interaction and gives Iranians such as Ebrahim a sense of membership in the community.

Membership in co-ethnic religious institutions also helps shield Iranian immigrants from further experiences of marginality or displacement in German society. When I asked Nasrin about faith and religious practice, she stated that she attended a Farsi-speaking church in Hamburg because members spoke her language and allowed her to pray in her own way. And after some traumatic experiences with a German church, where she was accused of worshipping in an "un-Godly" way, Nasrin felt forced to find another church, one that would understand her language and be culturally accepting of her style of worship. Nasrin believes that the mistreatment she experienced was caused by lingering racism in Germany.

When I further inquired whether there was anything that was significant about the church she found, aside from service in the Persian language, Nasrin replied:

It has a feeling that I can be comfortable and do work for everyone. . . .
Young kids who have just come from Iran and live in the immigrant shelters come to the church as well. Some of them came to my house for Iranian New Year and we celebrated it together.

In the Persian church, Nasrin feels purposeful and can help younger Iranians—especially those recently arriving from Iran. She considers the church to be a home, a place that provides her a sense of belonging and membership, one in which she can worship and praise God in a culturally acceptable manner without anyone doubting her intentions. For Nasrin, being a member of this co-ethnic church helps establish social bonds, networks, and a sense of membership, something Nasrin was unable to approximate in a German church.

Church attendance, in addition to developing social bonds with co-ethnics, is also a way for some Iranians to integrate and come closer to the dominant religious values of German society. It is not uncommon to hear Iranians speak of co-ethnics who had considered converting, or have converted,[11] to Christianity as a way to apply for political asylum and permanent residency. In my fieldwork, I encountered a number of Iranians of Muslim background who attended church services and were considering conversion. It is important to note that many of these individuals had recently migrated to Germany, as opposed to having lived in Germany for decades. Some of these individuals argued that they had always been interested in Christianity but feared conversion and religious persecution in Iran, while a few admitted that it was easier to be granted asylum and permanent residency if one has been religiously persecuted.

Conclusion

The findings of this research suggest that Iranians in Germany perceive and learn that German institutions mitigate the extent to which they can acquire further opportunities, mobility, and professional advancement. Importantly, there were no significant differences in how first- and second-generation Iranian immigrants assess and view German society and belonging. Although second-generation Iranians are fluent in German, are German citizens, and are educated in Germany, they still face discrimination. Both generations believe that the German national context, coupled with a highly prejudicial antiforeigner and anti-Muslim climate, promote structural and social disadvantages for those with foreign ancestry, especially Middle Easterners and Muslims.

The impact of racialization, prejudice, exclusion, and discrimination in German institutions is well captured in the narratives of first- and second-generation Iranians in this study. They provide a vivid picture for how ancestry, or race, and Germany's longer history of racialized belonging, citizenship, and social membership, continue to influence German national culture and identity as well as institutional arrangements and opportunity structures for those with non-German ancestry. When Iranians are denied job opportunities because of their ancestry, they do not feel themselves to be true members of German society. The recognition that being a foreigner is socially and professionally disadvantageous is central to their feeling of disconnect from German society. What is more, as demonstrated by some of the second-generation respondents in this study, no matter how integrated you are, you have to prove yourself (*beweisen*) to host society members and institutions, whether it be academically, professionally, socioculturally, or politically. The feeling of having to "perform" and to prove one's "fitness" to Germans has significant bearings on social and economic mobility, identity, quality of life, and belonging and membership. It is important to consider how, then, Germany's official definition of "persons with a migrant background" is linked to Iranians' narrations of "always feeling like a foreigner." If Iranians and their descendants are classified as foreigners, even after two or three generations in Germany, how can they feel attached to Germany and have a sense of belonging? By definition, Iranians, and other foreign populations, do not belong to Germany. They are in a state of not belonging, a state of *being without belonging*.[12]

This research speaks to the limitations of cultural competence and integration in facilitating access to structural resources and mobility as well as attachment and social belonging. It shows that conventional markers and measures of immigrant incorporation—such as language fluency, citizenship, educational attainment, and labor market participation—do not necessarily secure experiences of belonging or membership for immigrants and their children. It also highlights another important point that citizenship and civil participation, more broadly, do not necessarily indicate and promote belonging.

The findings of this research also highlight the power and implications of social boundaries and the value of the boundary framework for comparative empirical research on immigrants and their descendants. More specifically, it illustrates that the conception, erection, and institutionalization of social and racial/ethnic difference—the boundaries between "us" versus "them"—have significant impact on the quality of life of immigrants and their children. Importantly, the institutional approach, as seen in the scholarship of Crul and Doomernik (2003), Simon (2003), and Worbs (2003), has the potential to further address differences among the mobility patterns of second-generation Iranians in Germany and other Western nations. An exploration of the variations within Germany's education system and the ways in which transitions into the labor market take place may give us more insight into the mobility patterns of second-generation Iranians. It is important for future research to further explore how and in which ways the state and its institutions work to facilitate or curb mobility among second-generation Iranians.

Ultimately, this research shows that first and second-generation Iranians' assessments of generally not belonging are significantly influenced by the stigmatization, marginalization, and disadvantages that they experience as a result of being foreigners in Germany. These experiences do not help produce belonging; rather, they facilitate a sense of *being without belonging*. This research adds an important aspect to scholarship about Iranians in diaspora. Mainly, we have deeper insight into how racialized experiences in the labor market and larger state institutions influence and mitigate mobility, belonging, and membership among first- and second-generation Iranians and other immigrant groups in Germany.

Notes

1. The research presented in this chapter is based on my larger comparative dissertation project that examines the experiences of sixty-four immigrant and second-generation Iranians in the United States and Germany.

2. According to DeStatis (2015): "The migration status of a person is determined based on his/her own characteristics immigration, naturalisation and citizenship and the relevant characteristics of his/her parents."

3. Not surprisingly, these municipalities also tend to have a larger presence of Iranian organizations and associations. For example, nine of the organizations cited in the next section are located in Dusseldorf, the capital of Nordrhein-Westfalen; Cologne, also located in Nordrhein-Westfalen; and the city of Hamburg.

4. Notably, German citizenship is not a right by birth. Rather, in order for persons with a migrant background to become German citizens, they must prove that they are not dependent on state welfare assistance, such as unemployment benefits, demonstrate an adequate knowledge of the German language, possess knowledge of the German legal system, and have not committed an unlawful crime (Leise 2007).

5. These are initiatives put forth by the United Nations, such as eradicating extreme poverty and hunger, achieving universal primary education, promoting gender equality and empowering women, reducing child mortality, improving maternal health, combating HIV/AIDS, malaria, and other diseases, ensuring environmental sustainability, and developing a global partnership for development (United Nations 2016).

6. The works by Brubaker (1992); Gilroy (1992); Giroux (1995); Bonilla-Silva (2000); Green (2000); Alba (2005); and Mueller (2011) have addressed the importance of ethnocultural nationalism in the construction of the German state and its national identity. Blood-based conceptions of citizenship and belonging were crucial in the formation of the "Volk," the German people. These conceptions continue to influence Germany's national narrative, its national identity, and its ideal imagined community.

7. This was particularly evident among first-generation respondents who had difficulties in translating the educational and professional credentials in the German labor market, even if they were attained in Germany. Consequently, this causes many first-generation Iranians to feel excluded from opportunities and jobs that match their skills and qualifications.

8. In the interview, Siavash mentioned how he had heard of foreigners whose asylum or residency cases were rejected or jeopardized as retaliation for their complaints about discriminatory treatment.

9. The work of Bonilla-Silva and Mayorga (2011), Maira (2009), and Tehranian (2008) theorize and show the limitations of citizenship in securing equality, equity, and belonging for those of non-European racial ancestry in Western nations.

10. Being a "good foreigner" is about appealing to liberalism, modernity, and secularity as a way to demonstrate that a given population, in this case Iranians, are differentiated from and hierarchically placed above the "bad foreigners" who have not had a national history or culture of liberalism and progressive values, such as secularity. Importantly, the work of Mills (1999, 2011) is useful here. He argues that the Western liberal states have historically functioned as racial states, and thus the notion of liberalism is indeed a racialized (white) liberalism where whiteness is a prerequisite for the attainment of individualism, equal rights, citizenship, as well as moral equality. In this sense, we can also read Iranians' efforts of being seen as modern, secular, and integrated as appeals to (white) liberalism and as means of, ultimately, achieving equality with Germans.

11. It is important to point out that not all Iranian Christians that I encountered in Germany had converted to Christianity in Germany; some were a part of Iranian Christian communities in Iran, although they represented a smaller group than I had encountered in my fieldwork in the United States.

12. This term was conceptualized in my dissertation to describe and explain experiences of racialized belonging, namely: "racialization plays a key role in defining the *being without belonging* aspects of experiences of discrimination among Iranians in the US, and perpetual foreigner and stranger status of those in Germany" (Sadeghi 2014: 14). The concepts of being and belonging were articulated in the work of Levitt and Glick-Schiller (2004); they help to explain how Iranians experience belonging and social membership given global politics, as well as national contexts that facilitate stigmatized, politicized, and racialized identities.

CHAPTER 3

Challenges of Integration and Belonging: Iranians in the Netherlands

HALLEH GHORASHI

Two major political events in recent decades led to the emigration of a large number of Iranians, many of whom found new homes in the West. The first and most extensive source of emigration occurred immediately following the revolution of 1979. An increasing number of Iranians left the country beginning around 1981 because of personal political convictions or religious backgrounds. The second political event was the so-called Green Revolution in 2009. The focus of this chapter is on the narratives of first-generation Iranians (mainly women) who left Iran after the 1979 revolution and arrived in the Netherlands during the 1980s and early 1990s. Initially the Netherlands was not the most desirable country of immigration for Iranians, due to the language barrier and a lack of historical relations between the two countries. However, in the 1990s the Netherlands grew to be a more popular destination for Iranians because of its rather liberal asylum policy. For example, asylum requests filed by Iranians in the Netherlands increased in 1992 and 1993 and reached a record level of 6,000 in 1994.[1] This number decreased drastically because of the more restrictive asylum policies introduced in the mid-1990s. In 2013, 35,395 Iranians were officially counted in the Netherlands by the Central Bureau of Statistics.[2] This number excludes Iranians in refugee centers with pending applications as well as those who have been rejected and are currently residing in the country illegally. Including the undocumented Iranians and refugees with unresolved cases, I estimate the number of Iranians in the Netherlands to be close to 40,000, of whom less than half are women.

Until 1987, asylum seekers in the Netherlands were free to settle in any city of their own choice, and most preferred to live in larger cities such as Amsterdam, Rotterdam, and The Hague. After the introduction of a restricted housing policy in 1987, asylum seekers were first accommodated in special centers until asylum had been granted, then they were assigned housing throughout the country (Ghorashi 2005). As a result, Iranians who entered the country as asylum seekers after 1987 have not had much choice with regard to the place of residence and were dispersed throughout the country. Yet, the majority of Iranians continue to live in the western part of the Netherlands referred to as the *Randstand*, which includes the cities of Amsterdam, The Hague, Rotterdam, and Utrecht (Netherlands Institute for Social Research [SCP] 2011). Compared to other refugees in the Netherlands, Iranians have the highest income and level of education (Central Bureau of Statistics [CBS] 2012).

The data for this chapter was gathered through three sets of research projects. The initial research was based on narratives of identity and belonging and was conducted with twenty first-generation Iranian women living in the Netherlands between 1995 and 2001 (Ghorashi 2003a). The second dataset was based on a one-day seminar that was organized in 2013. Sixty first-generation (male and female) Iranians participated in this seminar. Participants were asked to reflect on the findings particularly in relation to themes such as identity, integration, and belonging. The final dataset was based on a focus group with eight first-generation Iranian Dutch women organized in 2014. The aim of the focus group was to gain a more indepth understanding of the experiences of the participants with the abovementioned themes. Based on these findings I argue that the integration process for migrants in general and Iranians in particular is very complex and goes beyond the binary division of success and failure. Integration, I argue, is a multilayered, ambiguous, and even paradoxical process and not a linear one as many assume. The conclusions of this chapter are primarily based on the narratives of Iranian women. There were a number of Iranian men included in the second dataset, but there was no primary focus on gender differences in that research. The main focus of the second research, which was collected as part of a seminar, was on integration challenges Iranians face in the Netherlands in general. There were also no particular differences noted in the narratives of men and women who participated in that seminar. This, however, does not mean that there are no gender differences in the positioning of Iranians in the Netherlands. Yet, the data from that particular seminar revealed that the ethnic marker (being the Iranian "other" in the Netherlands) somehow overshadows the gender differences. Having said that, it is important to emphasize that the data presented in this chapter are primarily based on the narratives of first-generation Iranian women and, in that sense, present a particular point of view in terms of both gender and generation.

Iranian Immigrants and the Integration Paradox in the Netherlands

A recent study on refugees in the Netherlands presented by The Netherlands Institute for Social Research in 2011 concluded that Iranians are generally highly educated and have earned more advanced degrees than the native Dutch. Almost 60 percent of Iranian immigrants have attained a higher education in the Netherlands (SCP 2011: 13–14). Another interesting finding was that, compared to other refugee groups in the Netherlands, Iranian refugees have the highest rate (29 percent) of interethnic partnership (both married and unmarried) with Dutch natives. In spite of this seemingly successful integration process, Iranians rank relatively high in unemployment and a sense of detachment to Dutch society. According to the report, one-fifth of the Iranian population in the Netherlands is unemployed, showing a great gap with the native Dutch. Also, a large number of Iranians have not been able to find suitable jobs compatible with their qualifications. In addition, Iranians are the most negative immigrant group in describing the Netherlands as a hospitable and open society and are quite pessimistic about their opportunities in their new host society. The report also suggests that, compared to other refugee groups in the study, Iranians are more likely to either believe there is discrimination in Dutch society or have personally experienced it. The SCP report refers to this as the "integration paradox." It is a paradox because more educated immigrants and refugees have more negative views regarding their migration experience and the acceptance and integration of migrants in the Netherlands.

Various qualitative studies have documented the nonlinear and layered dimensions of integration of Iranian immigrants in the Netherlands. Nekuee and Verkuyten (1999) note that, despite their successful integration, Iranians lack a sense of belonging to Dutch society. Also, my earlier study on Iranian women refugees in the Netherlands (Ghorashi 2003a) demonstrated that successful integration of Iranian women refugees in the Netherlands did not increase their sense of belonging to Dutch society. This paradox between integration and a sense of belonging has also been noticed for other immigrant groups in the Netherlands (Eijberts & Ghorashi 2016). Buijs et al. (2006: 202) use the concept of integration paradox to show that, when immigrants are eager to integrate into their new host society, they are most sensitive to feelings of exclusion. These authors show that the radicalization of Muslim youths is not due to their assumed isolation, educational backwardness, or antisocial attitudes. To the contrary, Muslim youths who are active, socially involved, sensitive to societal recognition, and eager to become successful and respected members of the dominant society are more prone to radicalization when confronted with unfair treatment, daily public insults, and disrespect for their parents, despite their parents' hard work in post–World War II Dutch society. To gain a better understanding of the processes behind the integration paradox of the Iranian Dutch, I present the results of the three earlier mentioned sets of data. But before that, I will elaborate on the theoretical framework of my research.

Identity and Belonging

Identity, as a narrative of the self, is a dynamic process: a changing view of the self and the other that constantly acquires new meanings and forms through interactions with social contexts and within historical moments (see also Giddens 1991). Identity, then, as a process of becoming, occurs through an intersection of various past and present experiences, which involve both elements of change and continuity. As Stuart Hall puts it: "Identity emerges as a kind of unsettled space . . . between a number of intersecting discourses" (1991: 10). These intersecting discourses include a certain amount of tension between, in Wekker's (1998) words, the images we have of ourselves and the images of us presented within the dominant discourse. In other words, the tension is between the self-image and the attributed image.

Identity narratives, thus, are positioned within a variety of discourses that individuals have been part of, and for that reason concurring discourses contribute to the ways individuals narrate their experiences in relation to those discourses. Individuals "actively construct their identities within a given social framework" (Räthzel 1995: 82). This "given social framework" or discursive space includes both the past and the present. Bourdieu's (1990) concept of "habitus" is useful regarding the past social framework. Habitus is not a mechanical, objectified past or a system of habits that controls individuals; rather it is a set of preferred and routine schemata, formed in the past, that obtain new forms through interaction with new settings in the present. In Bourdieu's own words:

> The habitus—embodied history, internalized as a second nature and so forgotten as history—is the active presence of the whole past of which it is the product. As such, it is what gives practices their relative autonomy with respect to external determinations of the immediate present. This autonomy is that of the past, enacted and acting, which, functioning as accumulated capital, produces history on the basis of history and so ensures the permanence

in change that makes the individual agent a world within the world. (Bourdieu 1990: 56)

This "embodied history" in the form of habitus gives the process of identity formation a certain amount of continuity or "permanence in change." The change becomes most visible when the habitus is challenged as old and new discourses intersect. For migrants and refugees, the tensions between the discourses of the past and the present are often quite salient because of their possible contradictory aspects. Being insider and outsider at the same time is identified by Edward Said (1993) as the condition of "in-betweenness." This condition means that past and present discourses remain simultaneously present in a migrant's life and are constantly negotiated (Said 1994). The duality of the insider/outsider position has the potential to make migrants, particularly the new generation, masters "of several cultural repertoires that they can selectively deploy in response to the opportunities and challenges they face" (Levitt 2009: 1226). Yet the capacity to negotiate this duality of position is quite different for various groups of migrants depending on their resources, possibilities, and inclusion in society. Societal inclusion and opportunities to deal with the challenges and tensions that result from intersecting discourses are crucial for the sense of belonging (Anthias 2006). Societal exclusion, in contrast, increases the tension between the self-image and the attributed image (Wekker 1998), resulting in a decreased sense of emotional connectedness and belonging to a new society. In the following sections I demonstrate how these societal tensions lead to experiences of inclusion and exclusion of Iranians living in the Netherlands.

From Multiculturalism to Assimilation

In most European states there has been what many call a "multicultural backlash." The Netherlands is often mentioned as one of the examples of this backlash because of its shift from a tolerant integration policy toward a restrictive assimilationist policy (Vasta 2007, Vertovec & Wessendorf 2009). According to Kennedy (2005), from the beginning of the 1960s until the mid-1980s, the Netherlands enjoyed the status of a *gidsland* (a leading nation). This term referred to its exemplary progressive public discourse in matters of sexuality, euthanasia, and drug consumption, as well as its inclusive approach to cultural diversity. This discourse and image were challenged as the turn of the century approached, yet its importance influenced progressive discourse in Europe and beyond. However, various data in this chapter (collected before and after 2000, considered to be the start of the backlash) show that the discursive shift (in terms of cultural diversity) was not as abrupt as it is argued. In my view, there have been continuities and changes within the Dutch discursive space in terms of inclusion toward migrants and refugees.

The narratives of Iranian women in the Netherlands that were gathered during my first study (Ghorashi 2003a) suggested that their first encounters (in the 1980s and early 1990s) with Dutch nationals were generally positive. Openness and enthusiasm to become part of this society was one of the points mentioned by almost all Iranian women in the study. Their enthusiasm and willingness were reflected in their attempt to learn Dutch in less than a year and moving on to pursue educational degrees in various fields. The initial positive feelings of Iranian women toward Dutch society were eventually replaced with frustration and disappointment. Despite their effort to become part of Dutch society, these women started to feel uprooted and detached. Their disappointments began when, contrary to their expectation, instead of being accepted and treated fairly they were treated as strangers. Iranian's feeling of exclusion and treatment as the "other" were experienced, similar to the experience of other migrant women in the Netherlands (Essed 1995; Lutz and Moors 1989; Lutz 1991). The experience of Iranian women in this study suggests the simultaneous paradoxical coexistence of exclusionary practices with the progressive discourse of cultural diversity in the Netherlands in the 1980s.

The Process of Othering in the Netherlands

The process of othering in the Netherlands involves the ways that images of the other are constructed and acted upon.[3] The fundamental ingredient in constructing the other is the immigrant's original culture. The immigrant's culture, including the religious practices and beliefs of migrants, is constructed as absolutely different from the culture of the natives. This practice, which I refer to as the "culturalist discourse of othering," has become increasingly dominant in most European nations. Prasad and Prasad (2002) argue that the contemporary discourse of othering in the West is informed by "the social and cultural construction of a fundamental *ontological* distinction between 'the west' and 'the non-west'" (2002: 61). The ways that migrants of color are approached in the present, the authors argue, can be traced to the colonial legacy (see also Wekker 2016). Within the constructed binaries of difference, the ethnic other is considered as not only absolutely different but also inferior to the norm of the ethnic Western self as well. The first large group of immigrants in the twentieth century that entered the Netherlands came from the former Dutch colony of Indonesia. They entered in three waves between 1945 and the mid-1960s (Bosma 2012). In the 1970s, immigrants from Surinam (the former Dutch Guyana) came to the Netherlands, followed by people from the Antilles and Aruba in the 1980s (Bosma 2012). Jones (2012: 27) argues that the legal status of migrants from the former Dutch colonies was less secure than they had expected. Schuster (1999) points out that in the Netherlands in the 1950s, some of the immigrant groups from former Dutch colonies were praised for their assimilation and were exemplars for other postwar immigrants (Schuster 1999: 81). However, Schuster also argues that the focus on crime among Surinamese immigrants by scholars and the media during the 1950s and 1960s contributed to the construction of negative images of the Surinamese (1999: 119–120), which influenced the Dutch immigration policy regarding this group.

The discourse on migrants in the Netherlands, however, has probably been most dominated by the arrival of so-called guest workers in the late 1950s. Postwar economic growth and the need for unskilled labor forced the Dutch government to look beyond its borders, fostering labor contracts first with Italy and Spain and later with Turkey and Morocco (Wilterdink 1998: 58). In the 1980s, the Dutch government shifted its policy regarding guest workers when it realized that this "temporary" migration had gained a more permanent character (Entzinger 1998) and that many temporary migrants had become "(im)migrants" (Lutz 1997). In spite of this legal shift, the general image of temporary migration related to former guest workers did not change. In the 1980s, the arrival of refugees, a new major migrant group in the Netherlands, reinforced and reinvigorated the temporary image of migration. Despite differences in the motivations of both groups, return remained an essential part of the constructed images for both. The key notion of return for guest workers and political exiles represented a strong bond with the past, giving both groups a distinctive temporary image. This image seemed to have remained quite persistent even when migrants and refugees decided to settle in the Netherlands permanently.

When considering different migration flows in the Netherlands, we observe the presence of two dominant views. The first is the sense of superiority toward the migrant other, which is inherited from the colonial past; the second is the notion of temporary settlement. These two views have contributed to the creation of an image of migrants that is entirely different from the native Dutch. This image portrays immigrants as individuals belonging to their home country to which they will, supposedly, eventually return.

Consequently, the identities of migrants are approached as fixed and rooted in their past, making them always feel out of place in their new country, because they *in fact* belong to somewhere else and can never be considered as "really Dutch." This process was present even at a time when it was generally believed that the Dutch lacked a strong national identity—perhaps as a reaction to the experience of World War II when national (German) identity served as a basis for exclusion and horrific violence. But this claim of nonidentity and manifest dislike of national identity did not mean that the notion of Dutchness was absent in public discourse and daily practice. As Prins (1997) puts it, "The essential trait of Dutch identity is assumed to be its non-identity, its fluidity, its openness to 'others'" (Prins 1997: 120). But this has a caveat: "By assuming that Dutchness is an unmarked category, a subject position that does not strike the eye because it does not differ from modern culture in general, it turns out to coincide with what is considered the norm or normal. Hence, everything not-Dutch gets marked as 'other,' as different from that norm" (Prins 1997: 126).

One of the major arguments of this study is that the Dutch national identity is too "thick."[4] This thickness renders it too narrow to embrace the diversity of cultures present in the Netherlands. The Dutch tolerance of the 1980s and 1990s was mainly based on indifference toward the migrant others, considering them by definition as outsiders (Ghorashi 2003a). The idea of tolerance based on indifference stimulated the process of othering between the Dutch and migrants as non-Dutch. Until recently, the Dutch national identity was barely explicit, though there were implicit and unspoken notions about codes of conduct and appearance that established who was and who was not a "real" Dutchman or Dutchwoman. The Dutch citizen is expected to be white and Christian (Wekker 1998). It is self-evident that migrants, with their "deviating" cultures, do indeed live in the Netherlands but can never be "truly" Dutch. At the very most, they can hope to be assimilated into the community of "solid citizens" that the Netherlands will tolerate. This unspoken yet "thick" notion of Dutch national identity has become more explicit in recent years, with debates about the Dutch historical canon being a case in point.[5]

The arguments above show the foundation of the process of othering in the Netherlands. Migrants are imagined and presented as absolute others within the Dutch dominant discourses on identity and migration. This was the case even in a time that the progressive discourse in terms of cultural diversity seemed to prevail. As indicated before, the manifestation of this process has led to the paradox of integration and belonging, even for Iranians with legal Dutch citizenship and full social participation. The following comment made by an Iranian woman clearly shows this paradox:

The Dutch do not consider us to be their equals; they consider us to be inferior to them. Some time ago I worked in a bank, and I had a relatively good
position there. . . . I had a female Dutch colleague who had more experience
than I had. . . . She said: "You are the first foreigner ever to start working
with us like that." . . . They do not have the understanding, or even if they
do, they do not want to accept that an Iranian has the talent and expertise
to rise to their level after living here for five years. That woman told me that
I would have had to start from the bottom, first by becoming a cleaner and
then work[ing] my way up. These are the things that bother me here. If you
want to study here or to work next to your Dutch colleagues and live with
them, then you have to put up with the contempt they have for you. (Ghorashi 2003a).

As this quote suggests, to be treated equally and fairly was one of the
most important points and concerns that was brought up repeatedly in the
narratives of Iranians in this study. The following section presents some of
the other major findings that came out of the discussions with Iranians in
the Netherlands.

Relational Aspect of Integration

The most striking finding of this study is the contrast between the way Iranians described their understanding of integration and the way they felt
they have been viewed by Dutch nationals. The question "What is your understanding of integration?" brought up several different answers from Iranian respondents in the study. The most prominent response was the willingness to participate in and give back to Dutch society as well as adapting
to it without ignoring one's own background. Other responses included developing oneself through education, participating in the labor force, and engaging in volunteer work. In addition, relating to others was also mentioned
as another core element of integration. Examples included being useful and
meaning something to others, avoiding labeling others, and accepting and
respecting others. Therefore, integration for most Iranians in this study was
not only considered as a form of personal development and social participation; it was also seen as a relational experience in social interactions with
others in the host society.

The next question was "What do you need to belong?" The one answer
that came up in all of the discussions was being treated with respect and being accepted as an equal. When participants were asked about their connection with Dutch society, in one way or another all respondents expressed

an ambivalent "love-hate relationship." On the one hand, freedom and opportunities for development were expressed as some important aspects that Dutch society offers. On the other hand, feelings of insecurity, loneliness, anger, and detachment were mentioned as negative aspects of living in the Netherlands. When asked to explain the reasons for these negative feelings, a majority of Iranians respondents listed unequal treatment and being treated as the "Other" and as a foreigner or as an *allochtonous* (non-native Dutch)[6] as the most common reasons. What became clear in these interviews was that Iranians were quite appreciative of the opportunities for personal growth offered by Dutch society. These opportunities have enabled them to participate in Dutch society at various levels and also made them more open-minded and receptive to others. Yet, the mixed love-hate feelings expressed toward Dutch society is very consistent with the integration paradox I alluded to earlier. Despite their high level of social participation and social engagement, Iranians in the study faced othering practices that led to feelings of detachment from the host society and its people.

Finally, another major concern about the feeling of attachment and belonging to their new host society brought up by Iranian women in this study was language. Consistent with my earlier study (Ghorashi & van Tilburg 2006) of Iranian and Afghani women in the Netherlands, highly educated Iranian refugee women in this study who had learned fluent Dutch while earning degrees from institutions of higher education that were entirely taught in Dutch had difficulty finding or keeping a job because they were repeatedly confronted with claims that their language was not "good enough." These narratives revealed that employers' presumed deficiencies of migrants (in terms of language, education, or culturally expected behavior) were considered the primary reason for exclusion of educated Iranian women from the job market. Being a minority woman overshadowed the achievements and qualities of these first-generation refugee women, who had arrived in the Netherlands when they were over 25 years old and earned a degree from a Dutch university. The deficit approach (e.g., fixation on the lack of migrants rather than their qualities) is so powerful that even educated immigrants who are fluent in the native language in the Netherlands face a wall of exclusion.

The Emergence of Exclusion Discourse in the Netherlands

By 2000, the implicit yet "thick" notion of Dutch national identity became quite explicit. Beginning in 1998, there was a turn toward mandatory civic integration, which was considered to be a move away from multiculturalism (Joppke 2004) or a shift toward assimilation (Vasta 2007). After September 11, 2001, it became clear that when a sense of threat becomes attached to the "absolute other" there can be no space left for tolerance; what is left in its place is fear, anger, and outrage (Ghorashi 2014). In spite of the persistence of this othering discourse concerning migrants, it has mainly been since 2000 that we observe extreme negative approaches toward the culture and religion of migrants (in particular Islamic migrants) in the public space. The 9/11 terrorist attacks awakened a latent discomfort toward migrants within Dutch society, which Entzinger (2003: 71) refers to as the feeling of "a silent majority tired of multiculturalism." Moreover, assassinations of Pim Fortuyn, an influential anti-Islam politician, by a native Dutch animal rights activist in 2002, and the filmmaker Theo van Gogh by a young Moroccan Dutch man in 2004 in the Netherlands added fuel to the existing anti-immigrant sentiments as well as the growing Islamophobia and the position of Muslim immigrants in the Netherlands. These events were the backbone of the growing restrictive immigration policy and anti-immigration discourse in Dutch society. The loyalty to the Dutch identity is increasingly presented as a dilemma for non-Western migrants, and they are asked to choose either the Netherlands or their home country (Wetenschappelijke Raad voor het Regeringsbeleid 2007). A country with a long-standing self-image based on promises of multiculturalism, openness, tolerance, and liberalism came increasingly under the throes of fear and protection of its "national identity" (Duyvendak, Engelen, and de Haan 2008). This shift in the Dutch discourse, from integration to assimilation, with an emphasis on loyalty to the Dutch national identity, is believed to be the result of the perceived failure of integration during the "multicultural era" (Vasta 2007; Schinkel and van Houdt, 2010). As indicated earlier, in my view the shift actually has its roots in the culturalist belief embedded in the dominant Dutch discourse on immigration and immigrants. In the progressive years, when the positive connotations of cultural diversity prevailed in the Netherlands, immigrants were still considered as "the tolerated others," living inside the nation yet not completely belonging to it (Ghorashi 2014). This level of tolerance existed when immigrants were not viewed as a threat to Dutch society and were not assertive about claiming equal citizenship. After the September 11 attacks, however, with construction of a new narrative and the image of immigrants as different and dangerous "others," the connotations of cultural diversity changed from positive to negative, and immigrants were considered as a potential threat to the state.

The shift in the attitudes of the Dutch toward immigrants was mentioned by some Iranian women in this study. As indicated by one of the respondents:

During the past three or four years, . . . lots of facilities were available! From 2010, 2011 onwards, they took these opportunities away. Currently, if you want to learn the language, you have to pursue it yourself, you can get a loan . . . to learn the language, if you don't do this, then it's your own problem because you won't get your residence permit. . . . This tells me "we have a number of expectations from you [i.e., immigrants—HG], it's your own issue, go solve it." This gives rise to a situation where those in need of assistance . . . will lag behind on these issues.

Another respondent added:

I think that . . . integration has lost its merit during the thirty years that we've been here. . . . Before it was free. Not in the sense that it didn't matter . . . they expected it, but it wasn't obligatory. Now that it has become compulsory, it's become heavier for both sides. Both for immigrants/foreigners, and for the Dutch.

Another comment by an Iranian woman emphasized the shift toward immigrants in recent years:

In the past, interaction with the Dutch seemed very significant to me. Now it's not like that anymore. . . . When the Dutch speak of integration, sadly, the best way I can describe it, is "nonsense." . . . They used to emphasize language a lot, but now you see, a person owns the language, is educated, has all these things, and still they create a distance. . . . We used to say that they [the Dutch] are open. But now they are not open anymore in their interaction with immigrants/foreigners. . . . They have become closed, and they seem to have become resentful of immigrants/foreigners. . . . My personal experience tells me that a lot has changed.

These women identified the policy changes from integration to assimilation and emphasized the impact of these changes on immigrants with less opportunities and fewer resources. In their views, Dutch society is becoming divided along both ethnic and socioeconomic lines. Consequently, immigrants and ethnic minorities with low socioeconomic status have more difficulties due to the increasingly strict state policies. Although the majority of Iranians in the Netherlands are not members of the low socioeconomic class, participants in this study were fully aware of this dire situation. Their narratives suggest that it is not only the notion of belonging that is at stake but also the resources and opportunities for integration. This was not the case before the turn of the century. This indicates a change for the worse when it comes to integration in the Netherlands.

Changing the Rules of the Game and New Expectations for Assimilation

The shift in Dutch immigration to a more exclusive discourse and restrictive policies has had a major impact on migrants and their children. Many studies show a sense of alienation even among second-generation immigrants who were born and raised in the Netherlands (Eijberts 2013; Omlo 2011; Van der Raad 2013). Migrants who are active participants in Dutch society at various levels feel that the rules of the game have changed as a result of the new assimilationist expectations. The focus and goal of integration have shifted toward the notion that migrants should assimilate by distancing themselves from their original culture (Vasta 2007) and, in case of Muslims, from their religion. For example, Buitelaar and Stock (2010) refer to the conflicting demands that Muslim migrants are confronted with as a "double bind." On one hand, they are called to relax their religious attachments. On the other, they are approached primarily as Muslims. This double bind is also related to language. While immigrants are obliged to learn Dutch in order to integrate, their fluency in the Dutch language is never considered adequate enough for integration and assimilation. There appears to be an unrealistic expectation of a native level of language perfection from first-generation migrants. The point of language perfection came up repeatedly in interviews and focus group discussions with Iranian women. As indicated in Jila's comment:

> When it comes to occupational cooperation, when they see, for instance, that you're better at some things than they are . . . they focus on your [level of Dutch] language—your weak spot—they'll want to, for instance, take my place. Especially when it gets tougher in society, we see this issue arises in a great deal of areas . . . that sensitivity toward foreigners/immigrants increases a lot.

Leila explored the same point more extensively and said:

> I've been in the Netherlands for 17 years now, I've been working for 12 years, and well, my language skills, I started off at a low level and eventually got better . . . until I reached a level which allowed me to communicate with

them [Dutch people] and well, ultimately I've been able to pursue my career. [. . .] with regard to the workplace, [then] you become their competitor. A foreign/immigrant competitor . . . "aha, her weak point is, that she can't speak the Dutch language like we can." . . . They zoom in on this matter so much, so much, that they demotivate you while you've endeavored for years. . . . The fact that they use our being an immigrant against us . . . our language skills, it's like a whip that they regularly smack in our face. . . . I'm caught up in it right now. . . . I stand up against them. But, I stand alone. . . . I stand alone against forty people.

Kobra continued:

> I see integration, just as the others said, as participation in society, not just by working, but also being socially engaged. So far, I've generally been very active, I've been involved in a movement, and it's been good. . . . I consider myself to be fully integrated. I've learned the language, however, I make mistakes, I have an accent, and I think that it is because of this that the Dutch always see me as inferior.

These quotes add new dimensions to the discussion on language fixation in Dutch society that was presented earlier. They describe the discrepancy between one's image of full integration and lack of recognition by Dutch nationals, mainly caused by a shift from integration to complete assimilation, including perfect acquisition of the Dutch language in the Netherlands. This point is very consistent with what Bjornson (2007) calls "fetishization" of Dutch language skills. Today, language no longer serves as a means to facilitate social participation and social interaction. Expectation of language perfection in Dutch now solely seems to be a mechanism for the exclusion of immigrants and refugees from entering the labor market and keeping jobs that match their qualifications. This is one of the alarming aspects of Dutch society that was reported by The Netherlands Institute for Social Research in 2011. The same report highlighted the difficulties that Iranian refugees, many of whom had higher levels of education than the native Dutch, experienced in the job market.

Having an accent is not just a shortfall for employment. It is also a manifestation of inferiority and an explicit and regular component in the process of othering on a daily basis.

Comments such as "fighting alone" or being viewed as "inferior" by the Dutch mentioned by Iranian women in the above comments suggest that having an accent and imperfect language skills gained an ontological meaning for Iranian immigrants that conveys inferiority in Dutch society. As one respondent mentioned, language has become "a whip that they regularly smack in their [immigrants'] face."

These findings show that the feelings of exclusion and nonrecognition held by Iranians in the Netherlands have increased over time. The more they have become part of society, the less they anticipate to be recognized. This has contributed to an even deeper sense of exclusion, feeling of inferiority, and treatment as the "other." The growing exclusionary discourse in the Netherlands that began at the turn of the century has certainly fueled this deeper sense of exclusion and othering. This feeling of inferiority adds an existential angle to the process of othering for these immigrant women. Consistent with the findings of others (Glastra 1999), the new findings in this research indicate that the linear assumption of the Dutch approach that suggests labor force participation and education are critical components of the integration of immigrants in the Netherlands does not hold up. To the contrary, immigrants' fluency in the Dutch language, achieving higher education, and participating in the labor process by no means guarantee social acceptance and recognition in the Netherlands. Even more so today, it is not integration that is at stake but the impossibility of absolute assimilation and being like the native Dutch. Therefore, all the ingredients that were believed to promote and facilitate integration have become the sources of exclusion of immigrants, many of whom are very successful in the Netherlands. What is left is a sense of insecurity and an impossibility to fight against an othering process that is beyond the control of these immigrants. Saideh, who has a good job and is active both in various communities and Dutch local politics, expressed this point powerfully:

> From the very beginning, I did feel a language gap, but on an intellectual level, I felt like I could interact with them. I never felt limited. But just like dear Parwin said . . . they remind you that "you're not one of us." . . . Coincidentally, they just made this joke before I came here [the focus group]. [Geert] Wilders was supposed to come visit at my workplace, he was planning to start his campaign there. . . . I told my colleagues "I'm leaving early, I'll see you Monday." They responded, "If you show up, they might mistake you for a Moroccan and send you back to Morocco" . . . not to Iran but to Morocco, this, this is what I mean, this sense of insecurity. When my son was 18, 19 years old and he'd go out, I was always afraid that they'd do something to him because they'd mistake him for a Moroccan.

The reference made by Saideh to Moroccans is linked to the fact that Moroccan immigrants have been the target of most of the anti-immigrant sentiments in the Dutch public space in recent decades. The most recent manifestation of this negative attitude toward immigrants is the controversy of the extreme anti-Islam/anti-immigrant politician Geert Wilders. On March 19, 2014, during local elections, Wilders asked his supporters in The Hague a question: "Do you want more or fewer Moroccans in this city and in the Netherland?" The public chanted back: "Fewer, fewer, fewer." Wilders replied: "We can arrange that."[7]

As indicated before, the 1980s image of the Netherlands as a leading nation for immigration in terms of ethnic tolerance and cultural diversity has shifted to a growing explicit and negative attitude toward immigration and immigrants. Despite this shift, however, there is an increasing collective public opposition against the ongoing anti-immigration backlash. Examples include the recent heated public protests against the "Black Pete" figure, which many feel is a racist element of the traditional Christmas festivities in the Netherlands.[8] Another example is the annual antidiscrimination demonstrations on March 22, 2014, which employed the slogan "We are all Moroccans,"[9] referring to the previously mentioned statement made by Wilders. In 2016 a Dutch court found Geert Wilders guilty for the anti-Moroccan comments he had made two years earlier.[10] These examples are an indication of the rise of antiracist alliances in the Netherlands in recent years.

Conclusion

As indicated earlier, today, in many European countries, including the Netherlands, culturalist discourse of othering prevails in public discussions. Immigrants, particularly Muslims, are viewed as problems or, even worse, as (potential) enemies. This study has revealed that the self-image of Iranian immigrants in the Netherlands as intellectual elites often does not coincide with the negative image of Iranians held by the host country. As articulated by some participants in this study, this homogenizing negative image of all immigrants and Iranians in Dutch society is so strong that there is little room left for differentiation, leading to tensions between self-image and publically perpetuated images.

As the data presented in this chapter suggest, one way to minimize and resolve this tension is for Iranians to present themselves to members of their host society as "engaged individuals" who are well integrated and contribute to their community and society. The high social integration level of Iranians in the Netherlands has been documented by other scholars (Van den Bos and Achbari 2007; Hessels 2002; Nekuee and Verkuyten 1999; SCP 2011).

Some of the women who participated in this study were political activists in Iran who redirected their efforts toward humanitarian activities in the Netherlands with a specific focus on women's issues (Ghorashi 2003b). In addition to their social activism, many Iranian women in this study formed strong solidarity with other disadvantaged groups in Dutch society and in other countries with a particular interest in the emancipation of women. This transformation is clearly a reaction to premigration political repression and legal barriers that prohibited Iranian women from acting upon their gender awareness and changing their social and legal status in Iran (Ghorashi 2003a). But after they began migrating to the Netherlands the new social space provided the opportunity for political and humanitarian activism as well as awareness of gender issues pursuant to their role as engaged citizens in society.

Despite their high level of integration, strong sense of engagement, and intention to become part of Dutch society, Iranians in the Netherlands feel that the rules of the game have changed and that the expectations of the Dutch regarding immigrants have shifted from cultural pluralism and tolerance to full assimilation. Although Iranians have tried very hard to integrate and fulfilled the expectations of the host society by learning to speak Dutch, earn a college degree, and participate in the labor market, it seems that the expectation bar is set so high (to be like natives) that overcoming it is almost impossible. Contrary to their belief that they are fully integrated immigrants, they are constantly reminded of their deficiencies in language skills and their lack of adequate assimilation in the job market and the larger society. The dominant negative discourse of othering at the social level, combined with frequent exclusionary remarks in daily interactions, contribute to a sense of insecurity for Iranian immigrants and their children in the Netherlands.

As stated earlier in the theoretical discussion of this chapter, the duality of the insider/outsider position has the potential to make immigrants "masters of several cultural repertoires that they can selectively deploy in response to the opportunities and challenges they face" (Levitt 2009: 1226). This study demonstrates that Iranians have a strong ability to capitalize on their dual insider/outsider position and to reach a high level of integration in terms of language skills, education, employment, and societal engagement.

In order for immigrants to feel a sense of attachment and security and to deal with the challenges and tensions that result from intersecting discourses in the Netherlands, it is crucial for the host society to provide migrants opportunities for social inclusion. Yet, the data presented in this chapter indicate that despite Iranians' high level of integration, the clash between their self-image and the prevailing images of Iran and Iranian immigrants is a source of tension, fear, and uncertainty for Iranian immigrant women in the Netherlands. Finally, even with the increasing alliances and social contacts with their Dutch friends, for many Iranians the dominant pattern in the narratives appears to be one of criticism toward Dutch society, particularly the insensitivity of Dutch colleagues toward immigrants, in addition to disrespectful public encounters. These experiences feed the "integration paradox," discussed at the beginning of this chapter. The SCP's 2011 report, and the growing criticism of migration discourse in the Netherlands, may create new possibilities and increase the reflective capacity of Dutch political leaders to promote a more inclusive society.

Notes

1. Thomas Hessels (2004) "Iraniërs in Nederland," CBS, www.cbs.nl/NR/ rdonlyres/85A9B7F7-8B56-4024-B535-A02470FEC5A4/0/2004k2b15p054art.pdf.

2. StatLine (January 1, 2017), "Population; Sex, Age, Origin and Generation," CBS, statline.cbs.nl/StatWeb/publication/?DM=SLEN&PA=37325eng&D1=a&D2=0 ,l&D3=0&D4=0&D5=104&D6=a&LA=EN&HDR=T,G1&STB=G5,G2,G3,G4&VW =T.

3. For more on this issue see Verkuyten et al. (1995), van Dijk (1993), and Essed (1991).

4. In making a distinction between "thin" and "thick" constructions of national identities, I was inspired by Rawls's (1971, 1980) distinction between thin universalism and thick particularism. In addition, Stratton and Ang's (1998) work also helped me to get a handle on the relation between cultural diversity and national identity. (For more on this, see Ghorashi 2003a.)

5. For an elaborate criticism of these developments, see Grever (2006).

6. According to the Dutch government's Central Bureau of Statistics (CBS), an *allochtonous* is defined as a person with at least one parent born abroad, as opposed to the native Dutch, who are referred to as *autochtonous*. (For more, see Yanow and van der Haar 2012.) The term "allochtonous" has a negative connotation in the Dutch public space.

7. Gerard Driehuis (March 20, 2014), "Dutch Politician Wilders Leads Anti-Moroccan chant," *Washington Post*, www.welingelichtekringen.nl/politiek/291280 /washington-post-dutch-politician-wilders-leads-anti-moroccan-chant.html. "Willen jullie in deze stad, en in Nederland, meer of minder Marokkanen? De PVV'ers riepen terug: 'Minder, minder, minder.' Daarop zei Wilders: 'Dat gaan we regelen,'" *Redactie* (March 20, 2014). "Wilders laat publiek scanderen: 'Wij willen minder Marokkanen,'" *De Volkskrant*, www.volkskrant.nl/vk/nl/2784/Verkiezingen/article /detail/3618750/2014/03/19/Wilders-laat-publiek-scanderen-Wij-willen-minder -Marokkanen.dhtml.

8. Arnon Grunberg (December 4, 2013): "Why the Dutch Love Black Pete," *New York Times*, www.nytimes.com/2013/12/05/opinion/why-the-dutch-love-black-pete .html?_r=0.

9. Republiek allochtonië (March 21, 2014), "'wij zijn allemaal Marokkanen!' Kom morgen demonstreren tegen racisme and discriminatie," www.republiekallochtonie .nl/wij-zijn-allemaal-marokkanen-kom-morgen-demonstreren-tegen-racisme-en -discriminatie.

10. DutchNews.nl (December 9, 2016), "Strong Reactions to Wilders Guilty Verdict on Inciting Racial Discrimination," www.dutchnews.nl/news/archives/2016/12 /98817-2.

CHAPTER 4

Integration, Cultural Production, and Challenges of Identity Construction: Iranians in Great Britain

KATHRYN SPELLMAN POOTS AND REZA GHOLAMI

This chapter introduces the Iranian population in Britain, focusing particularly on diverse experiences of integration, cultural production, and identity formation. Iranians in Britain are from a range of political, socioeconomic, religious, and ethnic backgrounds. The generational and gendered outlooks—as well as the varying degrees of social, political, and economic connections to Iranian society—are important factors for understanding the complexity and diversity of their experiences in Britain and their conceptions and narratives of "home" and "homeland."[1] This chapter focuses on interrelated themes, such as secular/religious subjectivity and identity formation; the maintenance and hybridity of cultural traditions and practices; and intergenerational change. We draw from ethnographic research to show how Iranians affectively hold multiple allegiances that shape and are shaped by an intersection of factors, including the socioeconomic and political conditions in British society, intradiasporic dynamics and ongoing relations with Iran. Although the experiences of Iranians in Britain vary among the different genders and internal ethnic and religious groups, they have shown positive signs of economic and social integration in British society. Many British Iranians have also continued to participate in local and diasporic networks and forums that place emphasis on the Persian language and the maintenance and renewal of Iranian cultural traditions and forms in British society.

This chapter is largely situated within the sociology/anthropology of ethnicity and migration, as well as transnational and diaspora studies. The empirical reality of the lived experiences of Iranians in Britain shows the limitations of conventional approaches in migration studies that suggest a linear and definitive assimilation of migrants into their new host society. This corresponds to the burgeoning research on the transnational dimensions of the migration and diasporic experience.[2] Indeed, improved modes of transportation and digital communication links have enabled many British Iranians to maintain social relations with people and activities in Iran and the wider diaspora. This, along with direct and relatively short flights (five hours and forty minutes) and competitive air fares (around £500) has made it possible for some British Iranians to build "social fields" that link together family and other networks between the two countries.[3] That being said, political circumstances continue to dictate the transnational connections and movement between Iran and Britain. The travel restrictions that softened during the 1990s and early 2000s, for instance, tightened when Mahmoud Ahmadinejad became president in 2005. Whereas many British Iranians have continued to travel back and forth between Iran and Britain, others feel uncertain of their safety upon return. While some British Iranians, as a matter of principle, have not returned to their homeland since the 1979 revolution, others in the second and third generations have never traveled to Iran at all. Therefore, the umbrella term "British Iranians" is being used here to encompass Iranian-born nationals, including asylum seekers, refugees, and voluntary migrants, as well as British-born citizens of Iranian descent.

Demographic Characteristics of Iranians in Great Britain

The 2011 British census results documented 84,735 Iranian-born residents in the whole of the United Kingdom with 79,985 residents in England, 1,695 in Wales, and 2,773 in Scotland.[4] This number does not include the children born to Iranian-born parents or those whose claims for refugee status are yet to be determined. The data generated from a new question in the 2011 England and Wales census—"If you were not born in the United Kingdom, when did you most recently arrive to live here?"—confirmed that the first peak of Iranian migration to Britain occurred in the late 1970s around the time of the Iranian Revolution. That makes 16 percent of the 81,680 Iranian-born residents arriving in England and Wales at that time. The new census question also identified a second peak in the 1990s when 22 percent of Iranian-born residents in 2011 arrived following the end of the Iran-Iraq War (1980–1990). The statistical data in the last four censuses (1981, 1991, 2001, and 2011) indicate exponential growth of Iranian migration to England and Wales since the Iranian Revolution. The 1981 population census recorded 28,617 Iranian-born residents in England and Wales, with 18,132 males and 10,132 females. The 1991 census logged 32,262 Iranian nationals resident in Britain, of whom 16,856 were living in inner and outer London. The 2001 census recorded 42,377 Iranian-born residents of England and Wales. This number has nearly doubled to 81,680 according to the 2011 census. The Home Office also released figures estimating that 16,000 to 20,000 temporary visas have been given to Iranians every year since 1990. The estimates of the Iranian population we heard among Iranians in Britain during interviews were greatly varied and usually much higher than the numbers recorded by the census. The guesses commonly fell in the range of 100,000 to 500,000.

It is worth mentioning the relatively new census question on ethnic identity, first devised in 1991. Although many ethnic groups in Britain welcomed the opportunity to be defined in the census, many Iranians felt unrepresented by the ethnic categories listed on the form. In the 2011 census, British Iranians ticked one of the following categories and/or wrote in by hand "Iranian" under all of the following categories: White; Mixed/multiple ethnic group; Asian/Asian British; and Other ethnic group. In Manchester, for instance, 165 Iranian-born residents ticked the "White" category and handwrote "Iranian"; 82 ticked the "Mixed/multiple ethnic group" category and wrote "Iranian"; 1,208 ticked the "Asian/Asian British" category and wrote "Iranian"; and 838 ticked "Other ethnic group" and wrote "Iranian." Some people identified themselves as "Persian" as well. Unlike British Arabs, who successfully campaigned to the Office of National Statistics for the category "Arab" to be listed on the 2011 census, Iranians have continued to struggle to work out which ethnic tick-box defines their ethnicity on official forms. This is further complicated by the British Iranians who identify with the wide range of Iranian internal ethnic and national identities, including Kurds, Azeris, Armenians, Assyrians, Jews, Balluchis, Lur, and so forth.

Additional data from the 2011 census found that there were 37,339 Iranian-born residents living throughout London's thirty-two boroughs and the City of London. They were mainly concentrated in the following boroughs: Barnet (7,055); Ealing (2,980); Westminster (2,704); Kensington and Chelsea (2,194); Brent (2,003); Camden (1,817); Hammersmith and Fulham (1,594); Enfield (1,552); Harrow (1,216); Richmond upon Thames (1,066); Kingston upon Thames (1,062); and Hillingdon (1,038).[5] Residency in several expensive London quarters, such as Kensington and Chelsea, Hammersmith and Fulham, Westminster, and Camden, indicates the prosperity of many British Iranians. In addition to the South East region of Britain, the following regions have more than 5,000 Iranian-born residents: North West, West Midlands and Yorkshire, and The Humber. There are large clusters of Iranian-born residents in the following cities and districts: Greater Manchester (6,186),[6] particularly Cheadle Hill; Newcastle upon Tyne (1,120); Sheffield (1,414); Leeds (1,452); Birmingham (2,762); and Brighton and Hove (1,043).

Research Methodology

The Iranian population has been subject to very few studies in the United Kingdom. This could be due to a number of reasons, including the relatively small number of Iranians in Britain, the fact they do not reside in concentrated areas (but in clusters based mainly on socioeconomic backgrounds), and because they do not tend to generate social problems for British society. This chapter draws on our respectively ongoing research among UK Iranians. The bulk of the data used here were collected during research projects carried out between 2011 and 2014 and funded by various UK funders, including the British Academy and the British Council. The projects' foci reflect our keenness to gain a deeper understanding of how secularism and religion (especially Shiism) inform individual and collective self-making in the UK Iranian diaspora. In this vein, we are also interested in issues of social, cultural, and political transmission and transformation, which also involves in-depth study of Iranian diasporic institutions such as schools and media.

Britain, and London in particular, has tended to occupy a central place in the modern Iranian cultural and migratory imagination. Along with a handful of other Western cities, London is considered a major social, cultural, and political hub of the Iranian diaspora. In fact, many Iranians from diverse backgrounds identify London as second only to Los Angeles in terms of its importance.[7] However, despite this centrality and the relatively large Iranian settlement in London and the United Kingdom, there have been surprisingly few studies of Britain's Iranian population. A few articles have been published since 2000 (Sreberny 2000, 2002; McAuliffe 2007). However, these have mainly come from media studies and at best offer only a glimpse into Iranian lives in the United Kingdom.[8] In this context, our work has been unique in studying the UK Iranian diaspora in a great deal of depth (see especially Spellman 2004a, 2004b; Gholami 2015).

Methodologically, therefore, we have relied primarily on long-term ethnographic research using participant observation, unstructured interviews, and focus groups in both Persian and English. We have employed ethnographic methods for studying Iranian diasporic media ("old" and "new") as a way to better understand how groups and individuals interact with media to produce and consume social, cultural, and political meanings, as well as the role that the media play in reshaping the structural, epistemological, and discursive contours of the Iranian diaspora in the United Kingdom and elsewhere. Finally, we have also used quantitative surveys and social network analysis to gain an appreciation of collective views on key issues such "community challenges," as well as to ascertain the nature and frequency of connections among Iranian organizations across the United Kingdom. The sampling method for surveys has been random, though we have also relied on "snowball" sampling to reach a larger number of organizations.

Iranian Settlement in Britain

Similar to the wider Iranian diaspora, the first substantial movement of Iranians arrived around the time that Mohammad Reza Shah was overthrown, in February 1979, and mainly consisted of families who benefited from the socioeconomic developments of the Pahlavi era and their political status at that time. Many were already familiar with the British way of life and the English language before their departure from Iran. After a relatively short period of infighting and political uncertainty in Iran, Ayatollah Khomeini and Islamic forces dominated the revolutionary process and its outcome. The threats and repression used to control the opposition, along with the beginning of the Iran-Iraq War in 1980, led to the second wave of emigration, which included both anti-Pahlavi and anti–new regime political activists, families fearing the military draft, intellectuals, and many others—notably women and members of ethnic and religious groups who opposed the Islamic Republic of Iran and the political, social, and cultural Islamization of Iran. It is worth adding that an estimated $40 billion from Iran ended up in Britain after the revolution.[9]

Throughout the 1980s and 1990s, intermittent migration from Iran to Britain continued and consisted mainly of economic migrants and religious minority groups who were seeking relief from declining political and economic conditions and religious discrimination in Iran. Hesse-Lehmann (1993) detected a similar migration pattern in her research on Iranians seeking asylum in Hamburg, Germany.[10] She also noted that many Iranians who gained asylum in Germany had their visas first rejected in England, France, and the United States. Those who were granted asylum in the United Kingdom spoke about the process of leaving Iran and resettling there during the 1990s. Some recalled how they gathered money (usually in the region of $5,000 to $10,000) from family and friends in Iran in order to pay smugglers to help them cross the Turkish border and ultimately reach the United Kingdom.[11] After officially claiming asylum (mainly at UK airports), they were granted political asylum; granted exceptional leave to remain[12]; or refused entry and deported. According to the Research Development and Statistics Directorate of the Home Office, between the years 1992 and 2000 1,395

Iranians were recognized as refugees; 1,420 were declined refugee status but granted exceptional leave to remain; and 3,875 were refused asylum and exceptional leave to remain.[13]

It should be noted that in 1991, the former president of Iran, Hashemi Rafsanjani, extended an invitation to the Iranian exiles to return to Iran. While a few returned or traveled back and forth between Britain and Iran, many did not believe it was safe to return or were unwilling to live in the strict political and social climate of Iran. Others wished to stay in Britain so their children could benefit from the British education system.

The most recent influx of Iranian migration to Britain occurred during Ahmadinejad's presidency (2005–2013), particularly after the heavily disputed results of his 2009 second election and the political movement that followed. Although systematic research is needed, most of these recent asylum cases have been political or ideological and are rooted in the political culture of the younger generations in Iran. Iranians of all ages, particularly youths, sought refuge in Britain for a wide range of reasons, including: human rights activities prohibited by the government; religious orientation and practices (particularly in Baha'i, Christian, and Ahle-haq faiths) and conversion from Islam to Christianity, Judaism, and Zoroastrianism; accusations of sexual behaviors deemed unlawful; forced marriage; and domestic abuse. According to statistical estimates by the United Nations High Commissioner for Refugees, during 2012 the number of Iranian refugees worldwide was 75,613.[14] The United Kingdom, Germany, Turkey, Australia, Sweden, and Austria were the six destination countries that received the largest numbers of new applications from Iranians. In these countries, of "21,310 decisions taken on Iranian asylum applications in 2012, including cases from previous years, some 10,327 resulted in refugee status, 447 decisions resulted in humanitarian status, 7,707 cases were rejected, and 2,671 cases were closed on other grounds."[15] Between the years 2001 and 2011 the United Kingdom was the top destination country of new asylum applications from Iranians, with a total of 35,359 applicants.[16]

Whereas earlier waves of Iranian migrants relied primarily on the family unit as well as Iranian political, ethnic, and religious groups to adjust in Britain, the newly arrived Iranians have made good use of the well-established Iranian diasporic networks and organizations, such as the Iranian Association and the Refugee Women's Association.[17] Nevertheless, the adjustment process and experiences for newly arrived migrants are also shaped by wider structural forces that impinge on their lives and the way they perceive and negotiate their presence in the host country.

Anglo-Iranian Relations and British Perceptions of Iran and "Persia"

The historical and current political, economic, and cultural relations between Iran and Britain provide important conditions for navigating migration and settlement experiences in the United Kingdom. Before the arrival of Iranians during and after the 1979 revolution, Britain was home to a small number of Iranian government officials, industrialists, and students who came to Britain during the nineteenth century, and more substantially in the twentieth century, in search of higher standards of living or higher education qualifications. However, Iran, or "Persia," has been evolving in the British imagination over centuries. British historians and travelers, missionaries, diplomats, and governmental agents have provided complex and often contradictory narratives of Persia and Persians, ranging from awe-inspiring and admirable to exotic and backward.[18] An interesting indicator of British perceptions of Iran and Persians during the Victorian era was the high-profile trip by Naser al-Din Shah (1848–1896) to Britain in the 1870s. The British press and Naser al-Din Shah's personal diary described the great fanfare and hospitality of Queen Victoria and her royal household. The crowds of British people who welcomed the Qajar Shah were also referred to in great detail in the reports. According to Afshin Marashi:

> The reaction of the crowd is difficult to judge. Their shouts of greeting might have stemmed from their perception of the Shah as an Asiatic oddity, on display like much of the other specimens of oriental culture in the museums and exhibition halls in London. Conversely their reaction might have been conditioned by the form of the encounter, in the style of the public rituals and ceremonies of that time.[19]

Although Marashi concludes that the Shah's status most likely lay somewhere between these two extremes, Queen Victoria's appointment of Naser al-Din Shah as a Knight of the Order of the Garter, the highest English order of chivalry, was presumably a sign of respect. The appreciation and even emulation of Persian culture and people was also evident in many classical writings and artistic productions. As Vanessa Martin states: "Iran or 'Persia' has had a part to play in the British imagination, in literature and myth, for many centuries and in particular has had a notable influence on British art and crafts bringing, on the one hand, new philosophies and images and, on the other, new designs."[20]

Relations and exchanges between Iran and Britain continued to evolve during the era of nation-state building. As both Ali Ansari and Reza Zia-Ebrahimi have convincingly argued, the idea of Persia in the British imagination should not be seen necessarily as a true reflection of Persia itself but in relation to the British or Western national narrative-making. The ancient origins and ancestral connections to what was constructed as the superior Persian "race," for instance, was used to authenticate and legitimize the foundation of many European (Aryan) nationalisms.[21] As positive narratives and mythologies of Iran's pre-Islamic past were used to construct European nation-states, the hegemonic discourses of Europe in turn entered the politics and culture of Iran's political and intellectual elites. As Ansari notes: "Indeed, for many Iranian intellectuals, this [Aryan] narrative was a means by which Iran could reintegrate itself into the narrative of the great (European) nations and they could extricate themselves from the decay and decline that was palpable around them."[22]

This Aryan discourse was effectively used by Iranians, particularly during the Pahlavi dynasty, to connect Iran racially to European nations and their political, economic, cultural, and technological dominance. As noted by Zia-Ebrahimi: "Nationalism discursively managed Iran's traumatic encounter with Europe and its modernity by portraying Iranians as inherently progressive and destined for a high rank among nations and as such was a mere shortcut to modernity."[23]

The propensity to draw on the superiority of the so-called Aryan race, and positive representations of Iran's heritage more generally, have continued over the years both in Iran and the wider diaspora. Some British Iranians, for example, identify with Iran's pre-Islamic past in order to transcend negative perceptions of Iran, the rise of political Islam, and the broader shift toward the Islamization of identity among many British Muslims.[24] The Salman Rushdie affair, Iran's nuclear power program, the volatile diplomatic relations between Britain and Iran since the revolution, the 2009 Green Movement protests and the death of Neda Agha Soltan, and the most recent closing of the British embassy in Tehran in 2011—these are some of the major political matters that have taken a negative toll on British perceptions of Iranian society. Indeed, according to a 2013 BBC World Service poll, "only 5% of British people view Iran's influence positively, with 84% expressing a negative view."[25] According to a 2012 Pew Global Attitudes Survey: "16% of British people viewed Iran favourably, compared to 68% which viewed it unfavourably; 91% of British people oppose Iranian acquisition of nuclear weapons and 79% approve of 'tougher sanctions' on Iran, while 51% of British people support use of military force to prevent Iran from developing nuclear weapons."[26] There are difficulties in measuring the limits of such attitudes and how they directly impinge on the lives of British Iranians, but these negative perceptions undoubtedly affect the ways in which Iranians navigate and negotiate their presence in the host society.

Conversely, there are key events in the political history of modern Iran that continue to foster mistrust toward Britain in the minds of some British Iranians.[27] For example, the one-sided Anglo-Iranian oil agreements, made in the early twentieth century, led to misgivings about Britain's economic intentions in Iran. These feelings were heightened by the British- and US-backed coup that removed Mohammad Mosaddegh, Iran's popular prime minister between 1951 and 1953, and still looms large in Iranians' collective memory. Indeed, Mosaddegh continues to be viewed as a national symbol of Iran's early attempt at democracy and a reminder of what is seen as the devastating impact of the meddling of Anglo-American agents. Finally, the BBC has been seen by many Iranians as merely the voice of British imperialism. However, despite such mistrust and bitter memory, many Iranian immigrants believe that the long-standing historical and cultural ties between Iran and Britain have created a sense of familiarity with the country and its people, and they regard their settlement in Britain as a good option for themselves and their families.

Economic and Social Integration

The economic and social integration of Iranians into British society depends on many factors, including age, gender, English proficiency, religion, ethnicity, and occupational and educational backgrounds. Similar to Iranians in the United States, many British Iranians have successfully obtained higher education degrees and professional or skilled jobs in fields such as medicine and dentistry, engineering, education, accounting, law, architecture, computing, filmmaking, and the arts. According to BBC Born Abroad, 24.19 percent of settled Iranians are employed in highly paid jobs, earning more than £750 per week.[28] Many Iranians are also self-employed, owning and working in businesses such as restaurants, property development and sales, florists, dry cleaning, and taxi companies. Some of these self-employed Iranians were unable to find jobs that matched their educational and occupational experience and qualifications in Iran. This concurs with the results of Vida Nassehi-Behnam's 2010 study showing that Iranians with higher occupational positions before exile have less opportunity to continue their professions in Britain.[29] This has particularly been the case for Iranian men. Her study also indicated a nearly equal gender ratio in employment, but with women having lower professional qualifications.[30] A considerable percentage of British Iranian women sampled in her study were employed in civil service jobs. According to Nassehi-Behnam, this is probably because women, often with more child-care and household responsibilities, tend to take on secure jobs with predictable hours. Nevertheless, there are many young, confident British Iranian women who have excelled in their education and have well-paid professional positions in the public and private sectors.

Iranian professional, ethnic, and religious associations and networks have played crucial social, cultural, and economic roles in the Iranian community in Britain. Some British Iranians, particularly nonprofessionals, have reported that Iranian informal networks and Iranian associations helped them negotiate the British job market. Many members of religious and ethnic subgroups, including Baha'is, Zoroastrians, Jews, and Christians (Armenians, Assyrians, and Protestants), also reported that they had help finding jobs from contacts in religious and ethnic organizations. Similarly, Iranian professional associations have played a major role in the Iranian community. During the 1990s and 2000s, a number of British Iranian professional organizations were also established. For example, the British Iranian Business Association, founded in 1994, claims that there are over 5,000 Iranian professionals and businesspeople affiliated with it and that its journal, *British Iranian Business News*, has a readership of 20,000. The British Iranian Business and Professional Society, also known as Anjoman, and the British Iranian Medical Association are further examples of professional organizations that aim to provide platforms to exchange ideas, facilitate networking across generations, and raise the profiles of British Iranians.

In addition to providing an opportunity for social networking, the Iranian professional organizations also serve as a social and cultural base. They regularly hold charity events, often for social causes in Iran, and organize events that commemorate special days in both British and Iranian calendars. It is worth adding that London is widely acknowledged as boasting the largest concentration of Iranian organizations and businesses in the United Kingdom (and probably in Europe).

British Iranians have also flourished in educational activity. The bulk of this activity is aimed at Iranian children and young people and takes place in the form of supplementary schools—though there is also some provision of adult education by community organizations such as the Iranian Association.[31] In London, schools such as Rustam School and Andisheh School are dotted across the city and offer Iranian children training in the Persian language as well as a range of mainstream subjects across all levels. This is underpinned by the philosophy that Iranian children, in order to succeed in British society, must be able to do well in mainstream education. Iranian schools state yet another aim: the support and strengthening of Iranian culture and community. In some cases, this goal is denominational and caters to a particular religious community—such as Tarbyat School, which emphasizes Baha'i teachings. By and large, however, ideas of culture and community are seen to be much more unified, espousing (or presupposing) a sense of common "Iranianness." Rustam School, for example, considers itself to be "more than a school. It is a community centre where families make friends and meet socially."[32] It often organizes Noruz and other Iranian celebrations as well as cultural events such as poetry evenings. Rustam also offers counseling sessions and coaching by a qualified therapist. These sessions are specifically offered for the treatment of depression and other emotional and mental-health issues and for improving parent-child relationships among Iranians. Finally, in addition to Iranian cultural celebrations, some schools also celebrate Christmas and other Western holidays. The idea, again, is that young Iranians—indeed, all Iranians—have to be well-integrated and well-versed in home *and* host cultures to be successful and that education must facilitate this.

Although education and the acquisition of social and cultural skills have been important in achieving integration, some Iranians have reported facing small doses of discrimination in Britain. For example, some non-professional and unskilled Iranians in particular have felt obliged to take on a Western name, especially for job applications, in order to increase their chances of securing an interview.[33] Note, however, that many Iranians who lived in other European countries before moving to Britain reported that British society was less racist and more tolerant to outsiders in comparison with their experiences in other countries. Emad, a thirty-five-year-old property developer based in London, stated: "Maybe it's just because London is so cosmopolitan, but I don't feel like a complete and utter outsider like I did in Norway." Fatima, a computer engineer based in Greater Manchester, noted: "In Germany, I only felt Iranian. Here I still feel Iranian, but I also feel Mancunian." These statements support responses to Nassehi-Behnam's (2010) findings on the consequences of September 11 on interethnic relations between Iranians and the British, which concluded that the event "did not have an important impact on the behaviour of English people towards Iranians."[34] Despite Nassehi-Behnam's findings, many British Iranians often feel misrepresented and distanced from the dominant discourses and negative stereotypes of Iran and Iranians, political Islam, and British Muslims.

The country's dominant model of citizenship in the twenty-first century has shifted from promoting multiculturalism toward so-called community cohesion, which is far more majoritarian. This shift stems from "ethnic segregation" becoming central to debates about integration and citizenship in the wake of urban unrest in northern English cities in 2001 that were closely followed by 9/11.

Iranians' Perceptions of Their Homeland

British Iranians' perceptions and narratives of their ancestral homeland rest on many factors, including personal biographies, group affiliations, and how they historicize and relate to Iran's social and political past. Homeland narratives are also shaped and reshaped by different interpretations of and engagements with key elements of Iranian culture and history such as: Iran's pre-Islamic heritage and legacy; the Arab defeat of the Sassanid Persian dynasty in the seventh century; the Persian language and Persian literature and poetry; Shiite tenets, practices, and politics; and wider religious, ethnic, and regional difference in Iran. Homeland narratives are also textured by different interpretations and stances toward key conjunctures and processes of state-building and modernization in Iran. The 1906 constitutional revolution; the Qajars' downfall in 1921; the rise of the Pahlavi dynasty in 1925; the departure of Shah Mohammad Reza Pahlavi; the fall of Mohammad Mosaddegh in 1953; the Shah's return; political struggles within and between nationalists, leftists, secularists, and Islamists; the 1979 revolution; the institutionalization of the *vali-ye faqih* (Guardianship of the Jurist or Providence of the Jurist); the turn to *shari'a* (moral code or religious law) and the enforcement of *hejab* (head, face, or body covering worn by Muslim women); contestations and strife between political factions in postrevolutionary Iran; and the Youth Movement—are all significant events and processes that are still widely debated, contested, and analyzed by British Iranians and the diaspora at large. While some British Iranians identify themselves enthusiastically with certain elements of Iranian culture and history, others feel embittered, alienated, or ambivalent. Some British Iranians long for repatriation while others have no wish to return.

Thus, it is through the different combinations of these enduring variables, together with experiences of negotiating entry to British society and its structures, that British Iranians' subjectivities and identities are negotiated, constructed, and maintained. Of course, the negotiating position, and the handling of multiple social identities, vary with length of residence in the host country and across generations. For example, the 1.5 generation and British-born Iranians, who have had less direct exposure to Iran's cultural and political landscapes, sift through and piece together fractured narratives of Iran as they simultaneously create and enable new voices and ways of being both British and Iranian. This might entail combining different parts of their cultural and political histories into new bricolages and assemblages, creating variations of their own. This process can be further complicated by the social exchanges between settled British Iranians, new Iranian refugees, and voluntary migrants to Britain, interaction with the wider diaspora, and ongoing discussion with networks in Iran. This communication leads to additional questions about authenticity, belonging, and attachment to Iran. Therefore, connections with Iranian heritage and contemporary life in Iran are multilayered, fluid, and context-specific.

To understand British Iranian identity construction it is essential to study the dynamics within and among the growing number of Iranian cultural, religious, media, and business activities in the host country, including the number of Persian-language schools and libraries, religious centers, charity organizations, community centers, cultural celebrations (particularly for *Noruz*, the Iranian New Year), poetry readings, music concerts and productions, academic conferences, film screenings and festivals, comedy shows, and so on. The many Iranian newspapers, magazines, and journals printed in London,[35] as well as internet-based newsgroups, blogs, and online dating sites, have also become a significant forum for communication and identity construction.[36] The ways in which Iranian identity is negotiated and performed through these cultural and media forms are complex and multifaceted and must be examined in relation to interrelated factors including gender, politics, generation, wealth, religion, ethnicity, and Iranians' social capital in British society. Indeed, among Britain's Iranians there are many contested and competing ways of *being* Iranian.

Secularism, Islam, and Iranian Identity

Perhaps unsurprisingly, contestations of Iranianness often revolve around questions of Islam and secularism, which continue to be divisive and decisive factors in community relations. It is important to bear in mind, though, that the various discourses and manifestations of Iranianness are not equally powerful. Nor do they equally present themselves as coherent and intent on social transformation. Gholami (2015) has argued that, in recent years, the contours and dynamics of "community" and "identity" have been increasingly redefined and reshaped by a particular form of intradiasporic secularism that marginalizes, excludes, and even eradicates the Islamic from "the Iranian"—he calls it "non-Islamiosity."[37] A detailed discussion of non-Islamiosity is beyond the scope this chapter.[38] Suffice it to say that it has had and is having a significant impact on how Iranians from diverse social, religious, and ethnic backgrounds live at the intradiasporic level. This is significant for two reasons. First, the particularities of migration flows to and settlement in Britain have been such that Iranians cannot take for granted a sense of a cohesive community or, indeed, positive community relations. Despite this, second, most Iranians desire a strong sense of community and often call for it openly. A reason commonly given by Iranians from diverse backgrounds as to why strong communal relations are important is that "this is the only way forward." However, Gholami's (2015) research on secular and devout Shiite Iranians in London found that both groups felt they had a great deal invested in intradiasporic relations. These investments were at once emotional, spiritual, social, cultural, political, and financial and encompassed highly intimate notions of past, present, and future. Because of these investments, some Iranians felt reluctant to show indifference to intradiasporic issues—such as devout Iranians being stigmatized by other Iranians for their religious beliefs and practices—whereas they could choose to treat relations with non-Iranians (including "British society") with relatively high degrees of apathy. In other words, they felt deeply implicated or tied up in intradiasporic relations. What is particularly interesting is that intradiasporic issues were experienced as immediately relevant and meaningful *regardless* of whether they were perceived to be positive or negative *and* regardless of how trivial they might seem to an outsider.

To give an example, one of Gholami's research participants, Ali (a pseudonym), a devout thirty-year-old male postgraduate student from London, described how one evening he and his family had been forced to finish their food quickly at an Iranian restaurant and leave sooner than planned because a scantily clad belly dancer suddenly started performing unannounced. A little more context is needed before we can fully appreciate the implications of Ali's experience. The restaurant in question, Persian Palace, is quite well known in London, and in recent years we have seen the establishment of many more Persian-style restaurants, including Persian Nights in Ealing and Prince of Persia in Harrow. As one would probably expect, the theme and décor of such establishments harken back to Iran's pre-Islamic heritage, making ample use of the usual symbols of the Persian empire—Persian Palace even offers a short history of the Persian empire on the back of its menu. As discussed earlier in this chapter, the Persian element is presented to evoke a unique sense of nostalgia—something mysterious and ancient yet strangely familiar and contemporary and, at any rate, desirable—to animate and drive Iranian desires for a yet-unfulfilled experience of identity and community. The nostalgia, therefore, is not for the past; it is for a particular sort of future (cf. Gholami 2015).

That is not the whole story, however. What also gives these emerging spaces of Iranian interaction and pleasure a sense of common identity is a careful exercise in selective inclusion and exclusion. Importantly, Iran's Islamic heritage is largely (often entirely) excluded. One might occasionally come across "something Islamic," for example a decorative piece of art such as a rug or a musical instrument. However, these references are immediately decoupled from Islam through a common recognition that they are part of Iranian (not Islamic) art and by being placed in an otherwise conspicuously un-Islamic setting. Furthermore, in higher-end restaurants it is increasingly the case that alcohol is served and the word *halal* is not displayed in the window. Of course, one may find exceptions, but the reason for this tends to be that those restaurants are situated in areas with a high concentration of (non-Iranian) Muslims whose business the restaurant tries to attract.

The flipside to this exclusion is an equally selective inclusion. Here, secular cultural forms from across Iranian and non-Iranian times and places are utilized to produce particular spaces in which certain types of individual and communal selves can be experienced and lived. From sassy pop music to live belly dancing (by mostly non-Iranian women!), from edgy music videos to antiregime sociopolitical programs from Los Angeles, most cafés and restaurants, explicitly or implicitly, champion and facilitate the consumption of a secular diasporic Iranian culture—a culture whose secularity is primarily characterized by its problematization and exclusion of Islam. On their face these secular forms do not have much to do with pre-Islamic Iran. (And let us not forget that the Persian empire can in no way be considered an irreligious place.)[39] But coupled with the Persian theme, they are especially potent in equating ideas of "true Iranianness" with neoliberal consumerism. Out of this conflation emerges an idea (or indeed a subject position) that has gained a great deal of purchase in recent years—that being a "true Iranian" implies having a sort of freedom to which Islam is essentially opposed.[40]

Let us now return to Ali: his experience of the surprise entertainment was, for him, a disconcerting one. Apart from the fact that his religious conviction forbade him to derive pleasure from looking at strange women (clothed or otherwise), he also said that some customers were giving this dancer money by sticking bills into her costume—which seems altogether inappropriate for a restaurant. This indicates that the moral/ethical boundaries of the British Iranian diaspora are in flux and raises the question of how and by whom they are being (re)defined. For Ali, as a devout Iranian Shiite, the answer was quite clear: he felt totally written out of "the community"—how it expresses and lives itself. Furthermore, given the fact that the belly dancing was unannounced, which is to say that the organizers took it for granted that their overwhelmingly Iranian clientele would simply accept it as entertainment, Ali also felt that "the community" did not want, or care about, practicing Iranian Muslims. To go back to the point that intradiasporic relations are experienced as significant regardless of positivity or negativity, Ali was unable to dismiss the incident with indifference. He could not satisfy himself, as he often did with other secular groups, that he simply did not seem to belong in such a (secular) setting—after all, he never went to the pub with his English colleagues. This is not to suggest that the secular Iranians in the restaurant had conspired to exclude Ali and his family. Rather, Ali felt sad and concerned that in increasingly secular (or non-Islamious) sociocultural relations, he was unable to express and live his Iranian identity freely without the fear of such surprises.

Whether Islam is treated with hostility or benign neglect, and whether pre-Islamic Persia informs fervent nationalism or is simply used to underpin ideas of Iranian heritage and culture, there is an emerging collective trend along the aforementioned lines. And it extends beyond restaurants and cafés into other spaces of sociocultural interaction such as the media and arts. In terms of media, British Iranians have access to a variety of television and radio stations, newspapers, magazines, and websites based both inside and outside the host country. We limit our discussion to UK-based media, the vast majority of which have a common "cultural," "national," and "secular" orientation that endorses noninvolvement in political issues pertaining to contemporary Iran and by extension issues related to Islam. (But this, as we will see, is not always adhered to or possible in practice.) For example, much of the programming of Manoto,[41] a popular London-based television channel, revolves around casting "ordinary" Iranians—they are in fact often quite eccentric!—to remake Iranian versions of popular British shows such as *Come Dine with Me*, where a group of seemingly perfect strangers host dinner parties for each other that they then grade. Manoto also shows dubbed versions of mainstream British programs such as *Downton Abbey* and *Mr. Selfridge*. As for politics, Manoto tends to limit its scope to global current affairs and, in line with most mainstream Western news channels, presents itself as impartial. Its dedicated news program, *otagh-e khabar* (*The News Room*), looks and feels very professional, with a group of journalists discussing current news stories and showing prerecorded reports. Interestingly, though, *The News Room* was recently mocked by Iranian state television.[42] A spoof sketch depicts the journalists quite crudely alongside caricatures of Barack Obama and "Israel" conspiring to stop Iran's nuclear program. Bizarrely, *The News Room*'s female host is played by an "effeminate" man in drag, ostensibly to be able to show "her" without a headscarf but clearly also to insinuate homosexuality. Iranians commenting on the sketch on YouTube were clearly dismayed by the crude depiction and used very explicit language to express their anger. This compels us to think seriously about the impact that a British Iranian medium is having around the world and not least inside Iran. But the point here is that this is one way in which—whether intentionally or not, and however secular and nonpolitical they claim to be—diasporic media become embroiled in Iranian politics, which inevitably is linked in sensitive ways to issues of religiosity and secularity.

Another way for British-Iranian media to become caught up in Iranian politics is by choosing to involve themselves in particular events. The many freely available magazines and newspapers are a good case in point.[43] Again, these media describe themselves as secular, cultural, and in the service of all Iranians, which of course implies impartiality and equal inclusion. However, during times of crisis for the Iranian regime, the tinge of their rhetoric tends to change markedly to show support for the opposition. For example, during Iran's election crisis in 2009, *Persian Weekly* printed special election editions carrying headlines such as "The Lump in Iran's Throat [Iran's Grudge] Has Burst (*Boghz-e Iran Tarekid*)."[44] Similarly, the front page of *Ava*'s June issue was green, the color of the opposition, with a black strip across the top left corner in honor of the casualties of the demonstrations. For these media, too, "secularity" often simply means excluding the Islamic aspects of Iranian culture and history. On the whole, these media tend to be almost entirely silent in commemorating key Islamic events such as *Eid-e fetr* and *Ashura*. However, they are very active in celebrating and advertising popular non-Islamic religious/cultural events such as *Mehregaan*, Christmas, and Valentine's Day. We can also include here London Persian Radio,[45] which plays pop music around the clock. However, the majority of the songs espouse a deeply nostalgic sort of nationalism that revolves around tropes of "saving our land" and "freedom" as well as references to mythic Persian heroes such as Arash Kamangir.

Of course, all this is not to suggest that Shiism has no place in the diverse landscape of Iranian sociocultural production in the United Kingdom. For instance, there are a number of British Iranian Sufi orders—such as the *Nimatullahi* Order and the MTO *Shahmaghsoudi* Order—that serve as a contemplative social, religious, and cultural base for some British Iranians.[46] Interestingly, like the Iranian media discussed above, many Sufi orders in the host country believe that the spiritual pathways of Sufism are rooted in the "reality" of the pure and authentic Islamic tradition and surpasses the "contaminated" religion promoted by elements of the Islamic regime and other Islamic groups around the world. In addition to the Sufi orders, there are many networks of devout (non-Sufi) Iranian Shiites who also actively practice their faith in the United Kingdom. For example, women-only ritualized gatherings, called *Sofrehs*, which have a long history in Iranian society, continue to be held by networks of British Iranian women in their homes and at religious centers.[47] The point made here, however, is that it is not Shiite religious discourses and practices that significantly animate emerging notions of diasporic Iranian identity and community. British Iranian Shiites are nonetheless major players in the emerging British Shiite community, which has become more established and integrated with non-Iranian Shiites in recent years.

Iranian Shiites in the United Kingdom and the Wider British Shiite Landscape

London is known to be the international headquarters of Shiism.[48] Nearly all of the prominent Shiite ayatollahs and *marjaje'* (sources of emulation)—such as Seyed Ali Khameneh'i, Seyed Ali as-Sistani, the late Seyed Abu al-Qasim al-Khu'i, the late Seyed Mohammed Husayn Fadlallah, Seyed Sadiq Al-Shirazi, and Ayatollah Naser Makarim Shirazi and Ayatollah Saafi Golpayegani—have representatives and offices that are largely based in northwest London.[49] Moreover, many prominent Shiite Iranian scholars, including Sheikh Shomali and Sheikh Bahmanpour, have studied and worked in the United Kingdom while actively engaged in transnational networks and activities of Shiites and their centers around the world. Indeed, there is a trend for Shiite scholars to receive religious training at the Islamic seminaries in Iran or Iraq; obtain a British postgraduate degree at the University of London, or Oxford, Cambridge, Exeter, or Manchester; and then teach at the Islamic College for Advanced Studies in London (or one of the other Shiite religious centers around the country). It is not unusual for Iranian Shiite leaders—and devout Iranian Shiites at large—to have strong, bonding, transnational networks. In addition to participating in religious, political, and economic activities among Iran, Britain, and other Western countries, making a pilgrimage to Karbala in Iraq has also become an important calendar event for British Iranian Shiites.

In recent years, networks of religious men and women, across ethno-national backgrounds and generations, have also started to see themselves as a part of wider British Shiite Muslim community.[50] Around 15 to 20 percent of the nearly three million Muslims in Britain are thought to be from Shiite backgrounds, making approximately 450,000 in total.[51] The majority of British Shiites are Twelver or *Ithna Asheris*.[52] The first substantial numbers of Twelver Shiites in the United Kingdom were men from South Asia, eventually joined by their families, who came as guest laborers following World War II. During the 1970s and 1980s, adverse political situations in Iran, Iraq, and Afghanistan brought the largest number of Shiites to the United Kingdom, followed by the Khojas, who left East Africa owing to the political turmoil in the newly independent countries. As such, Shiites in the United Kingdom come from diverse ethnonational, linguistic, educational, and class backgrounds and have different religious practices that are rooted in their ethnonational background and theological tradition. Some British Shiites, for example, endorse Khamenei, the Iranian supreme leader, and the doctrine of *Valayet-e faqih*.[53] They would be more inclined to attend gatherings and events at religious organizations such as the Islamic Student Association (Kanoon Towhid) and the Islamic Centre of England (Markaz-e Islmai-ye Englis) that are closely aligned to the Iranian government. The Islamic Universal Association (Majmah Eslami), which is financially independent from the Iranian government, mainly attracts devout Iranian Shiites who wish to stay clear of Iranian politics. Ayatollah Golpayegani, currently based in Qom, Iran, is the *marja* who represents and financially supports this center. Other British Shiites who do not believe in the doctrine of *Valayet-e faqih* and follow such *marjas* as Sistani or (the late) Fadlallah attend the religious programs at the Shiite centers that are linked to their rulings.

The proliferation of Shiite leaders and centers around the host country has made it possible to cater to Shiite ritual practices and jurisprudential rulings.[54] This is not to say that no internal differences exist within the British Shiite Muslim community. On the contrary, Shiite networks in Britain are diverse and highly competitive. Despite these internal differences, a wider British Shiite community has emerged in recent years. This is partly due to larger external forces, including the Iranian Revolution, the global influence and impact of Wahhabi and Salafi anti-Shiite campaigns, the fall of Saddam Hussein in Iraq in 2003, and the increasing sectarian and political violence in the Middle East and Pakistan. The British "Shi'a Awakening" has also been bolstered by greater coordination among the well-funded British Shiite institutions to deal with important life events such as weddings, divorces, and funerals. Internal debates among Shiites about the quintessential and debated Shiite customs, such as Ashura commemoration[55] and Muta marriages,[56] have also brought about greater communication, as well as the need for a united Shiite voice to counter Islamophobia and anti-Shiite campaigns. Finally, young British Shiites have developed novel ways to negotiate a Shiite religious belonging in light of and despite their other personal allegiances. For devout Iranian British Shiites, the expanding "Shiite diaspora" has become an additional base of belonging in British society.

British Iranian Ethnoreligious Groups

The non-Muslim Iranians, including Zoroastrians, Jews, Christians (Armenians, Assyrians and Protestant—Anglican and Evangelical converts), and Baha'is, also rely on community resources for additional support and solidarity in Britain. Unfortunately, very little research has been carried out on these communities and on how they relate to the wider Iranian diaspora. Based on interviews with members of these communities, we see that the Iranian ethnic and religious minorities are numerically smaller in size compared to their cohorts in the United States. Nevertheless, they have established strong institutional bases and social networks and have made inroads into British academic, political, business, and cultural sectors. These observations are similar to Bozorgmehr and Sabagh's work on ethnoreligious minorities in the Los Angeles.[57] Although religious minority groups, namely the "People of the Book"—the Zoroastrians, Jews, and ethnic Christians—are guaranteed religious freedom in Article 13 of the Constitution of the Islamic Republic, they have faced various degrees of discrimination in Iran and have often been accused of being linked to foreign countries such as Israel, Britain, and America.[58] It has been particularly difficult for Baha'is and Christian converts, who have faced death, imprisonment, and deprivation of jobs, pensions, and educational opportunities.[59] Not surprisingly, these subgroupings have been actively involved in exposing human rights issues and abuses in Iran.

The administration of the Baha'i community estimates there to be over 6,000 Baha'is in the United Kingdom with 127 local communities around the country. They do not reveal, however, the percentage of those coming from Iranian descent. The presence of Baha'is began with an American who settled in London in 1898. As D. Wheatley states:

The community grew from a single person in 1898 to the degree that between 1911 and 1913 when Abdul Bahá, the head of the Bahá'í community from 1892 to 1921, made two visits to the UK, the early Bahá'ís in these islands were sufficient in number, resources and organisation to arrange visits for him to several churches in London, and the Shah Jahan *masjid* in Woking, as well as trips to Bristol and Edinburgh.[60]

Although small in numbers, Baha'is are known for their governmental and international human rights work on the freedom of religion or belief, on discrimination and equality, and the protection in international human rights law. Their international human rights work correlates with the central theme of Bahá'u'llah's religious teaching that the future of humanity will be united in one global society. It is worth adding that their human rights activism connects them to the much wider and prolific human rights organizations and activities, many of which are internet-based. Interestingly, these online activities are obviously hard to pin down nationally and therefore blur the distinction between national diasporic groupings.

Much like the Baha'is, organizations supporting Muslim converts to Christianity facing harassment and persecution in Iran have a strong global online presence that highlights human rights abuses in Iran. There is no space to elaborate here, but the research carried out by Spellman (2004b) and Miller (2014) sheds light on the growth of Iranian Muslim conversion to born-again Christianity in England and Scotland and how the process of conversion is linked to the positive evocations of Iran's pre-Islamic past. Other Iranian religious and ethnic groups have found additional ways to negotiate and express their various identities and allegiances in the host society.

The Iranian Zoroastrian community is tight-knit and well organized, although it is small in number, with an estimated 500 people in the United Kingdom.[61] According the 2011 census, which includes Parsi Zoroastrians, there are 4,015 Zoroastrians living in England and Wales, with about 2,235 residing in London.[62] Their main fire temple is located on Rayners Lane, northwest London, and the World Zoroastrian Organisation is also based in London. The Iranian Zoroastrian community, along with Parsi members, were recently placed in the limelight with the high-profile exhibition *The Everlasting Flame: Zoroastrianism in History and Imagination*, mounted in the Brunei Gallery at the School of Oriental and African Studies. Despite the internal differences between members of the Zoroastrian community (in terms of theological differences, membership, class, and ethnicity), the arts have been a significant way for them to integrate in and contribute to British society.

The majority of Iranian Armenians are thought to live in west London and a smaller number in Manchester. Despite the fact that many Iranian Armenians travel to Iran periodically because they either have financial interests or family links, generally speaking they do not have a strong emotional affinity with Iran or the Iranian diaspora. That being said, several people reported that the regional differences among Armenian communities in Iran continue to play a role in the diaspora. For instance, Armenians from Tabriz tend not to socialize with those from either Tehran or the region around Isfahan, and vice-versa. On a larger scale, there has been greater effort by British Iranian Armenians to nurture a sense of affinity with the wider Armenian diaspora. As stated by the anthropologist Susan Pattie: "While transnational religious, social and political institutions have kept Armenians connected to post-genocide and dispersion, an increasingly diverse use of the arts among Armenians in the diaspora and the Republic of Armenia has encouraged exploration and dialogue about identity."[63] The performance organized by the Armenian Institute in London in 2013, *Salon Mashup: Displacement and Regeneration, Armenian Perspectives of Loss and Resettlement*, which brought together Armenian artists, performers, and audience members to interactively explore the tensions between "the dualities of separation and assimilation, remembrance and comprehension, memory and the present" was a case in point.[64]

Similar to Iranian Armenians, British Iranian Jews are also keen "to preserve and renew collective memory and culture of earlier times when the region, or its cities, were much more diverse and cosmopolitan than they have become after decades of ethno-religious pressures against difference."[65] Although the vast majority of Iranian Jews in the Western world live in the United States, some have found a home in Great Britain, and most live of them in London or in Manchester. British Iranian Jews also see themselves as part of wider Jewish networks; many are also active in the cosmopolitan networks in the United Kingdom and beyond. A famous example is Dr. Nasser Khalili, a prominent figure in the art world and education sector and a renowned philanthropist. He is well known for having the largest private collection of Islamic art. He is the cofounder of the Iran Heritage Foundation (IHF), which will be discussed in more detail below.

As the British Iranian ethnoreligious groups continue to be rooted within their family and communal networks, some participate with wider networks of sociability that include other Iranians with whom they might share the Persian language and cultural memories of the Iranian homeland. Many, of course, participate in wider British and cosmopolitan circles through their cultural, intellectual, and professional interests and affiliations.

British Iranian Cultural Production

The United Kingdom is known internationally for being a global center for cultural production and commerce. British Iranians, making the most of Britain's well-developed cultural industries, have flourished in terms of artistic and educational activities. Although London and New York City have been hubs for Iranian artists since the 1960s, the diaspora has provided a particularly important forum for Iranian artists to freely express their artistic visions, which has obviously been limited in postrevolution Iran. Some British Iranian cultural organizations, as well as individual artists, have also found creative ways to maintain connections to their histories and homeland while establishing a strong public presence in their host country. Let us turn to a few examples.

The Iran Heritage Foundation was the first diasporic cultural organization in the United Kingdom, and perhaps in the wider diaspora, to invest systematically in the preservation of Iran's culture and heritage. Drawing from aesthetics rooted in classic Persian and Islamic history, art, architecture, and literature, it has developed hundreds of projects aimed at preserving the past. It also supports Iranian academics and artists living in both the diaspora and in Iran to redefine "Iranianness" in contemporary language.[66] IHF was established in 1996 as a nonpolitical, British-registered charity by a group of affluent Iranians based mainly in London. According to Farhad Hakimzadeh, the founding chief executive officer from 1996 to 2008, "The motivation was to promote the culture and heritage of Iran and introduce Westerners to the little-known nuances of Iran and its people."[67] IHF's main sources of funding have been annual pledges from their trustees and the money generated at lavish gala charity events, particularly the annual *Noruz* celebration. The following list of lecture/film events in the 2014 program is a good indicator of IHF's activities and interests: "Persepolis: the Life and Afterlife of a World Wonder," a lecture by Dr. Ali Mousavi; "Recollections of Archaeology in Iran," a lecture by professor David Stronach, OBE, FSA; *Iran's Natural Heritage*, a screening of documentary films; "Modern Iranian Art," a lecture by Morad Montazami; Iranian food events and panel discussions, followed by a buffet. The archetypal themes of exile, such as homeland-diaspora relations, collective memory, belonging, and cultural authenticity, are often explored through IHF commissions.

It is fair to say that the IHF has become part of the British establishment (and in the United States, too, with the development of IHF America). Taking stock of the currency of the arts and education, IHF has managed to galvanize partnerships with key British figures and institutions. Board members include Lord Lamont of Lerwick and the Conservative Party MP (now prime minister) Theresa May, and it has built partnerships with prestigious arts and educational organizations, including the British Museum, Tate Modern, the Barbican, Oxford University, Cambridge University, and the School of Oriental and African Studies. Similarly, IHF America collaborates with US institutions such as the J. Paul Getty Museum in Los Angeles, the Freer and Sackler Galleries of the Smithsonian Institution based in Washington, DC, the Metropolitan Museum of Art in New York City, and the Asian Art Museum in San Francisco.

Although occasionally reproached by some British Iranians for monopolizing the British Iranian arts and cultural scenes, IHF has been central in preserving, innovating, and showcasing Iran's cultural and intellectual traditions in the diaspora. In turn, IHF members have generated social capital and made important inroads into their respective host societies.

There are plenty of other examples of British Iranians' engagement with the arts and education sectors. In Scotland, for example, the annual Edinburgh Iranian Festival (EIF) has been taking place since 2009. Affiliated with Edinburgh University's Persian Society, the organizers' aims are to

> introduce the tremendous breadth of Iranian history and culture to adults and children living in Scotland; integrate the Iranian community into Scottish society through a broad range of interactive events spanning across a wide range of art forms; and encourage interaction between British and Iranian artists, performers and historians.[68]

The EIF is clearly very ambitious, and successful, in terms of the sheer number of events it sponsors,[69] ranging from plays and films to lectures and concerts and even bazaars, tea houses, and "rug villages." It is also very well attended, with the 2009 festival being visited by 2,500 people. What is particularly interesting to note here is that, although the majority of Britain's Iranians live in London,[70] a similar cultural festival has never been organized in London. That is to say, London does not host such a consistently large-scale and annually recurring celebration of Iranian culture. What is also interesting is that the EIF addresses *Scotland* very specifically—rather than Great Britain or the United Kingdom generally. Further research is required to learn more about the extent to which Scottish Iranians feel connected to, or would identify themselves as, "British Iranians."

Iranian live performance has also been taking off in recent years. Iranian theater companies such as the Saam Company, based in north London, have become increasingly active both locally and globally. For instance, in

2013 Saam collaborated with the celebrated Iranian playwright Iraj Janati-Attaei to produce *A Private Dream*, a play featuring the acting icon Behrouz Vosoughi, who lives in California, and the young actress Golshifteh Farahani, who was involved in controversy when she posed topless for a French magazine. The play was extremely well received by British Iranians. These activities are also gaining wider recognition as they manage to attract funding from national sources. Since 2013, Saam has been organizing the London Persian-English International Theatre Festival. With funding from Arts Council England, this five-day festival brings together and showcases Iranian actors and playwrights from all over the world. The company also periodically receives funding from the National Lottery Fund for some of its community projects, which include acting classes coupled with English-language training or education and tend to place emphasis on family participation. One of its previous projects encouraged Persian-speaking families to perform their narratives of migration and offered participants, in addition to English lessons, counseling sessions. Clearly, Saam believes its role is also to support and somehow improve the lives of diasporic Iranians.

Another important area for Iranian live performance is stand-up comedy. The popular London-based Iranian satirist Hadi Khorsandi used to perform (in Persian) frequently but seems to have become less active in recent years. However, stand-up is arguably the art form in which Iranians have had the most success, managing to break fully into the British mainstream. Khorsandi's daughter, Shappi, is notable in this context. She has become a household name in Britain as a result of appearing on popular TV comedy shows such as *Live at the Apollo*, shown on BBC1. Her repertoire is quite varied (thus appealing to mainstream audiences) and ranges from material about marriage and being a woman to technology and racism. However, she also has jokes specifically about Iran and being Iranian. Arguably, these jokes tend to play to (or appease) the expectations of contemporary Western audiences by reinforcing common stereotypes. For example, Shappi tells of her cousin Mohammed having to change his name to "it wasn't me." In another joke, she says that the "real" difference between Iran and Iraq is that "we [Iranians] are the ones *with* weapons of mass destruction."

This sort of self-deprecating and stereotyping humor is also a noticeable part of the work of Omid Djalili, another Iranian comedian popular with mainstream audiences. Having been raised in a middle-class family in the affluent London borough of Kensington and Chelsea, Djalili has appeared in Hollywood blockbusters including the *Pirates of the Caribbean* series and *Gladiator*. He has also starred in West End plays and had his own show on the BBC. However, he often portrays himself and other Iranians as quite crude and vulgar. References to Islam play a big part in these depictions. For example, during one of his shows he made a "genuine confession" to the audience: "I am as alarmed as anybody in this room by the sight of Arabs at the airport—even family members!" In another show, he talked about making a soap opera titled *Middle-East Enders*.[71] Its theme song, which Djalili made up on stage, was a series of random repetitions of the word "Allah" and ended with the word "Hezbollah"; the characters (who for some reason retained their Western names) kept refusing alcoholic drinks because they were Muslims and it was Ramadan; the Islamic call to prayer substituted for the last call for alcohol in a pub; and a "Muslim" man tried to haggle over a £500 computer by offering £1 and a glimpse of his wife's ankles. Another comedian worth mentioning here is the Irish Iranian Patrick Monahan. Similar to Khorsandi and Djalili, Monahan derives a great deal of material from stereotyping his Iranian background and from his knowledge of the Persian language. In one joke, for example, he begins speaking Persian to an unsuspecting group of Iranians in his audience. He asks them trivial questions such as if they are well and what they do for a living, to which they reply truthfully in Persian. He then translates this to the rest of the audience as a warning that the building is about to be blown up and they only have a few minutes to evacuate.

Judging by this trio it does seem that, in order for an Iranian comedian to break into the British mainstream, he/she is almost expected to perform crude, stereotypical, and self-deprecating material—despite the fact that this is misrepresentative of Iranians both inside and outside Iran (as these comedians also acknowledge sometimes). Moreover, it seems as though their Iranian identity not only adds "authenticity" to this material but also allows them to push the envelope, as it were, further in terms of controversy than any non-Iranian mainstream comedian could. All this notwithstanding, many British Iranians are greatly supportive of these comedians because they have managed to break into the mainstream and as such are believed to ultimately help give Iranians a better image in the eyes of the Western majority.

Conclusion

This chapter has looked at the diversity and complexity of Iranian lives in Britain. It has demonstrated that finding a distinct Iranian place in, and adapting to, British society are two processes at work—processes driven by differing degrees of willingness and assertiveness in terms of the integration or preservation of various religious, secular, national, ethnic, and gendered subjectivities. However, during these processes the subjectivities themselves often also become redefined, giving rise to entirely new modalities of living, power structures, and sociocultural relations. We saw, for example, how a particular deployment of secularism and Persian identity have impacted the ways in which some Iranians interact in the wider Iranian diasporic community in Britain. Spellman Poots's recent work (2012) provides evidence to suggest that devout Iranian Shiites may increasingly be seeing themselves as part of an emerging, cross-ethnic British Shiite community, in addition to an Iranian one. The extent to which there is a correlation between these trends is an interesting question for future research.

There are other pressing questions that future research on UK Iranians has to explore. As we have seen throughout this chapter—in the case of restaurants, schools, and cultural organizations, for example—issues of community, especially in relation to institutional practices, must take center stage in this context. In a survey carried out by Sreberny and Gholami (2016) of 262 UK Iranians, 64 percent of respondents said that there is such a thing as "an Iranian community" in Britain—implying a degree of felt cohesion— while 25 percent said that multiple Iranian communities exist. Less than 8 percent believed that a community does not exist (Sreberny and Gholami 2016). This is an interesting finding given the scattered nature of Iranian settlement as well as the fact that received knowledge often holds that Iranians are not very communal. How is this community being developed, defined, and lived? What do its power structures look like? What modes of sociocultural belonging does it offer or limit? These, and no doubt more, are key questions. And although our own recent work has begun to answer them— see Gholami's argument that non-Islamiosity is playing a huge role in "community" formation—there are still many dimensions left to explore.

The question of British Iranians' interaction with Iranians elsewhere is particularly relevant for scholarly endeavors and poses an interesting theoretical conundrum. This chapter has shown that the British Iranian diaspora has features and processes that are unique to the British context. As such, we have tried our best to write with an awareness of Britain's social, political, and historical realities. However, the fact that British Iranian lives are thoroughly interlaced with the rest of British society raises a question about the extent to which we can usefully talk of *one* global Iranian diaspora. In fact, Graham and Khosravi (2002) have suggested that, given the sheer degree of heterogeneity found among diasporic Iranian voices and positions online, we should be thinking in terms of multiple Iranian diasporas. The merits of this argument notwithstanding, members of Britain's Iranian population—in their mind-boggling heterogeneity—have deeply meaning-ful connections with Iranians across the globe that play a significant part in shaping their lived realities. Apart from private family and business con-nections, for example, many of the restaurants mentioned earlier, as well as other public spaces of interaction, expose their customers to live TV from Los Angeles and Dubai. Discourses and practices of "community" come to exist to a large extent in such consumption patterns. Furthermore, the fact that the Iran Heritage Foundation has expanded its activities to the United States demonstrates its belief that the "Iranian diasporic project" is global in nature and is relevant to, and resonates with, Iranians outside the United Kingdom. By the same token, there can be little doubt that the connections are mutually productive and that British Iranians help to shape the experi-ence of Iranians elsewhere—the reactions to Iranian state television's mock-ing of Manoto's news program, and the international success of British-Iranian artists like Omid Djalili, being cases in point.

Theoretically, therefore, we would argue that the Iranian diaspora can be usefully viewed within the framework offered by Pnina Werbner (2002) in which she draws on an analogy with the Visa credit card and conceives of diasporas as "chaordic." Such a theoretical stance would mean acknowledg-ing that the Iranian diaspora is not singular or unified in terms of having a central command structure. Rather, as we have seen throughout this chap-ter, it comprises a multitude of local, translocal, transnational, and global positions, activities, and networks. Of course, these are often discontinuous and contradictory. But they are also all buying into, identifying with, and competing to produce and represent the *Iranian* diaspora. Importantly, tak-ing this approach allows us to examine and better understand the ways in which various groupings and movements impact each other directly or in-directly; as we saw above, irrespective of their differences, many Iranians care a great deal about what is happening at the intradiasporic level, even if they disagree with it or are negatively affected by it.

Notes

1. We conceptualize "homeland" not only as a territorial site from which people claim to have originated but also as the feeling of belonging to a geographical site and how the site is remembered, made meaningful, and/or symbolized. The concept of "home" may refer to multiple physical locations and/or feelings that can be con-nected to certain people, cultural objects, familiar smells, and familiar habits. See Brah (1996); Al-Ali and Koser (2002).

2. The approach we take to diasporas and identity is informed by Hall (2002: 31); Gilroy (1994); Naficy (2001); Bhabha (1990); Tololyan (2007).

3. See Basch et al. (1995: 1).

4. The census information cited in this section is taken from the Office for National Statistics, 2011 Census: aggregate data (England and Wales) [computer file], and National Records of Scotland, 2011 Census: aggregate data (Scotland) [computer file]. UK Data Service Census Support, infuse.mimas.ac.uk. This information is licensed under the terms of the Open Government Licence, www.nationalarchives.gov.uk/doc/open-government-licence/version/2.

5. www.nomisweb.co.uk/query/asv2htm.aspx.

6. Greater Manchester consists of the following districts: City of Manchester, Stockport, Tameside, Oldham, Rochdale, Bury, Bolton, Wigan, City of Salford, and Trafford.

7. Gholami has often asked interview participants to list the most important cities to the Iranian diaspora. Los Angeles and London have most frequently occupied first and second position, respectively. London's centrality is also well documented in pre- and postrevolution cultural outputs, both domestic and diasporic.

8. For a discussion of these works, see Gholami (2015).

9. See Haghighat (2012: 54).

10. See Hesse-Lehmann (1993: 3–7).

11. See Spellman (2004a: chap. 4).

12. Exceptional Leave to Remain (ELR), according to the Refugee Council, "was a form of immigration status in use before April 2003. It was granted to asylum seekers who the Home Office decided did not meet the definition of a refugee as defined in the Refugee Convention but it decided should be allowed to remain in the UK for other reasons." See Refugee Council, *Terms and Definitions*, November 24, 2014, www.refugeecouncil.org.uk/glossary#E.

13. webarchive.nationalarchives.gov.uk/20110220105210/rds.homeoffice.gov.uk/rds/pdfs/hosb1701.pdf.

14. UNHCR defines refugees as "individuals recognised under the 1951 Convention to the Status of Refugees in its 1967 Protocol; those recognised in accordance with the UNHRC Statute individuals granted complementary forms of protection; or, those enjoying 'temporary protection.'" See UN High Commissioner for Refugees, *UNHCR Global Trends 2012: Displacement, The New 21st Century Challenge*, June 19, 2013, www.refworld.org/docid/51c169d84.html, 39. Asylum seekers are individuals who have sought international protection and whose claims for refugee status have not yet been determined.

15. www.irainc.org/iranref/statistics.php.

16. Ibid.

17. Although not exclusively Iranian, the Refugee Women's Association was set up by an Iranian woman, Parvin Paidar, and continues to be run by Simin Azimi.

18. See, for instance, Sir Anthony Sherley, *His Relation of His Travels into Persia* (London, 1613); Sir John Chardin, *Travels in Persia*, ed. P. Sykes (London, 1927). J. Fraser, *History of Nader Shah* (London, 1742); D. Wright, *The English amongst the Persians* (London, 1977) and *The Persians amongst the English* (London 1985); M. Rollin, *The Ancient History of the Egyptians, Carthaginians, Assyrians, Babylonians, Medes and Persians, Grecians and Macedonians* (Edinburgh, 1832); E. Gibbon, *The History of the Decline and Fall of the Roman Empire*, vol. 1 (London, 1776); J. Malcolm, *The History of Persia from the Most Early Period to the Present Time*, 2nd ed., vol. 1 (London, 1829); R. W. Bullard, *Letters from Tehran* (London, 1991).

19. Marashi (2008: 24).

20. Martin (2011: 2).

21. Ansari (2005: 16).

22. Ibid.

23. Zia-Ebrahimi (2011).

24. See Roy (2004).

25. downloads.bbc.co.uk/mediacentre/country-rating-poll.pdf.

26. Pew Research Center, Washington, DC, "Global Views of Iran Over-whelmingly Negative," June 11, 2013, www.pewglobal.org/files/2013/06/Pew-Global-Attitudes-Project-Iran-Report-FINAL-June-11-2013.pdf.

27. This mistrust was popularized by Iraj Pezeshkzad's 1973 novel, *My Uncle Napoleon*, which was turned into a hugely successful TV series directed by Nasser Taghvai in 1976. Iranians still quote famous lines from the series to describe "the British" (or "the English") in their everyday conversations about British society, British foreign policy, and life in Britain generally.

28. Pew Research Center, "Global Views of Iran Overwhelmingly Negative."

29. Nassehi Behnam (2010: 79).

30. Ibid.

31. The Iranian Association claims that it annually deals with between 14,000 and 20,000 requests for support in a host of issues ranging from education to migration. In terms of education, it responds to the community's needs by providing classes on English language (ESL), how to pass the UK's Citizenship Test, job searching, general literacy and numeracy, health and hygiene, and so on: www.iranianassociation.org.uk/index.php/services.

32. rustamschool.org.uk.

33. See Spellman (2004b).

34. Nassehi-Behnam (2010).

35. Mass-media forms are aimed at and marketed to various socioeconomic, political, religious, and ethnic networks in the United Kingdom. The main newspapers—*Kayhan*, *Nimrooz*, and *Etela'at*—mainly carry news from Iran; they also advertise, for Iranians, services and events around the diaspora. Magazines and newspapers such as *Banu*, *Niazmandihah*, *Nameye Digar*, and *British-Iranian Business News and E-run* focus(ed) more attention on problems and issues facing Iranians outside Iran and circulated information about Iranian cultural events. Iranian TV channels from Iran and Los Angeles, and more recently the United Kingdom, are also readily available.

36. Many interviewees reported that the internet is ideal because they do not like to attend Iranian cultural events but they like to talk anonymously in chatrooms about topics such as Iranian identity, dating, marriage, and politics. It is also an important medium for the organization and expression of political opposition and resistance in the Iranian diaspora. The internet and other sorts of media have also been used in creative ways to reinforce the aims and objectives of the religious organizations.

37. Gholami (2014).

38. See ibid. and Gholami (2015).

39. On the issue of religion in pre-Islamic Persia, see, inter alia, Davaran (2010).

40. See Gholami (2015).

41. Informal form of *man va to* (me and you).

42. www.youtube.com/watch?v=tiOijoOSCxY.

43. Established publications include: *Persian Weekly, Ava-ye Landan, No Bahar Weekly, Persian Herald, Barg-e Sabz*, and *Bazaar-e Hafteh*. These are available at most Iranian outlets. They are also a major source of communication, as Iranians advertise a range of goods, services, and opinions in them.

44. *Persian Weekly*, issue 101, June 19, 2009, front-page headline.

45. londonpersianradio.net.

46. See Spellman (2004b).

47. Ibid., chap. 3.

48. This research is based on Spellman Poot's ongoing ethnographic study centered on young British Shiite Muslims, funded by the British Academy.

49. In the absence of Mahdi, *marja'e*, who are mainly based in Iran and Iraq, are deemed to be the most learned juridical authority figures in the Shiite community and have the highest authority to make binding decisions for those who acknowledge and commit to their rulings.

50. We are using the term "community" as used by our interviewees themselves.

51. See 2011 census results.

52. Twelvers, or *Ithna asheri*, are Shiite Muslims who believe in twelve Imams, descending from the Prophet Mohammed through his daughter Fatima and son-in-law, Ali. The twelfth Imam is believed to be in occultation and will come again.

53. *Valayat-e Faqih*, or Guardianship of the Jurist, is a concept purporting that religious scholars have the exclusive right to interpret Islamic law. It was first applied as a form of government when Khomeini came to power in 1979.

54. See Spellman-Poots (2012).

55. Ashura, which falls on the tenth day of the month of Muharram, is a significant holy day for Shiites to commemorate the martyrdom of Imam Hussain, the grandson of the Prophet Mohammed.

56. *Mut'a* marriage, also known as *Sigheh* in Persian, is a form of marriage in Shiite jurisprudence that allows a man and women to be legitimately married to each other for a specified period of time and in exchange for a specified amount of money or material reward for the woman.

57. See Borzorgmehr and Sabagh and Der-Martirosian (1993).

58. See Sanasarian (2000), www.fidh.org/IMG/pdf/IrandiscrimLDDHI545a.pdf, and iranprimer.usip.org/blog/2013/sep/03/iran-minorities-1-diverse-religions.

59. See Spellman (2004), www.refworld.org/cgibin/texis/vtx/rwmain?page=search&docid=51371a3c2&skip=0&query=A/67/369, and www.refworld.org/docid/51371a3c2.html.

60. Wheatley, in *Middle East in London*, a magazine published by SOAS.

61. This estimate was provided by Malcolm M. Deboo, president of the Zoroastrian Trust Funds of Europe, Harrow, UK.

62. www.nationalarchives.gov.uk/doc/open-government-licence/version/2.

63. Pattie (2013).

64. Ibid.

65. Spellman-Poots and Zubaida (2013: 7).

66. Over the past eighteen years it has commissioned and supported thirty-six multidiscipline events and exhibitions; sixty-two film and performance arts events; nine academic and travel grants; forty academic conferences; seven university fellowships; and sixty-five cultural and academic publications.

67. farhadhakimzadeh.wordpress.com/2013/02/25/iran-heritage-foundation.

68. Quoted from the festival's official website, www.ediranfest.co.uk/about_us .html.

69. In 2009, thirty-five events took place.

70. According to the 2011 census, 36,250.

71. Spoofing the popular British soap *EastEnders*.

CHAPTER 5

Transmigration, Proximity, and Sociopolitical Disconnection: Iranians in the United Arab Emirates

BEHZAD SARMADI

Studies of Iranian migration, despite their growth in recent years, continue to train our attention on the social worlds of Iranian émigrés residing in the "Global North." The contemporary travels and transnational connections of Iranian populations around Iran's orbit and in the "Global South," therefore, have been largely neglected.[1] This chapter is an attempt to remedy this by offering ethnographic analysis focusing on the Persian Gulf. I examine the shared imaginings, lived experiences, and structural circumstances of working-class Iranians in Dubai. I do so in order to contribute an alternative analytic lens to the broader study of Iranian migration, specifically one that foregrounds *impermanence* and *proximity* rather than *permanence* and *distance*. This research grew out of an interest in examining Iranian experiences with Dubai's recent urban transformation, especially as they varied based on class. What initially led me to engage with the working-class Iranians who are the subject of this chapter was the fact that the area of the city where they worked and lived was marked for demolition. I have opted to focus on their reality rather than those of their middle-class counterparts because I wish to emphasize the structural vulnerabilities that produce impermanence, as well as the interpersonal connections that rely on proximity.

I was fairly confident about the focus of my research project before I left for the field in early 2010. My confidence was not misplaced. "After all," I thought, "I grew up in Dubai; who better to know where to look and what kinds of questions to ask?" It was not long, however, before I was humbled by the task ahead of me. An early lesson in humility came in the form of a question from one of my working-class interlocutors: "You're here to study us, well then, can you speak our language?" He posed the question in Persian, but he wanted to know if I spoke Achomi, a Persian dialect prevalent in the smaller cities and towns of some southern provinces in Iran. "Unfortunately not," I said, "it's no longer taught at the University of Toronto." My interlocutors appreciated this attempt at humor and explained: "That's because it's a *dāhāt-i* language." *Dahat-i* is the adjective form of *dāhāt*, or "village." In Iranian vernacular, it bears connotations of backwardness or a lack of sophistication. Their point was to explain why my preparations for fieldwork had neglected to culturally differentiate this kind of Iranian migrant from others in Dubai.

I refer to this episode because I believe that my anthropological blind spot was indicative of a larger blind spot in the literature on Iranian migration. These working-class Iranians in Dubai are part of a particular "transnational social field" that links their hometowns in southern Iran with cities on the southern shores of the Persian Gulf. In analyzing this social field, I ask questions about the "ordinary ethics" (Lambek 2010) that sustain it; that is, their shared understandings of "the good life," the hardships to be endured while striving toward it, and the moral geography that encompasses them. What kinds of persons, or moral subjects, did these working-class Iranian men imagine that traveling to Dubai enabled them to be? How was this mobile personhood justified according to their sense of place about Dubai and Iran? In answering these questions, I take up their shared conceptions of *gheirat* (honor) and *sakht-ī keshīdan* (enduring hardship) as the ethical criteria underpinning their precarious life as transmigrants.

I begin by explaining my research methodology and the caveats that accompany ethnographic research in Dubai. I then situate this research in relation to the larger scholarship on Iranian migration, and I critique what I take to be its geographic bias. This is followed by a brief history of migration from Iran to Dubai, including a sketch of the current state of Iranian society in this city. This is followed by an elaboration of the social world of these working-class Iranians. I take up their moral geography to shed light on the particular kind of transnational mobility they practice and the kind of personhood they associate with it. To this end, I focus on a particular articulation of this personhood: the *ziāratī*. I argue that this figure crystallizes both the precariousness and moral striving that these men associate with life in Dubai. The overarching theme running throughout these sections is the lived significance and structural circumstances of proximity and impermanence.

Research Methodology and Setting

This chapter draws from fifteen months of ethnographic fieldwork in Dubai, intermittently conducted between 2008 and 2012. I relied primarily on extensive participation-observation with working- and middle-class Iranian residents. With regard to the former, I chose to focus on a particular inner-city area known for its concentration of small retailers staffed and managed by Iranians. Due to the nature of participant-observation, it was the crews of seven such Iranian retailers whom I regularly interacted with so as to culti-vate the intimacy and trust that this research aimed for. After a few months, I relied on snowball sampling to conduct semistructured interviews with members of their extended social network in the area.

These crews numbered between five and eight men, mostly hailing from cities and small towns in the southern Iranian provinces of Fars and Hor-mozgan. They also varied in age: from the seventeen-year-old who had left high school to pursue work as an apprentice mechanic, to his *arbāb*, or "manager," who was in his midforties.[2] Their shops specialized in auto parts and services, which this particular area was known for. To their operators and their Iranian customers, these shops were either called *pancharchi* (an auto shop offering mechanical services and repairs) or *taz'inat-i* (an auto shop specializing in the customization of car interiors and bodies).

The urban milieu of these working-class Iranians is also worth noting, as it highlights the circumstances of my access to them and the rhythms of their everyday life. Running through this area was a long and bustling thor-oughfare situated between low-rise buildings on either side. These buildings featured small shops opening onto the sidewalk. The goods and staff of these retailers sometimes extended onto the sidewalk, mingling with the throngs of passersby. Our meetings often took place later in the afternoon, when the crowds and cars were beginning to descend on the strip. This was also when crewmembers were returning from their apartments, located either in the same building as their shops or one nearby. Soon, they would be attending to their customers and their vehicles while hunched over the hood, tinker-ing with the radio settings, installing new tires, replacing the black tint on the windows, applying decorative stickers, and so on.

Late into the evenings, when the crowds subsided and the shops were shuttered, we would retire to their small apartments for dinner. These apart-ments were homosocial spaces. They had just a couple of bedrooms, and each of these had several bunk beds. Before dinner was served, there was the little ritual of recapping the day over drinks and cigarettes.[3] These conversa-tions thus provided an occasion for these men to talk, joke, and vent with-out the regular interruptions from customers. Reasons for actions could be given, challenged, and reconsidered, rendering explicit moral conventions that are otherwise implicit during the stream of everyday practices. It was often here that an Iranian Canadian could befriend crewmembers and learn of their shared knowledge.

Like all major social scientific research projects conducted in Arab societies of the Persian Gulf, my research project also has its share of limitations. My analysis in this chapter requires the mention of three. First, demographic data on the national composition of foreign residents is a matter of political sensitivity and not readily available. I have thus been unable to acquire official data or estimates on the size of the Iranian population in Dubai. As I explain in the last section, the context informing this sensitivity is a significant numerical discrepancy between citizens and foreign residents, as well as the ethnonational politics that continues to regard it as a threat to the nation.[4] Second, as I focus on a section of Dubai's population that is regularly targeted for policing—dragnets seeking to arrest undocumented workers—I have decided to omit the name of the inner-city area that concerns this chapter. Third, this structural vulnerability severely limited my capacity to undertake random surveys from which to better generalize about the structural circumstances of working-class Iranians in Dubai. Whether it was expressions of skepticism, or outright accusations of being a "spy" (*jāsus*), I was ultimately met with a refusal to participate.

Of Other Destinations

Scholarship on Iranian migration continues to examine the cultural production, shared vocabularies, and structural circumstances of Iranian immigrants in Europe, North America, and Australia. To these ends, scholars have relied on a variety of analytic tropes—such as "exilic haggling,"[5] "identity control,"[6] "cultural hybridity,"[7] and "liminality"[8]—so as to examine the lived experiences of reconciling life *away from* Iran, with discourses and policies that continue to mark these populations as *derived from* Iran. However, studies of Iranian migration remain overwhelmingly focused on the Global North. This geographic bias reflects that of the broader scholarship on transnationalism that coalesced in the 1990s, which often eschewed South-South migration.[9]

In this section, I explain how focusing on Iranian émigrés living in the Global North forecloses our knowledge of transnational experiences and imaginings that are born of proximity to Iran and impermanence of residency. I begin by offering a brief overview of some key currents in the literature on Iranian migration. Despite important theoretical shifts, I argue that this literature continues to take for granted the regulatory logic of liberalism that prevails in the settings under study. I then elaborate the regulatory logic of ethnocracy, which underpins the everyday lives of migrants in the United Arab Emirates (UAE), as it does in all Arab states of the Persian Gulf.

In a review of the burgeoning scholarship on Iranian immigrants, Karim and Elahi (2011) adopt the concept of "diaspora" as especially well suited to understanding the increasingly diverse ways in which "Iranians have . . . reinvented themselves as a distinct national and ethnic group outside of Iran."[10] They explain its suitability by noting the ongoing incorporation of Iranian émigrés into the societies in which they live, as well as the recognition of their "ethnic legitimacy"[11] that this process has involved. Indeed, much recent scholarship has examined various ways in which different generations of Iranian émigrés actively participate in the civil societies of these (liberal) polities as its hyphenated members. Such participation, to list a few examples, includes the public celebration of Iranian cultural heritage,[12] the cultivation of nostalgia among second-generation youth mobilizing on university campuses,[13] the mediation of "home" and dual nationality through blogging,[14] the production of literary works such as memoirs,[15] and the development of cultural organizations relying on policies of multiculturalism.[16]

These recent studies and their concern for diasporic practices and identitarian hybridity mark a departure from earlier scholarship on Iranian émigrés and refugees. The latter—largely focused on the United States—was often more concerned with the socioeconomic profile, intra-ethnic divisions, and enclave economies of Iranians arriving in the 1980s.[17] Yet the struggle with identity was not absent from these works. In addition to ambivalence about assimilation,[18] and alienation from fellow Iranians,[19] we learned of organized efforts to craft an "exilic" identity through cultural production. The latter, of course, refers to Naficy's groundbreaking 1993 analysis of the televisual culture produced by Iranians in Los Angeles. Informing this televisual culture, he explained, was a "considerable tension between the resistive communitas and incorporative structuration."[20]

This tension continues to reverberate in the cultural activities of 1.5- and second-generation Iranian émigrés, the focus of recent scholarship. It also points to two socially mediated moral imperatives that underpin the lives of migrants in liberal polities: living as a member of such a polity, while also claiming the heritage of another. However disparate the immigration policies of liberal democracies may be, they do not limit formal citizenship to ethnic criteria.[21] Political membership, in other words, is officially disarticulated from ethnicity, allowing for the possibility of naturalization. What is more, to varying degrees immigrant populations are also afforded the rights and resources required to assemble cultural organizations and ethnic lobbies.[22] Indeed, whether we read earlier or more recent studies of Iranian migration, we often find that their Iranian subjects are already naturalized or live as permanent residents of these (liberal) societies. If these Iranian immigrants assemble cultural associations, orchestrate public festivities, change their names, or encourage their children to speak Persian at home, it is because "incorporative structuration" in these societies structures toward permanency. It is the possibility of permanence and the frictions of distance (e.g., the higher cost of travel) that ostensibly qualify the lives of these Iranian immigrants as "diasporic" and informed by the familiar trope of nostalgia for a distant "homeland."

Yet what of other destinations in the circuits of Iranian migration? What is the stuff of "diasporic" life—its social practices and moral vocabularies—when *impermanence* and *proximity* rather than *permanence* and *distance* are the circumstances of reception and the thresholds of settlement? What about modes of transnational mobility that never lead to the multicultural imperative of "creat[ing] a space of difference"[23] as minority members of a "host" nation?

Dubai, like other Arabic societies of the Persian Gulf, does not grant permanent residency and naturalization to noncitizens (regardless of the duration of their stay). In this reception regime, the arrival of migrants is regulated according to a sponsorship system, the *kafala*, which ties residency status to employment. Employers thus double as sponsors.[24] Migrants arrive as expatriate laborers or, in official-speak, "guest workers." Moreover, they are required to renew their sponsorship every two years.[25] The lives of foreign residents in such societies, therefore, are formally mediated to remain in a state of "permanent impermanence."[26] This sponsorship system is part of a broader ensemble of policies, discourses, and social practices that regulate social difference in terms of a highly regimented distinction between citizens and noncitizens. For example, while citizens enjoy state largess in the form of cradle-to-grave social rights, foreign residents are left to manage risk according to their financial capacities in the free market or the services that their respective governments make available to them, if any. The rights of assembly and association for noncitizens are also highly restricted. The formation of cultural organizations—independent of government affiliation—is largely absent.

The result is not a democratic but "ethnocratic" polity wherein citizenship is conflated with ethnicity.[27] Despite the hustle and bustle of transnational movements in peoples, customs, and commodities, Emirati society provides a social context where the imperative for "incorporative structuration," as Naficy puts it, is absent.

Finally, the normative hierarchy of belonging by which this ethnocratic politics functions is worth elaborating in order to explain how these working-class Iranians are constructed as especially transient. As a raft of recent scholarship has noted, this politics not only focuses on distinguishing an ostensibly homogenous nation from a large population of foreign residents—about 90 percent of Dubai's population—but is also informed by a postcolonial racial hierarchy that values foreigners of Anglo-Saxon descent over their African and Asian (especially South Asian) counterparts.[28] In addition, the presence of family is a marker of permanence. Thus while these Iranian crews *formally* shared a similar residency status to other Iranians in Dubai, they were *socially* registered as representing a more transient segment of Dubai's foreign population for residing in Dubai without family. The moral logic that is on display in much official discourse and news media conflates "family" with "the nation" and regards the presence of a concentration of single men as especially transient for eventually reuniting with families elsewhere, and thus especially morally dubious.[29] This separation from family was also regulated in terms of economic standing. Foreign residents can obtain residency visas for family members only if they earn a minimum monthly income of AED 4,000 (roughly US $1,100). In effect, then, the labor brokerage systems or networks of chain migration in "sending" countries that link individual émigrés to lower-income work opportunities in Dubai are complemented with reception policies and social norms that render them transient and expendable residents.

Migration History of Iranians to Dubai

Migration from Iran to Dubai is hardly new. Since the late 1800s, there have been several episodes of mass migration from the coastal towns and port cities of the northern Persian Gulf to its southern shores. These port cities were already established entrepôts and key nodes in Britain's trade network linking the Indian subcontinent to markets in Europe and North America. Iranian governments looking to consolidate their political control and regulate national identity triggered earlier episodes of mass migration from Iran. Those leaving Iran behind were not departing for disconnected social worlds but often were joining their extended kin on the other side of the Persian Gulf. These movements, therefore, were often a consequence of soft boundaries solidifying.

An early episode came with an increasing push by Iran's Qajar government in the late 1880s to exert more control over these port cities in order to directly manage their tax revenues. This extension of Tehran's author- ity over these port cities involved the dislodging of the Qawāsim, an Arab tribe that had been ruling in this region since the late 1700s. It was especially their authority over the lucrative port city of Lingeh (a majority Sunni Arab town) that was challenged. The capture and imprisonment of the Qawāsim ruler in 1887, and the tribe's decisive military defeat in 1899, each triggered an emigration of Sunni Arab communities.[30] It was not only persecution they were escaping from but also the imposition of more taxes. In 1902, a new customs tariff was imposed on British trade in Iranian ports, precip- itating the emigration of several major trading families to Dubai, whose ruler at the time waived tariffs to further facilitate this process. As a result, for example, the Bombay and Persia Steam Navigation Company bypassed Lingeh for the first time in 1903 and directly shipped cargo to Dubai.[31] The demise of Lingeh thus proved a major boon to the emergence of Dubai as a regional entrepôt.[32]

The next major episode of Iranian migration came in the 1930s on the heels of the modernization schemes of Reza Shah, Iran's first Pahlavi mon- arch. On the one hand, his government considerably raised customs duties on food staples that happened to flow through Iran's southern trade sys- tem to help fund ambitious infrastructure projects.[33] On the other hand, the modernization programs of Reza Shah also involved a disciplinary project targeting "traditional" moral norms. One manifestation of this was a law passed in 1936 that banned the practice of veiling in public. Officially known as the *kashf-i hijab* ("the opening of the veil"), it was presented as an at- tempt to unfetter Iranians from the burden of ostensibly outmoded tradi- tions. This law was also intended to diminish the political authority of the *ulema* (clerical establishment). Together, these interventions initiated a pe- riod of emigration from towns in southern Iran to what was then called the Trucial Coast (the UAE).

The next notable period came in the 1960s and 1970s. My working-class interlocutors trace their history in Dubai to this period. I was often told of an earlier generation of fathers and uncles, now back in Iran, who had set up a shop in Dubai. These decades coincided with the discovery of oil in Dubai (1966), the dredging of Dubai's creek, and the first master-planned urban development projects.[34] This time, however, the migration of Irani- ans was no longer predominantly Sunni or ethnically Arab in character.[35] Rather, it was part of a broader influx of "unskilled" labor—from the Middle East, India, and Pakistan—that serviced Dubai's budding economy. Dubai's population nearly doubled, from 59,000 to 120,000, as a result of this influx between 1968 and 1974.[36] Following the UAE's independence in 1971, many

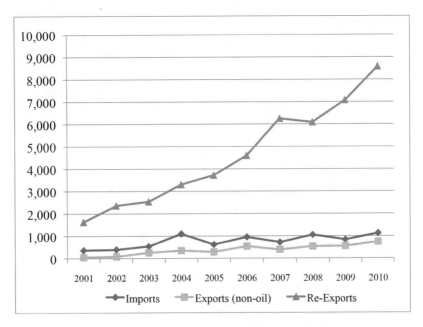

Figure 5.1. UAE Trade with Iran, 2001–2010 (in millions, US dollars)
Source: Ministry of Economy, United Arab Emirates (2015)

Iranian traders who had settled in Dubai during these years were offered citizenship, especially Achomi-speaking Iranians of southern descent.

The last major emigration of Iranians to the UAE in the twentieth century occurred in the early 1980s. It followed the 1978–1979 revolution and the start of the Iran-Iraq War in 1980. Unlike much of the Arab world, Dubai remained neutral during the war and quickly began to serve as a major economic conduit for the Iranian economy. A re-export market thus developed, allowing Iranian businesses to continue accessing global markets in goods and services despite the imposition of embargos and sanctions by the United States. An early indication of the strategic significance of this economic dependency on Dubai was the formation of the Iranian Business Council in 1982. This institution also represents the first endeavor by Dubai's Iranian residents to establish an organized presence in local civil society.

Dubai's re-export economy remains a cornerstone of diplomatic relations between Iran and the UAE. It rapidly expanded during the global boom in credit and commodities during the 2000s (figure 5.1). In fact, according to statistics from the International Monetary Fund, it has consistently placed the UAE as the highest-ranking origin of imports into Iran since the late 1990s.[37]

However, the imposition of new sanctions on Iran by the United States and the United Nations in 2010 took their toll on Iranian businesses in Dubai.[38] The UAE Central Bank also froze the assets of forty-one Iranian businesses, while UAE-based banks began to deny letters of credit to Iranian businesses.[39] Meanwhile, the Iranian Business Council was publicly raising the alarm over a precipitous decline in the number of Iranian businesses in Dubai.[40]

Iran (Dis)connections in Dubai Today

Like many other urban contexts in which the Iranian diaspora has been studied, the identity politics and socioeconomic divisions that prevail in Iran are reflected in Dubai as well.[41] While a detailed elaboration of these divisions is beyond the scope of this chapter, it is worth highlighting some of its key characteristics and their spatialization so as to better situate Dubai in relation to these other diasporic contexts.

The wave of emigration from Iran in the 1980s significantly expanded and diversified Dubai's Iranian population in terms of ethnicity and class. There arrived Iranians from throughout Iran. They often exhibited the social and cultural capital that identified them as middle-class foreigners: possessing a postsecondary education, arriving with their families, and pursuing work in white-collar professions. This wave of migrants diversified Iran's economic links to Dubai and the region through the re-export market. Consequently, the end of the Iran-Iraq War did not see an Iranian exodus back to Iran. Rather, it further embedded these newcomers, living and working in Dubai, as transnational participants in an Iranian economy that began to normalize and expand its presence in global markets.

The Iranian population in Dubai has steadily grown since then and is popularly estimated to be around 400,000.[42] Despite this relatively large population, there is no Iranian "ethic enclave" in Dubai. This suggests that the formation of enclaves is not an inevitable outcome of sustained immigration.[43] As I explained above, lack of multicultural policies and long-term residency in the UAE structurally inhibit this process. Yet ethnic enclaves exist in Dubai: there are, for example, enclaves of Indian immigrants in the inner city (e.g., Karama). My research suggests two more reasons that shed light on the absence of sociospatial concentration among Iranians. First, the wide-ranging presence of the Iranian state in this city works to relieve many Iranians from the sustained and structural barriers to employment and civic participation that have been associated with the formation and utility of ethnic enclaves among immigrants.[44] For example, the Iranian government has funded the establishment of a host of civic institutions catering to Iranian immigrants, including the Iranian Hospital, five secondary schools, and the Iranian Club.[45] The Iranian Club, for example, was established in 1990 and offers a sweep of large and well-maintained cultural facilities, from a soccer stadium to a cinema. The presence of the Iranian state also extends to a network of highly capitalized businesses that are either subsidiaries of parastatal Iranian organizations—such as the Islamic Revolutionary Guard Corps—or are de facto subsidiaries for being owned or associated with individuals who are well placed in the Iranian state.[46]

Second, my research also suggests that this proximity to Iran is the source of a shared anxiety among Iranian immigrants, especially those who plan to inevitably return to Iran at some point. Put simply, this is the concern that lifestyles radically at odds with moral norms in Iran—regardless of whether these norms are the implicit stuff of cultural convention or the explicit prescriptions of government ideology—might be relayed to social networks back there through gossip and thereby harm one's social standing in Iran. When discussing the benefits of living in Dubai with middle- and working-class Iranian immigrants, a recurring theme was the availability of greater "social freedoms" (āzādi-hāyeh ejtemā'ī). Participant-observation, particularly among middle-class Iranians endowed with the disposable income that these (often consumerist) freedoms required, confirmed that many do indeed practice the kinds of activities that they lamented were unavailable in Iran (e.g., the consumption of alcohol, public intimacies between men and women, a lack of mandatory veiling, etc.). The practice of these social freedoms, however, required some judgment about whether and to what extent they ought to be flaunted among fellow Iranians, as well as the kinds of Iranians with whom to mutually pursue them. As one interlocutor put it: "Of course, you have to be careful. There are a lot of Iranians here, and many of them are 'government types' (dowlatī)." This sense of vigilance about straddling two divergent moralities was all but common knowledge among Iranians in Dubai. I found this to be especially the case among middle-class Iranian youths and young professionals. Thus the same socioeconomic exchanges linking Dubai to the Iranian economy and state that so many of my interlocutors relied on to sustain their everyday lives in Dubai also resulted in a shared anxiety about other Iranians as potential sources of risk. Put simply, the company of fellow Iranians is inevitable in Dubai, but not always invaluable.

This anxiety resonates with recent analyses highlighting social tensions within populations of Iranian immigrants. Such a tension, for example, has been attributed to divergent practical orientations toward their host society between Iranian "exiles" and "emigrants" in Sweden.[47] More recently, Mohsen Mobasher has observed feelings of ambivalence and outright disappointment among Iranian Americans with their migrant "community" in Texas owing to ideological differences (2012: 79–84). While these tensions are affectively similar to the anxiety that I am describing in Dubai, it is critical to note that in Dubai they are informed by a sprawling presence of the Iranian state's socioeconomic apparatus, something that cannot be said of Stockholm or Dallas.

The transnational connections that feature in the everyday lives of Iranian immigrants in Dubai today orient them toward not only Iran but also the larger Iranian diaspora as well. Dubai's superlative transformation, beginning in the late 1990s, featured a rapidly expanding tourism infrastructure. An early milestone was the launch of the Dubai Shopping Festival in the summer of 1996, aimed at attracting retail tourism from the region. This event not only marked the beginning of Dubai's status as a popular recreational destination for tourists from Iran (table 5.1); it also became a node in the transnational circuit of Iranian cultural production and consumption. Since 2005, for example, Dubai has steadily become a globally recognized hub for Iranian art. Established and upcoming Iranian artists travel to Dubai from Iran and around the world to exhibit their works.[48] Similarly, the combination of entertainment infrastructure and proximity to Iran regularly attracts celebrated Iranian musicians and disc jockeys based in Europe and the United States to perform for large Iranian audiences in Dubai. These performances are known to draw large numbers of fans from Iran as well. In fact, since the early 2000s, Iranian tourism to Dubai represented a veritable cottage industry for travel agencies and guided tours. Not geographically as far afield as Europe or North America, and yet a world apart from Iran, Dubai thus sits at the crossroads of the Iranian diaspora, offering opportunities to fashion identities outside the realm of moral possibilities prescribed by the Iranian government while still living within the regional orbit of Iranian society.

Finally, it is worth noting how Dubai's emergence as a key node in the Iranian diaspora has coincided with its urban transformation, along with the rearrangement of social boundaries among Iranian residents. Like other rapidly developing cities in the Global South, this process further splintered the city in terms of class. Underlying Dubai's urban transformation was the introduction of property ownership for noncitizens in 2002.[49] A nascent "freehold" real estate market boomed, and a constellation of residential megaprojects took shape on the city's periphery. These projects were in-

Table 5.1. Iranian Visitors to Dubai

2000	2001	2002	2003	2004	2005	2006	2007	2008
192,230	212,161	284,675	342,571	358,954	348,125	361,876	413,721	476,124

Source: Dubai Department of Tourism and Commerce Marketing (cited in Hassan et al. 2010).
Note: Hassan et al. 2010, 41. These numbers capture arrivals on "Visit" visas. As such, they are inflated to some extent because they include Iranians who were traveling to Dubai to work informally, or unofficially residing in Dubai by conducting so-called visa-runs (i.e., crossing the border in order to simply cross back with a renewed Visit visa).

formally known as "New Dubai," and middle-class Iranian residents were among its earliest and most active consumers.[50] By one account, Iranians represented 10–30 percent of purchases in new developments by 2005.[51] In terms of total value of transactions, Iranians were officially ranked fourth by 2009 when this real estate market collapsed, and fourth again in 2012 when it was rapidly recovering.[52] This resulted in a steady flow of middle-class Iranian residents toward New Dubai. The master-planned, largely high-end, privately guarded, and often self-contained spaces of this region were disconnected from the hustle and bustle of the urban core and the broader socioeconomic diversity that it featured. Indeed, my working-class Iranian interlocutors were hardly familiar with this world. Likewise, most of my middle-class Iranian interlocutors who resided in New Dubai claimed to travel much less to the inner-city districts of Deira or Bur Dubai since moving there. Ironically, while Dubai's rapid development expanded the *transnational connection* of Iranian culture and commerce, it has also expanded the *urban disconnection* among its middle and working-class Iranians.

The Khaleej-boro and His Moral Geography

Between my visits to their places of work and residence, I grew to understand how these working-class Iranian men and youths conceived of their presence in Dubai. Travel to Dubai was understood as a moral project, that is to say, a deliberate undertaking toward becoming a certain *kind of person* or moral subject. This was the *khaleej-boro* (literally, "Gulf-goer"). This moral persona was a category of practice[53] among these inner-city crews of Iranians, and it was invoked to identify what they imagined to be *their* segment of Dubai's Iranian population. Specifically, the *khaleej-boro* referred to Iranian males who hailed from the south of Iran, spoke Achomi, and typically followed paths of chain migration in search of menial labor to financially support their dependents back in Iran.

The *khaleej-boro* thus represents a distinctly gendered Iranian transnational migrant who relies on a moral geography that presumes proximity to Iran. This kind of person is more of a "transmigrant"[54] than the kind of hyphenated member of liberal polities often featured in studies of Iranian immigrants. He originates in Iran's orbit, visits Iran regularly, and is expected to eventually return to Iran. His is not a *centrifugal* exit from Iran in search of destinations far afield in which to permanently settle and assimilate into, but rather a *centripetal* one that effectively renders the *khaleej* (the "Gulf") as a "transnational social field."[55] This social field enables a moral project, because assuming the life of a *khaleej-boro* is associated with achieving respectable masculinity. This life demonstrates one's willingness to endure hardship and distance from family in order to support them financially, eventually begin a (conjugal) family of one's own, and return to Iran permanently.

This eventuality is often viewed in the long term. Until then, however, return visits to hometowns in Iran are not uncommon. With the exception of some younger crewmembers, most of these men would travel to Iran once a year, usually for a couple weeks. The older crewmembers, especially the *arbāb* (manager) of the store, might even stay for a month or two to reside with their (conjugal) families. By contrast, an apprentice would be expected to visit less often; enduring longer periods of separation is part of their moral training as *khaleej-boro*. The frequency and length of stay, on either shore, are thus tied to the social status of crewmembers. In fact, as I elaborate in the next section, one modality of being a *khaleej-boro* even includes short stints of informal work on a seasonal basis.

Successfully inhabiting the life of a *khaleej-boro* thus involves a circular and ongoing movement between Iran and Dubai. It is worth emphasizing that this circularity of travel and its moral connotations inform one another. Iranian tourists, for example, are not referred to as *khaleej-boro* simply for traveling to Dubai (they are called *gardeshi*). Nor are Iranian immigrants who reside with their families in Dubai worthy of the epithet, because their lives in Dubai are not removed from their immediate dependents. The *khaleej-boro*, instead, resides in Dubai but is oriented toward Iran as he labors to meet his familial obligations by remitting part of his monthly earnings. These remittances thus valorize his travel as a form of care.[56] In this way, the moral project of the *khaleej-boro* is imagined as a distinctly masculine form of care. Such, at least, is the normative conception informing the persona of the *khaleej-boro*.

Yet the moral connotations of this transnational migration are also informed by broader conceptions about Dubai and Iran as certain kinds of places. Indeed, this imagined geography arising between these two places is inextricably linked to the life of a *khaleej-boro* as a moral project. Dubai is viewed as a place where opportunities lacking in Iran are abundantly available, thus warranting a removal of oneself from family and nation (Iran) in order to pursue them. Dubai is a place where the capital required for realizing the good life in Iran could be earned (the cost of a dowry, of home improvements, of a parent's retirement, etc.). Then again, it is also often discussed as a place of hardship and danger: a place that does not lend itself to the endurance of social bonds and requires one to always be on guard lest one is taken advantage of by people who do not mean what they say. This sense of place about Dubai is often captured with the category of *nā-mardi*. Depending on the context, this notion of *nā-mardi* could refer to "unmanly," "dishonor," "unfairness," or "injustice."[57]

Furthermore, the notion of *nā-mardi* and its associated concepts of dishonor, unfairness, or injustice are almost always discussed in relation to Iran. Explanations or even passing references to the kind of place that Dubai is—its opportunities and demands—are juxtaposed with anecdotes about the state of life in Iran. These anecdotes usually involved explanations of why life in Iran is increasingly untenable, thereby justifying resettlement on "this side of the *khaleej* (Gulf)." Iran is understood to be a place where economic security and social standing were less about individual actions than they were about nepotism, a place where social welfare was less a concern for the government than were political security and loyalty. This sense of place about Iran was captured by the oft-repeated notion of *fesād* (corruption).

Here, then, is a transnational moral geography: a shared knowledge about Dubai and Iran as discrete and morally charged places requiring travel between them, and certain kinds of conduct while doing so. This correlation between places, actions, and their reasons is imagined in terms of proximity. An early conversation I had with an auto-shop manager, Reza, is worth drawing from:

Reza: "Our customers have more money here. So earning money here is easier."
Another crewmember: "There are a lot of 'lord[s]' here (using the English word; *inja lord zīāde*). So they spend more money, and they don't haggle as much. In Iran if people see some of these prices, they'll laugh at you. But here people pay it."
Reza: "Even when they haggle you, they still pay more than over there."

Behzad (author) [later on in the conversation]: "Is it necessary to travel to the Gulf?"

Reza: "What do you mean?"

Behzad: "If a man doesn't go to the Gulf to work, is this frowned upon?"

Reza: "No. Many go to other places, like Shiraz. It's common."

Behzad: "So it's not expected to travel to the Gulf."

Reza: "Many come here, but others make money elsewhere."

Behzad: "What if they don't go anywhere?"

Reza: "That's not good. I mean, if they don't have adequate income (*darāmad-e kāfī*) there . . . then those who stay, we say that the guy doesn't have honor (*migim yāroo gheirat nadāreh*); that they're not willing to endure hardship (*nemīkhān sakhtī bekeshan*)."

These two categories of *gheirat* (honor) and its demonstrations through *sakhtī keshīdan* (enduring hardship) are central to this shared moral geography that understood traveling to Dubai as a venture toward respectable masculinity. Here, in other words, is a migratory sensibility that hinges on the notion of *honor-as-endurance*.

As I came to learn, there was much that required enduring. Here I focus on a particular circumstance that is associated with honor-as-endurance; the risk of legal ensnarement for undocumented work. I contend that this risk is especially indicative of the extent to which impermanence could be experienced here, and that such experience is derived from structural exclusion rather than "incorporative structuration" that Naficy (1993), for example, notes to be the case in contexts of liberal pluralism. This kind of *khaleej-boro* is known as the *ziārat-ī*. It is toward examining this particular experience that I now turn.

A Precarious Pilgrimage

In standard Persian, the term *ziārat* means "pilgrimage." In standard Arabic, it may be deployed as the noun form of "visit" or in attributive nouns such as "visit-visa" (*t'shira-ziāra*). It is this latter bureaucratic category—the official title of short-term visas granted, for example, to tourists—that these men index when they qualify it with the attributive suffix "i." A *ziārat-ī*, then, is a crewmember that officially traveled to Dubai as a tourist but actually did so to work. This kind of *khaleej-boro* is most often associated with younger recruits. New to this circuit of migration, they often seek employment for just a few months to demonstrate their worth as a worker who would merit the costs of sponsorship and formal employment.[58] Yet I also observed it among older crewmembers, despite their history of legal employment and residency in Dubai. I was informed that this is usually the case when a work permit could not be obtained in time or its application was (temporarily) denied.[59] This practice of short-term travel for informal work thus smacks of being a seasonal sojourner. If I refer to the *ziārat-ī* as a participant in this transnational social field and identify him as a certain kind of *khaleej-boro*, it is because my interlocutors understood and experienced him to be so. It was common knowledge that this persona represented a condition, or way of being in motion through this social field, that many of them will inevitably experience, whether as a young recruit or an older crewmember transitioning from one period of residency in Dubai to another. The *ziārat-ī*, then, is not only born of this transnational social network—linking recruits and their managers to each other and their mutual acquaintances in hometowns back in Iran—but represents its practical continuity in the face of legal limitations.[60]

In this section, I continue to ethnographically unpack how proximity and structural impermanence informed the shared knowledge and lived experiences of these working-class Iranians in Dubai. I focus on the virtue of honor-as-endurance as a key aspect of the way in which this life in Dubai was understood as a masculine undertaking. It is to this end that I seize on the figure of the *ziārat-ī*—a certain kind of *khaleej-boro*—through the experiences of a particular crewmember. These experiences, to be more specific, highlight the moral struggle involved in navigating the vulnerabilities produced by this structural impermanence and how such struggles implicate these Iranians in a (proximal) transnational social field.

This *ziārat-ī* was Amir. He was in his late thirties and had been working and living in this neighborhood for several months by the time we met. Like his fellow crewmembers, he had a history of traveling and working in Dubai. His stint with this particular crew, in fact, was the result of his long-standing relation with the master's brother. He too was away from his wife and children in Iran. Unlike his crewmembers, however, he was residing alone. He invited me over for dinner sometimes. Roasted chicken from a nearby rotisserie, and playing cards would preoccupy us until well past midnight.

It was while observing Amir attend to the everyday demands of servicing customers that I came to appreciate how mundane banalities could risk exposure to legal ensnarement. Working outside the prescribed limitations of a visit-visa, as a *ziārat-ī*, made him vulnerable to arrest and deportation. This vulnerability was socially mediated in such everyday interactions with the help of his crewmembers. Amir was limited in his range of activities. Driving long distances to pick up supplies, intervening in a crew-member's dispute with a customer, or participating in the occasional prank on a passerby are among those activities understood to be beyond their ca-pacity as they invite the possibility of interacting with law enforcement. Like most *khaleej-boro*, he endured life away from his family. And like most *ziārati*, he endured not only the *sakhti keshīdan* involved in manual labor and long hours but also the added vigilance required to limit the risk of le-gal ensnarement. Under these harsh and legally risky working conditions, in other words, honor (*gheirat*) and the capacity to endure (*sakhti keshīdan*) was called for and tested.

I soon came to learn that Amir had already encountered the police. One evening, while sitting outside the shop, we were alerted that undercover po-lice were roving the neighborhood. With this Amir suddenly lunged out of his chair and disappeared into the alleyway. The next time I saw him, he explained:

> They got me a while ago. The guy parked his car . . . when I went to talk to him he suddenly showed me that he was police! He wanted to see my pass-port . . . and when he found out that I didn't have a [working] visa, he ar-rested me. . . . I was in jail for a few nights, but I still refused to admit that I was here (Dubai) to work. . . . I told them I had come here to see some friends and I was just helping the guys because I was staying with them. So they took my passport and gave me [a] court date.

This hearing was scheduled for several months after his arrest, but by now only a few weeks remained. When it came, it resulted in yet another court date. It was scheduled for four months later. This was because Amir had in-sisted that he was not working illegally.

Those four months took their toll on Amir. He increasingly lapsed into melancholy. He had not planned on being apart from his family for so long and clearly missed them. His presence at the shop became more sporadic. His crewmembers teased him simply to take his mind off his legal limbo. His master encouraged the crew to assume some of his share of work so as to lessen his fatigue. He was even considering smuggling himself out of the country at one point but decided against it. Despite his exhaustion with the whole affair, he remained adamant about not confessing the truth to the court: "So long as my story doesn't change, they can't prove anything." It was during our last dinner together—though we didn't know it at the time—that he told me he wasn't sure what kind of ruling to expect or whether to expect one at all.

Once again, his appointed court date approached. It passed, and Amir was not returning my calls. A couple of days later when I reconvened with his crew, I was told that he finally confessed; that he could not muster another denial. As his *arbāb* put it:

He's in *ou'jil* now. That's your "Out Jail" (*īn "Out Jail-e" shomā hāst*). He caused a scene too. They wanted him to shave his head but he refused and started pushing them away, so I think they'll be holding him longer.

Amir stubbornly held out for almost a year because he was caught between moral obligations that precluded one another and yet were no less significant to his standing as a *khaleej-boro*. Since he was first arrested, the ethics of honor-as-endurance expanded beyond the toleration of routine hardships. It now included the expectation that he would limit the potential liabilities that his arrest posed for others, that is, those who depended on him and those whom he depended on in turn. On the one hand, there was his family. Amir wanted to leave open the possibility of returning to Dubai for future work in order to meet their needs, as respectable men would. A guilty verdict would have ensured his deportation and a permanent ban from reentering the country. It would thus deprive him from a significant source of future revenue and remittances, thereby diminishing his capacity to effectively care for his dependents. On the other hand, his refusal to confess was also directed toward a more immediate obligation: care for his master (*arbāb*). A confession might cause his master to face a significant penalty for knowingly hiring someone without due process. His living alone may be better understood in this light. If a follow-up inspection had found him residing in an apartment occupied by employees, it would have certainly implicated his master.

Amir's moral struggle, I contend, underscores the proximal nature of the transnational social field in which he moved. This field is organized according to networks of extended kin and their mutual relations between Persian Gulf cities like Dubai and hometowns in southern Iran. More specifically, the maintenance and activation of these networks—their capacity to facilitate the physical movement of these men and conscription of their labor— requires both the relative ease of travel across the Persian Gulf as well as the moral obligations at once linking transmigrants to their dependents and their masters. These networks, then, are embedded more in interpersonal relations rather than the mass mediation of Iranian culture that can cultivate identitarian forms of belonging across much greater distances. Whereas the latter relies on fiber-optic infrastructure linking various publics, the former relies more on "social infrastructure,"[61] or the interpersonal channels of communication that carry personal reputations and mutual obligations.

A Regime of Removal

Amir had encountered a deportation regime.[62] This was a federally orchestrated policing of working-class transmigrants that was informed by ethnonational politics. Official discourse often identifies this segment of Dubai's population as an excess of foreigners and a source of moral pollution. Variously referring to them as "scores of criminals and beggars," "illegals," "visa overstayers," and "infiltrators," this discourse amounts to a moral panic about undocumented transmigrants or those contravening their visas.[63] While this deportation regime targets the more economically marginal segments of foreigners, it corresponds with the fundamental premise of the larger regulatory regime that precludes permanent residency and naturalization to all migrants: the ideological conflation of citizenship with shared descent.[64] My working-class Iranian interlocutors, and the figure of the *ziārati* in particular, were simply more vulnerable to the same structural impermanence that underpins the everyday lives of noncitizens here. Here I briefly analyze the political economy that produces this vulnerability and informs their sense of disenchantment with Dubai as a place of *nā-mardi*.

This moral panic was provoked by the population surge that Dubai experienced during its recent boom: roughly doubling between 2001 and the onset of the financial crisis in 2008.[65] The ethnocratic identity politics according to which the nation is imagined in the UAE is trained on the distinction between citizens and noncitizens. A readily understood indicator of this distinction—and one that came in for increasing public discussion during the later years of the boom—is the notion of "demographic imbalance" (*khalal sukkāni* in Arabic). This "imbalance" emerged with the discovery of oil in the 1960s and the influx of foreign labor required for its production and derivative economies. This more recent surge in population, however, is not only manifested in labor encampments in the outer city. Rather, it is also visible in the inner-city neighborhoods with populated retail and wholesale industries. It is this visibility that informed this moral panic of "demographic imbalance" and "illegals" impinging upon Emirati society. The end goal of the state's intervention to diffuse this problem was deportation from the nation altogether, rather than the relocation or redistribution of this foreign population within the city.

Amir's "illegal" status and arrest, I contend, was ultimately derived from a contradiction inherent in the sponsorship system (*kafala*).[66] As I noted above, this system functions as a regulatory framework for receiving migrants and conscripting their labor. As such, residency status is dependent on employment. This effectively works to inhibit the possibility of unemployment or even part-time work. Termination of employment triggers a formal countdown toward the termination of one's residency visa. The formal "freedom" of working-class transmigrants to seek employment, therefore, is largely constituted abroad, and "unskilled" jobs in Dubai largely rely on those labor brokerage systems in the sending counties. Changing jobs while already residing in the UAE requires an official release from the current employer, called a "No Objection Certificate." With the exception of certain white-collar professions, a mandatory waiting period of six months is imposed if the employee quits prior to the termination date in the contract.[67] Together, these provisions work to preclude a legally enduring pool of unemployed foreign labor immediately available for exploitation.[68]

All of this, furthermore, is compounded by the administrative costs and process required to legally conscript noncitizens. These prove to be economically unfeasible for smaller retailers who are especially dependent on short-term seasonal demand. Indeed, the costs that the employer must bear amount to hundreds of dollars: obtaining an entry visa, obtaining a work permit, converting the entry visa into a residence visa on the basis of employment (lasting two years), paying for the employee's medical screening, covering the cost of their flights, or paying a hefty fee to a recruiting agency to facilitate all this.

This structural contradiction between the formal configuration of labor laws under the *kafala*, versus the need for immediately exploiting a pool of "unskilled" labor, has resulted in reoccurring accumulations of working-class foreigners residing in the UAE informally, be they employed or not. One strategy the state has relied on to address this is periodic amnesties. Running for several months at a time, they have seen significant numbers of largely South Asian and East Asian men and women coming forward to their embassies in order to either receive "out-passes" or to reconcile their visas with their current employment (i.e., to "legalize" their status). The magnitude of these numbers (table 5.2) attests to the widespread reliance on informal labor in Dubai. The numbers also suggest that the real value of this strategy seems to be the continuation of *kafala* as a socioeconomic order by defusing this contradiction through removal en masse, not by adjusting its underlying policies. The other state strategy has been the dragnet, especially following amnesties. The fanfare of local news coverage regularly reports of-

Table 5.2. Foreign Residents Applying for Amnesty, UAE

	1996	2002	2007	2012
Deported	200,000	300,000	247,000	62,000
Legalized	—	—	95,000	—

Sources: See Jandaly (2012) for 1996 and 2002 figures, UAE Ministry of Labor (2007) for 2007, and Ahmad (2013) for 2012 (table by author).
Note: With the exception 2007 figures, the UAE Ministry of Labor has not released official reports documenting amnesty results. These numbers are based on official statements given to the media and are approximations.

ficial campaigns targeting "illegals" in surprise inspections of workplaces, border crossings, and even bus stations.[69] Amir was ensnared in one such surprise inspection.

Amir's arrest was indicative of how this regime of removal localized the danger of moral pollution in Emirati society by conflating it with the category of low-income foreign men. For his fellow crewmembers, however, it was indicative of the omnipresent danger of the state. Indeed, his identification as a *ziārat-i* was itself informed by this ever-present threat of removal.

Conclusion

Amir's experiences—while inhabiting the moral persona of the *ziārati*—can hardly be said to exhaust the diversity of experiences and daily circumstances according to which his peers dwell in Dubai as *khaleej-boro,* much less those of Iranians in Dubai inhabiting other social categories altogether and living in other parts of the city. Still, his predicament does much to distill the moral geography shared between the social category of *khaleej-boro,* and the way in which it was animated by notions of honor (*gheirat*) and endurance (*sakht-ī keshīdan*). In Dubai, in other words, there is a sense of living well with and for others that is highly gendered and necessarily mobile.

With regard to the scholarship on Iranian migration, Amir's narrative captures the shared cultural logic and structural arrangements that frame this transnational social field in terms of proximity and impermanence. The mobility of these working-class Iranian transmigrants does not result in being formally incorporated into another polity. It is always imagined as dwelling in Iran's orbit and activates a social infrastructure that links the northern and southern shores of the Persian Gulf. Analyses of the Iranian migration, then, would do well to travel a little closer to the homeland and the Global South more generally. There are other circuits in which Iranians move through as transmigrants—from Turkey to Malaysia—and variously encounter or evade that diasporic tension between incorporation and ethnic solidarity.

Notes

1. For a rare exception, see Nadjmabadi (2010).
2. The managers of these retailers were distinct from their owners. The latter were Emirati nationals and were often absent from the day-to-day operations of the shop. Commercial regulations stipulate that businesses incorporated in the UAE require an Emirati to hold least 51 percent of the ownership. These Emirati partners of Iranian retailers in this neighborhood were often of Iranian heritage, representing earlier periods of migration from the south of Iran. As a result, these Emirati owners also spoke Achomi.
3. This consumption of alcohol was informal and depended on the black market.
4. Sarmadi (2013).
5. Naficy (1993: 9).
6. Blair (1991: 148); Mobasher (2006: 112).
7. Ghorashi (2004: 334).
8. Malek (2006: 355).
9. A temporal bias also informs studies of Iranian migration insofar as the 1979 Iranian Revolution is often treated as "the formative moment" (McAuliffe 2008: 65) of the Iranian diaspora. Indeed, the geographic and temporal biases are correlative.
10. Persis and Elahi (2011: 382).
11. Elahi and Karim (2011: 386).
12. Malek (2011).
13. Maghbouleh (2010).
14. Alinejad (2011).
15. Fotouhi (2015); Malek (2006).
16. Malek (2015).
17. For example, see: Ansari (1992), Bozorgmehr and Sabagh (1988), Chaichian (1997), (Fathi 1991).
18. Chaichian (1997: 616).
19. Ansari (1988: 80). For a more recent observation of this sentiment see Mobasher (2012).
20. Naficy (1993: xvii).
21. I follow Holston and Appadurai in distinguishing between "formal citizenship" and "substantive citizenship" (1999: 4). Whereas the former refers to official membership in a polity, the later refers to the actual (and often unequal) capacity of citizens to fully participate as such members.
22. For an excellent comparative analysis of this capacity between Canada and Sweden, see Malek (2015).

23. Ghorashi (2004: 335).

24. Longva (1999).

25. Until a policy change in 2010, residency visas lasted for three years.

26. Ali (2010: 162).

27. Longva (2005: 118–119).

28. Among these are ethnographic analyses by Anh Longva (1997), Ahmed Kanna (2011), Neha Vora (2013) and Andrew Gardner (2010).

29. The Dubai Municipality, for example, regards any adult man or woman residing in Dubai without the accompaniment of immediate family—regardless of whether or not they are actually engaged in conjugal relationships—as "single" (Glass 2007).

30. Abdullah (2007: 230).

31. Heard-Bey (1982: 244); Abdullah (2007: 232).

32. Al Sayegh (1998: 89).

33. Abdullah (2007: 247).

34. For a history of this period and Dubai's earlier urban development schemes, see Ramos (2012).

35. Abdullah (2007: 276).

36. Heard-Bey (1982: 269).

37. International Monetary Fund, Direction of Trade Statistics (www.imf.org).

38. These new sanctions were decidedly more comprehensive, as they banned Iran from the international SWIFT network (Society for Worldwide Interbank Financial Telecommunication), a first in the history of any modern sanctions regime.

39. See, repectively: Habibi (2010: 7); Shaheen (2010).

40. Al Arabiya News, 2010.

41. Kelly et al. (1993), Bozorgmehr (1997), and Chaichian (1997).

42. Snoj (2015). For reasons that I explained in the methodology section, this figure remains speculative. It is certainly exaggerated. Even during the height of the boom, Dubai's population was only just reaching 2 million. This oft-cited figure of 400,000 would imply that two out of every ten people in the city were Iranian, which was decidedly not the case!

43. Brettell (2003: 109–125).

44. Portes and Manning (1986); Zhou (2004). This relief from structural barriers in the UAE does not mean that Iranian businesses necessarily enjoy the official support of the Iranian government. My interviews with Iranian entrepreneurs in Dubai suggest that there is no shortage of grievances with the Iranian government (especially with regard to administrative protocols and transparency).

45. These schools in Dubai are administered by the Directorate of Iranian Schools (located in Dubai), which is responsible for other Iranian schools in the UAE as well.

46. Sadjapour (2011). According to one estimate (Ramezanpour 2009), about 60 percent of the Iranian capital invested in Dubai during its boom was by companies affiliated with parastatal financial institutions ("Bonyads"), such as the Sitād-e Ejrā-ye Farmān-e Emām.

47. Graham and Khosravi (1997).

48. Rahbar (2015).

49. This was a first in the recent history of any Arab society of the Persian Gulf and technically violated federal property laws of the UAE.

50. This was a universal observation among the thirty-two professionals in the real estate sector whom I interviewed during my fieldwork in 2010.

51. Fattah (2005).

52. Respectively: Reidin (2010) (cited in Futurebrand 2010), and Dubai Land Department (2012). These numbers, however, also include nonresident Iranians.

53. Brubaker (2004: 31–33).

54. Bruneau (2010: 49).

55. Basch et al. (1994). I posit this concept of "transnational social field" slightly differently here. Its original formulation was intended to critique analyses of transnational processes that too often described them in bounded terms, enclosing them within a particular territory (Glick Schiller 1999: 97). I too wish to avoid the conflation of place with process, as well as the danger of methodological nationalism that it invites. These working-class transmigrants were not cut off from the global Iranian diaspora. However, while this particular "field" is traversed by broader flows, it is *not* indefinite in its geography. The *khaleej* represents a practical nexus linking hometowns in Iran with Arab cities on the southern shores of the Persian Gulf.

56. This practice varied widely and generally reflected the economic circumstances of dependents in Iran and the capacities that these men and youths had to meet them.

57. At its most literal, *nā-mardi* translates to "un"(*nā*)–"manly"(*mardi*). It refers to either an act or condition of being "unfair" or "dishonorable" in standard Persian. Insofar as it is couched in terms of the negation of manliness, it may be viewed as indicative of the patriarchy underpinning normative gender relations in Iranian society more generally.

58. Men with years of work experience in the network of petty trades and retail in Dubai are better situated to secure a residency visa by relying on the relationships that they have accumulated.

59. Applications are sometimes denied because these small businesses are judged to have exceeded their allowable limit of employees.

60. It is not unusual for a single crew to accommodate two *ziārati* during the spring and summer months, coinciding both with higher demand in Dubai and school holidays in Iran.

61. Elyachar (2010).

62. De Genova and Peutz (2010).

63. For example, see Salama (2008).

64. Longva (2005: 119).

65. Krane (2009: 119).

66. In making this point I rely on Gardner's (2010) analysis of how the sponsorship system produces "illegality" in Bahrain.

67. Al Jandaly (2012).

68. These provisions have received minor modifications since 2008, but the net effect to which I refer continues to prevail.

69. Hassan (2011).

PART II

CREATIVE CULTURAL ACTIVITIES AND (RE)CONSTRUCTION OF CULTURE AND ETHNIC IDENTITY

The essence of ethnicity consists of culture and history (Nagel 1994). Not only do culture and history construct and provide meaning to ethnicity; it is also through culture that the content of ethnicity (i.e., language, religion, art, music, poetry, beliefs, and traditions) is established and preserved. As indicated by Nagel, rather than viewing culture as a historical legacy loaded with cultural goods, we should perceive culture as an individual and group construct through which cultural items are selected, "borrowed, blended, rediscovered, and reinterpreted." Cultural (re)construction and rediscovery are more vital and pronounced for immigrant groups in diaspora due to the clash of cultures in exile and the need for ethnic identity confirmation. This is particularly the case for immigrant groups such as Iranians whose culture has been traumatized and their ethnic identity devalued and scorned. The Iranian Revolution and the ensuing sociopolitical national and international crisis, including the American hostage crisis, constituted a major traumatic experience for the majority of Iranians inside and outside Iran. The most immediate traumatic outcome of the Iranian Revolution for a large number of Iranians, particularly high-ranking members of the former regime, intellectuals, and opponents of the new government, was indefinite exile. Other troubling consequences of the Iranian Revolution were total Islamization of Iranian culture and society based on strict Islamic principles and the accentuating and promoting of Islamic values, identity, and heritage while downplaying the Persian cultural heritage. Nagel's (1994) discussion of cultural construction sheds light on the processes of adoption of "Persian" as an ethnic identity choice, the glorification of pre-Islamic cultural celebrations, the creation of new cultural forms, and the revitalization of Persian history and poetry among many Iranian immigrants in diaspora (Mobasher 2012). It also helps us to understand the functions of cultural activities, ethnic cultural associations, political organizations, ethnic language classes, ethnic poetry and literature, and ethnic festivals and concerts in perpetuation of Iranian culture in diaspora.

The three chapters in Part II explain the role of literary production and cultural activities such as poetry reading and film festivals in coping with challenges of integration in exile as well as (re)constructing, perpetuating, and maintaining attachment to Iranian ethnic heritage and culture. Some of the chapters, particularly chapter 6, address these issues and how cultural, religious, national, and ethnic identities are perpetuated and maintained through collectively shared cultural activities and practices. Shared cultural activities and practices become even more significant for immigrants and minorities in diaspora as they are disconnected from their taken-for-granted cultural habitat. Sanaz Fotouhi's chapter, "Construction of National Identity through Ethnic Poetry, Film, and Play: Iranians in Australia," illustrates the significant role that such Iranian cultural activities as poetry reading events, film festivals, and drama workshops play in the Iranian community for reproduction of Iranian culture and the formation and negotiation of diasporic Iranian ethnic identity in Sydney. These cultural activities, according to Fotouhi, not only strengthen cultural continuity and cultural belonging but also help Iranians to connect and remember their historicized past and restore their ethnic/cultural identity. The significance of poetry nights as an important marker for maintaining a sense of Iranian identity, Fotouhi adds, is rooted in the Iranian culture's high regard for poetry. Poetry, she notes, has always been an inherent part of the Persian discourse for communication, with an identifiable and historical, and unchanging and continuous, presence in the Iranian understanding of cultural identity. What makes traditional and classical Persian poetry a significant element of cultural identity (aside from carrying timeless and universal human ideologies) is its symbolic role in cultural resistance and pride. While Iranian poetry nights offer a social space for Iranians to come together and maintain a sense of ethnic community, it is the themes in the poetry that reconnect Iranians to their heritage and their current condition as displaced people in diaspora.

Unlike the poetry nights that provide a collective site for connecting to the past, film festivals are social sites for negotiating Iranian ethnic identity with members of the larger Australian society. Moreover, the Iranian film festivals in Sydney are sites where Iranians and non-Iranians can engage in a cultural dialogue and reciprocal recognition through universally understood and recognized visual images. They are also platforms for the expression and introduction of cultural experiences and mediums through which a connection has been made between the Iranian experience and the rest of the world. Although film festivals provide a social space for recognition and cross-cultural negotiation between Iranians and Australians, they may not be enough for Iranians to regain their ethnic identities and voices lost in the process of migration. To reconstruct the identity and the voices that were silenced in diaspora, Iranians participate in drama performances and run stage production shows in Sydney.

Chapter 7, "Diaspora and Literary Production: Iranians in France," by Laetitia Nanquette, focuses on literary production of Iranians in France since the 1979 Iranian Revolution. Based on participant observation, ten years of personal involvement with the Iranian community, and interviews with dozens of Iranian writers, translators, publishers, and bookstore owners, Nanquette traces the evolution of literary texts produced by Iranians in France and the cultural connections to Iran and other Iranian literary institutions and communities in diaspora. Adopting Nanquette's typology of diaspora as her starting point, Nanquette categorizes the Iranian diaspora as a victim diaspora, mainly because of forced migration of the many Iranians who opposed the new government after the revolution. The presence of political opponents to Iran's government among the French Iranian community has created a politically diverse, fragmented, and divided diaspora characterized with less association and interaction between community members. Despite their small population size and political divisions, Iranian immigrants in France have played a crucial role in the cultural, political, and intellectual landscape of the Iranian diaspora. France has been an important site for the production of Iranian texts outside Iran since the revolution, written predominantly by secular intellectual writers. During the first thirty years after the revolution, literary texts by Iranians in France were dominated by works in Persian narrating the anxieties of exile. After 2009, production in the French language increased, and a generation of newly arrived intellectuals from Iran slowly changed and diversified the literary production, through their texts and through their work for literary institutions such as bookstores and publishing houses. The literary production of this new generation has gone beyond the theme of the agony of exile and is more concerned about one's diasporic identity. This is particularly the case for those who write in French. Paradoxically, this generation, Nanquette points out, has more connection to Iran than the postrevolutionary migrants of the first generation whose political engagement prevented them from returning to Iran. Nanquette's historical analysis reveals that the social and political characteristics of the Iranian diaspora not only influence the ways that Iranian culture, and particularly literature, circulates in

France but also makes Iranian French texts unique and distinguished from other diasporic literary productions. Nanquette's analysis also indicates that external factors, including international sanctions against Iran, censorship, and strong control over cultural matters in Iran by the home regime, as well as the structure of Iranian diaspora, have limited the flow of goods, individuals, and money between Iranian communities in diaspora as well as between diasporic communities and Iran. These external and internal forces have disconnected Iranian writers in diaspora from readers in Iran. Despite this disconnect, however, Nanquette describes how the new digital technology has empowered Iranian literary scholars and agents of literary production such as bookstores with a national/ethnic orientation to function as diasporic political spaces for the perpetuation of political activism. They also function as cultural centers and create links between literary production, the maintenance of cultural identity, and political activism.

In chapter 8, "Diaspora and Ethnic Identity Construction and Negotiation through Literary Production: Iranians in Italy," Alicia Miggiano provides another example of how Iranian ethnic identity in diaspora is constructed, maintained, and negotiated through literary production. Much like Iranian intellectuals in France, secular Iranian intellectuals in Italy have also channeled their experience of exile and nostalgia into a vast production of literary works in Italian. After describing the functions of cultural activities, ethnic cultural associations, political organizations, ethnic language classes, and ethnic festivals and concerts in perpetuation of Iranian culture in exile, Miggiano analyzes the narrative production in Italian by Iranian authors. In her view, just like the literary production of Iranians in other European countries, most of the literary production of Iranians in Italy is also dominated by emotionally intense themes such as nostalgia, longing, displacement, and the distinct feeling related to the sense of separation caused by exile. In fact, for a great number of Iranian intellectuals in exile, she adds, writing represents an immediate response to the "shock of events," an attempt to re-create the facts and the details related to the life left behind in Iran and a tool to maintain links with their origins and their cultural roots. The most important challenges for Iranian writers in this process are coping with alienation, creating a new identity, and writing and expressing in a foreign language. According to Miggiano, Iranian authors in exile live in a continuous process of identity negotiation in choosing to write in Italian to express their displacement. Miggiano's review and analysis of a sample of literary production, mainly novels and short stories written in Italian by Iranian nationals since the turn of the century, reveal some common elements and patterns, including portrayal of the Persian landscape, depiction of Iranian protagonists at a crucial time in Iranian history, and constant references to Persian traditions, habits, food, culture, and literature. Miggiano concludes her chapter with a remarkable analysis about the current state of Iranian literary production and the reasons for Persian translations of some novels by Iranian authors. In her view, unlike in past decades when Iranian writers in Italy deliberately maintained a low profile and visibility and their work was unknown to Iranian readers in Iran and other diasporic communities, Iranian writers today are more self-confident and receive more publicity and recognition in both Italy and Iran. She attributes this shift to improved diplomatic relations between Iran and Italy in recent years, changes in Italian society, change in the relationship and establishment of new linkages between Iranians in diaspora and Iran (including more frequent trips to Iran), and enhanced communication among Iranian diasporic communities. Nevertheless, Iranian literary production in Italian neither enhances social solidarity among Iranians nor reconstructs and strengthens the Iranian community in exile. Rather, it remains either as a medium to construct and maintain Iranian ethnic and national identity, or as a political rhetoric or ideology to educate ordinary Italian readers about the social and political situation in Iran.

In conclusion, the three chapters in Part II together reflect the significance of literary and creative cultural productions for Iranians in diaspora. As indicated in these chapters, it is through the collective work of first- and second-generation Iranian writers, poets, filmmakers, and playwrights that Iranians in diaspora express their experience in exile, chart their past, stay connected to their native land and culture, and (re)construct and articulate their ethnic identity. Moreover, the diasporic literary productions of Iranians, particularly classical Persian poetry, not only serve as a medium for political resistance against censorship in Iran but also function as a catalyst for community gathering, interethnic dialogue, and connection across different Iranian communities in diaspora.

CHAPTER 6

Construction of National Identity through Ethnic Poetry, Film, and Play: Iranians in Australia

SANAZ FOTOUHI

According to recent census records,[1] Australia is home to nearly 35,000 of the almost 4 million Iranians living outside of Iran.[2] Despite their small population, Iranians in Australia have managed to construct a low-key sense of community among themselves. This has been created partially through establishing and participating in cultural and creative activities. Over the eleven-plus years that I have lived in Australia, I have observed these activities in conjunction with the ever-shifting nature of Iranian communities. As a researcher and a scholar interested in the literature of the Iranian diaspora in English, I have been particularly interested in examining how creative and cultural activities correlate with how diasporic communities define and redefine themselves and their sense of identities. Over the years, as I participated in and organized some of these activities, I noticed their significance in maintaining, constructing, and negotiating the diasporic Iranian cultural identity.

The fact that members of the Iranian diaspora draw on creative cultural activities to define a sense of cultural identity is nothing new. As Stuart Hall (1996) argues, everyone's sense of cultural identity—"those aspects of our identities which arise from our 'belonging' to distinctive ethnic, racial, linguistic, religious, and, above all, national cultures"[3]—is constructed through a sense of maintained connection with specifically shared elements and cultural activities. This connection becomes more important for those who have migrated because migration suddenly cuts connections to those cultural elements. That is why, for diasporic people, engagement with cultural elements of the past, as well as association with people who also share that cultural understanding, becomes even more significant. This chapter explores how creative cultural activities contribute to the ways in which the Iranian sense of cultural identity is constructed, maintained, and negotiated in Australia. It also points toward how they contribute to countering stereotypes associated with Iranians in Australia.

The Iranian community in Australia partakes in a number of cultural and creative activities. Annually there are many recurring events that attract Iranians of diverse backgrounds. They include celebrations of non-religious national events such as Chahr Shanbe Souri, Sizdeh Bedar, Shab Yalda, as well as Mehregan. There are also numerous concerts each year by Iranian artists in Australia and by those living elsewhere. Additionally, there are many small and informal groups, including writing groups and book clubs, that have over the years started various ongoing creative and cultural activities. Given the large number of activities that take place each year, I have limited this analysis to examining a few recurring events, including poetry nights, film festivals, and drama workshops.

I have chosen to focus on these for several reasons. First, these are recurring popular activities, well-established, and consistent. This means that they have been ongoing for a few years and have an avid group of participants. This gives us a trajectory for tracing their history alongside the changing nature of the Iranian community. Second, these activities are nonspecific and inclusive. By this I mean they are not catered for people of certain ethnic backgrounds, or with specific religious and political views, and therefore they are attended by a cross section of Iranians. This inclusiveness allows for analysis of their importance in relation to the general Iranian population in Australia.

Finally, my personal involvement, interest, and engagement with the Iranian community gives me a unique ability and vantage point for the analysis and examination of the aforementioned activities. Though not officially an anthropologist, I have kept an active interest and have been involved, both as participant and as organizer, in numerous activities in the community. As a participant, I have actively attended dozens of various Iranian events across Australia such as poetry nights, film events, and book clubs, some on a regular basis. As an organizer, I was one of the founding members of the Persian Film Festival. My managerial role in the festival, as its codirector and later marketing manager for over four years, has given me a distinct opportunity to engage with the community and understand its needs and desires.

Data Collection and Methodology

Part of the data presented in this chapter comes from participant observation as well as the collection of informal short video interviews, audience feedback surveys, and long chats with supporters and sponsors of Iranian film festivals. My engagement with the Persian Film Festival specifically provided me with a set of information and data that I draw on for this chapter. In addition to participant observation and video interviews, I have conducted a series of formal and informal interviews with members of the Iranian community over the years. Lastly, I designed an opinion-based survey and collected information from some thirty Iranians of diverse backgrounds living across Melbourne and Sydney. I also conducted a number of informal interviews and discussions through email with some leading members of the community about some of the issues addressed here.

Literature Review

Given the relatively short period of Iranian settlement, there have not really been many sustained studies or examinations of the Iranian diaspora in Australia.[4] Among the few that have been conducted (Tenty & Housten 2013; McAuliffe 2007; Adibi 2003; Khoei et al. 2008; Share-Pour 1999; Aidani 2010), except for Aidani, the rest offer either overall perspectives or snippets on specific issues affecting particular groups within the Iranian community. In his study, for instance, Adibi (2003) offers a demographic and sociological analysis of the size and distributions of the Iranian community in Australia. In another microstudy, Tenty and Housten (2013) and McAuliffe (2007) address a narrow perspective by focusing on small parts of the Iranian community in relation to religion and religious identity. While Tenty and Housten address racial and religious discrimination (specifically in relation to Islamophobia) against Iranians in Sydney, McAuliffe touches on how religious identity affects ethnic identity construction among second-generation Iranian Muslims and Baha'is in London, Sydney, and Vancouver. Others such as Khoei et al. (2008) take on a different approach and examine sexuality and health among Iranian women in Sydney. One of the very few studies on the issue of Iranian identity formation in youths has been Mahmoud Share-Pour's (1999) sociological and ethnographical study of adolescent Iranians in Sydney and Wollongong.

Of the studies on Iranians in Australia, Aidani's work has been the only one with attention to the intersection of community, creativity, and issues of identity. In his fieldwork conducted on the Iranian community in Melbourne for his PhD, he observes the significance of cultural and creative activities among a group of Iranian refugees and asylum seekers. Aidani's research also highlights the significance of specific activities, such as reading and writing poetry, singing, as well as participating in drama and performance, in the way they maintain and construct a sense of cultural identity among Iranians. By drawing and elaborating on some of the issues raised by Aidani and others, this chapter offers a unique and broad perspective for understanding the link between cultural and creative activities—specifically poetry nights, film festivals, and drama performances—and the construction, maintenance, and negotiation of Iranian identity in Australia.

Migration History of Iranians to Australia

According to Australian historical records,[5] the first people of Iranian background to be accounted for in Australia were in the 1891 census, which counted seven Iranian-born people living in Victoria. Records show Iranians started coming to Australia in greater numbers since the 1930s and 1940s, but their number increased dramatically after World War II, especially in the 1950s and 1960s, with people in the oil industry being among the first to settle in Australia.[6] But Australia was not really known to many Iranians until the two countries entered into trade agreements in the 1970s.[7] It was the Shah's visit to Australia in mid-1970s and the performance of Australian athletes in the Munich Summer Olympics that brought Australia to the attention of Iranians.[8] It was after this that Iranians saw Australia as a potential country for migration, work, and study, and by 1976 there were 390 Iranian-born people living in Victoria.[9]

Soon after the Islamic Revolution of 1979, however, this number began to increase dramatically, as many Iranians escaped persecution, civil unrest, and the war between Iran and Iraq. Consequently, in the early 1980s Australia, after North America and Europe, became one of the major destinations for Iranian migration, especially after the Australian government began a humanitarian assistance program in 1981 to aid those who were being religiously persecuted in Iran, aimed specifically at the Baha'i.[10] This led to a dramatic increase in the number of Iranian emigrants; according to the 1991 Australian census, there were some 12,914 Iranian nationals living in Australia.[11] This number gradually increased in the 1990s and early 2000s due to the continuing politically tight situation in Iran, as well as Australia's acceptance of a large number of people under the Skilled Migration and Family Stream visa programs.

In the late 2000s and early 2010s, however, this pattern of migration changed. Following the 2009 disputed presidential elections and political unrest in Iran, and Australia's lessening of skilled migrant intakes, there was a sudden influx in Iranian asylum seekers who came to Australia by boat. While there are no accurate records on the exact numbers of Iranians who came this way to date, there were only approximately seventy Iranian-identified refugees who came illegally by boat in 2004.[12] However, since early 2000, this number has increased dramatically with Iranians numbering the highest in the refugee population coming to Australia by boat in recent years.[13] The combination of these push and pull factors led to a 52.8 percent increase in the Iranian population in Australia between 2006 and 2011. By 2011 this number increased to a recorded 34,543. The majority of Iranians lived in New South Wales with 15,463 (44.9 percent) and 7,447 (21.6 percent) in Victoria, followed by Western Australia with 3,722 (10.8 percent), South Australia with 2,822 (8.2 percent), Australian Capital Territory with 545 (1.6 percent), Northern Territory with 360 (1 percent), and Tasmania with 197 (0.6%).[14]

Over the years, Iranians have established a sense of community for themselves through community and nonprofit organizations. These are usually groups who come together to run various events, often on a small scale, and usually operating out of community centers in the city where they are based. Sometimes they register themselves officially as associations and manage various events. Almost every major city in Australia has an Iranian association. Given that the larger number of Iranians live across New South Wales and Victoria, these states are also home to some of the most active community groups. In New South Wales, especially in Sydney, there are a number of Iranian associations that provide community services such as translations, legal advices and referrals and that organize events and programs. The most established of these includes the Australian Iranian Community Organization, founded in 1986, which aims to "maintain the unity of Iranians living in NSW, assist Farsi speaking individuals to settle more quickly in Australia, and develop social and cultural activities based on three pillars of good thought, good words and good deeds."[15] There is also Kanoon Aknoon in Hornsby, one of the northern suburbs of Sydney with a large number of Iranians. Established in 2007, one of the aims of this association has been to cater to the growing population of Iranians in north Sydney.[16] Aknoon is also the umbrella for a number of ongoing activities, including the Ayla Drama Group, writing workshops, and reading groups. In addition, Aknoon and its volunteers run Farsi-language and dance classes and maintain the Persian Library in Hornsby. In Victoria, too, there are a number of similar associations such as the Iranian Australian Society of Victoria[17] and House of Persia (HoPe), which has been one of the main organizers of the annual Melbourne Persian Fair every October.[18] Melbourne is also home to Australian-Iranian Youth Society of Victoria.[19] In addition, Melbourne accommodates the Australian Persian Arts Centre,[20] which runs workshops and arts and cultural events.

Aside from these community associations, universities also have their own Iranian gatherings across New South Wales. For example, in Sydney most major universities have student organizations that bring Iranians together to play games, watch films, or celebrate cultural events. Similarly, in Melbourne there are a number of active student-run initiatives such as the Iranian Society at Melbourne University and one at Swinburne University. However, in addition to organizations, most of the major recurring cultural activities have been initiated and run by individuals and independent groups. For example, in Sydney the Persian Poetry nights, the Persian and Iranian Film Festivals, Cinema Azadi, the Ayla Drama Group, and the major Persian newspapers have all been initiated and managed by individual Iranians rather than as collectives.

Poetry Nights: Maintaining Cultural Connection

Poetry nights, where people gather to read Persian poetry, are one of the oldest community activities in Sydney. While there are multiple poetry nights around town, the most popular is Shab She'er Iraaniane Chatswood. This is a monthly event held in a community center in one of Sydney's affluent suburbs with a large Iranian population. It attracts between 50 to 150 or more people each session, depending on the time of the year. My interviews with some of the participants revealed that Shab She'er is independently organized by a committee that changes regularly. For their first event in 1986, they attracted some 500 people of the 3,500 people of Iranian background living in Sydney.[21]

Persian Poetry nights are not unique to Iranians in Australia. There are numerous such events across Europe and North America with a longer history than the ones in Australia. What makes them unique, however, is that these events highlight the significance of poetry as a unique marker of cultural identity for Iranians in diaspora. The significance of poetry nights for maintaining an Iranian cultural identity is rooted in the high regard for poetry in Iranian culture. So undeniable is poetry in the Iranian cultural identity that, as Hamid Dabashi (2011) writes, "If jazz is the cadence of American culture then Persian poetry is the pulse of Iranian culture, the rhyme and rhythm of its collective memory."[22] If we look at Iranian history, poetry has always been an inherent part of the Persian discourse of communication, with an identifiable, unchanging, and continuous presence in the Iranian understanding of cultural identity.[23]

The importance of poetry as a marker of cultural identity, both in Iran and beyond its borders, has deep historical roots that go hand in hand with the spiritual nature of classical Persian poetry and the fact that its essence can overcome the diversity that makes up the Iranian society today. This dates back to the time of the Arab invasion of Persia 1,400 years ago. As Seyyed Hussein Nasr (1991) argues, "The current Persian language and the literature written in it were born from the wedding between Islam and the soul of the Persian people."[24] Although the invasion, according to Nasr, "affected deeply all facets of life of the Persians" including their social, political, artistic, religious, and even linguistic dynamics, its effect was different in other countries in the region. In contrast to the lands to the west where Arab domination brought "Arabization," so that many countries from Egypt to Morocco speak Arabic even to this day, in Persia Islam spread without its citizens losing their Persian identity and becoming Arabized. Contrarily, after the invasion, the Persian language expanded and became infused with the vocabulary of Quranic Arabic. Consequently, it formed "a major Islamic language while also making major contributions to Arabic."[25]

Aside from carrying timeless and universal human ideologies, what makes traditional and classical Persian poetry a significant element of Iranian cultural identity is that it is viewed as a symbol of cultural resistance and pride. Despite the many sociopolitical changes that have affected Iran over time, Persian poetry has surpassed, survived, and retained its most distinguishing attributes over centuries. The fact that Persia, after the Arab invasion, managed to retain its own language and even develop a unique literature has always been a source of historical pride. It is these qualities of Persian poetry that have made it such a significant marker of Iranian cultural identity and an element, according to Nasr (1991), "of utmost importance . . . for Persian culture and the nourishment of the Persian soul."[26] This is why, as Jahanshah Rashidian (2010) observes, this literature "fosters Iranian identity by establishing Persian as a common language of all Iranians."[27]

More important, Persian Sufi poetry, with its emphasis on the spiritual/ esoteric aspect of Islam, is perceived as a form of resistance against the current Iranian regime. Despite the fact that Sufi poetry has generally been frowned upon by the government for various reasons, it continues to form a significant part of Iranian literary discourse and cultural identity. Despite the Iranian government's attempt to marginalize Sufism as a practice after the revolution, Sufi poetry, with its aspirations to mysticism and the spiritual aspects of Islam, became a more favorable point of identification for those who have resisted the government's forced Islamization of the country. As such, engagement with this poetry as a shared element of cultural heritage opens up a space for many, both inside and outside of Iran, to maintain a connection to each other through universally appealing ideas devoid of any particular nationalistic, religious, or political attachments.

It is for this reason that Persian Poetry nights are conceivably significant sites for the maintenance of a sense of Iranian identity in diaspora. As Hall (1996) argues, an important aspect of cultural identity rests on "one, shared culture, a sort of collective 'one true self,' hiding inside the many other, more superficial or artificially imposed 'selves,' which people with a shared history and ancestry hold in common."[28] Here, cultural identities reflect the common historical experiences and shared cultural codes that provide us, as "one people," with stable, unchanging, and continuous frames of reference and meaning, beneath the shifting divisions and vicissitudes of our actual history.[29]

With its emphasis on true and universal realities, Persian poetry in diaspora provides a space not only for the reflection of those human ideals but also one where Iranians can connect to each other and maintain their Iranian cultural identity. Cut from their homeland, in their new country they are left with only a few markers of cultural belonging. As Andrew Davidson and Khun Eng Kuah (2007) describe it, "Migrants experience a sense of deterritorialization and dislocation where the break with the country of origin with its familiar social practices and cultural icons means these are no longer available to these migrants in their adopted country."[30] Consequently, many "consciously seek to retrieve and reproduce some of these social practices and cultural icons"[31] that remind them of their sense of belonging and cultural identity. Remembering and drawing on certain elements of a cultural past, according to Hall (2003), "offer[s] a way of imposing an imaginary coherence on the experience of dispersal and fragmentation, which is the history of all enforced diasporas."[32] This is why, despite their ethnic, religious, and political diversity, Persian poetry for Iranians in Australia is a shared cultural heritage that provides an opportunity to maintain and connect with their past and current condition as migrants and displaced people.[33] In short, themes in much of classical Persian poetry are those that reflect a sense of migratory fragmentation and displacement. As Aidani (2010) observes, "[This] poetry communicates what is otherwise ineffable about oppression, marginalization and displacement and the feeling of being a stranger both at home and in a foreign land. [It] speaks to them about fragmentation, which is seen as a critical theme of their recent history in its splintering of their lives."[34]

For the Iranian community, as Aidani maintains, poetry "echo[es] their social world, their ethics, their politics, their longing and desires."[35] Aidani concludes by saying: "When everyday language fails, the language of [poetry] has a potency, vigor and depth through which they can express their own emotions surrounding displacement and being a stranger in a foreign country. This literary heritage . . . gives profundity to their loss—of friends, memories, home—and the ambivalence of being a stranger."[36] This is partially why Persian Poetry nights play such an important role for the reconstruction and maintenance of Iranian culture in Australia and in other Iranian diasporic communities.

Film Festivals: Negotiating Presence

While there have been some regular movie screenings organized by independent monthly film clubs and student organizations, it has only been recently that Iranian films were screened in specialized film festivals in Australia. The Iranian Film Festival Australia (IFFA) and the Persian Film Festival (PFF) both started independently by different individuals in 2011 and have both been running annually since then. Unlike IFFA, which screens films only from Iran, PFF screens content from Iran and Afghanistan and from across the global diaspora and aims to reach a more diverse range of general Australian audiences to be a platform for cultural expansion and negotiation through the medium of film. This is reflected in their choice of programming. IFFA's program is usually inclusive of mainly more contemporary and some popular Iranian films, while PFF aims for a wider range of both popular and art-house films, including documentaries, from Iran and Afghanistan. The choice in programming, which is lined up by PFF director Amin Palangi, who himself is one of the few successful Iranian Australian filmmakers, is reflective of PFF's ethos. As stated on the PFF website, the festival's aim is not only to attract Iranian audiences but also to "be a leader in shifting views and misconceptions of Australians about Iran and Iranians and creating spaces for new and alternative voices."[37] As such, PFF has been featured on mainstream Australian national media (ABC, SBS, and major newspapers) and international media (including CNN Spanish). No other Iranian cultural event has achieved this level of publicity in the history of Iranian migration to Australia.

To maintain visibility, PFF's social media marketing tries to reach new non-Iranian audiences each year. This is why the festival has been continuously picked each year and mentioned repeatedly as one of Sydney's top ethnic film festivals. This has brought PFF to the attention of top cultural organizers and prominent individuals in the film industry in Australia for support and funding. Just like with poetry nights, Iranian viewers find the festival's significance in creating and maintaining a sense of community. However, most audiences are also aware of the festival's significant impact beyond the community, and within the Australian society at large, as a social space for identity negotiation. The importance of both aspects of the film festival has been reflected in the survey conducted for this chapter. For example, Shokoufeh Kavani, a translator, artist, active community member, and organizer of a regular event called Persian Morning Tea, observed:

> They [both IFFA and PFF] create a sense of belonging from the culture that we have been separated from. It is also important to get to know more people and create a network, especially for helping new arrivals and migrants and breaking the isolation of Iranian highly educated and giving them the opportunity, space and time to represent their work and make the community to become stronger and have a voice in Australia.

Others participants also highlighted the significance of the festival as an event for negotiating Iranian cultural identity within the larger Australian society. Mohammad, a PhD student who also organizes film night events at a university himself, said,

> [The festival] is very good as it fosters dialogue between Iranians and many other non-Iranian attendants of the festivals. This might lead to friendship and more dialogue and communications.

He continued,

> Also, these festivals held in Australian cinemas are effective in terms of portraying a positive and internationally active image of Iran which will eventually enhance the self-image of the Iranian in Australia.

Similarly, Nima, a financial adviser, believes that film festivals "play [a] really important role as a cultural product to show different aspects of Iranian arts, lifestyle and cultures." And as Seina, a photographer and engineer who has grown up in Australia, wrote:

> As a young Iranian/Australian, I think it's great to see events about our culture that invites not only Iranians but also non-Iranians into life in Iran and bridges the culture gap between our two worlds.

Although in any diasporic group there is a deep-seated desire for maintaining a connection to the homeland through shared cultural elements such as poetry for Iranians, there is also the desire to create and negotiate a space for mutual understanding and belonging in their host communities. Through this social space, diasporic groups find an opportunity for integration based on a sense of universal human experiences. As Aidani observes (particularly in relation to the situation of the Iranians in Australia), there is "a significant and clearly articulated cultural self-awareness in regard to a relationship between two cultural milieus (Anglo-Australian and Iranian) that marks them as migrant, refugee, *gharibe* (stranger), *mohajer* (immigrant), *koly* (gypsy) or *khareji* (foreigner)."[38]

This sense of being the "other," or the outsider, often marred in stereotypical myths as theorists of identity and subjectivity, like Kelly Oliver (2001), observe, can appear to be oppressive because it is based on emphasizing the difference rather than the similarity of human experiences. This is so because our sense of identity and subjectivity are constructed intersubjectively, especially by how others perceive us and we perceive ourselves. As Oliver (2001) puts it, "A positive sense of self is dependent on positive recognition from others, while a negative sense of self is the result of negative recognition or lack of recognition from others."[39] This operates on a social level, where positive recognition from a dominant culture leads to emergence of positive self-perception. As she indicates, "Recognition from the dominant culture is necessary to develop a strong sense of one's own personal and group identity."[40] Stereotypes based on lack of understanding and cultural differences construct an antagonistic relationship and further the gap between the self and the other. This has the ability to objectify a group of people, and "objectification undermines subjectivity [since] objects are not subjects."[41] For immigrants, this can lead to a difficult process of being accepted, understood, and assimilated into the dominant culture of their new countries.

Much like other immigrants, the Iranian diasporic community in Australia faces the difficulty of overcoming their otherness. Aside from the general sense of misrecognition associated with the process of migration, Iranians face the additional negative stereotypes associated with Iran stemming historically from the onset of the Islamic Revolution, the American hostage crisis, the events of 9/11 and America's declaration of Iran as part of an axis of evil, Islamophobia, and the violation of human rights and persecution of political dissidents since the 2009 elections in Iran. While these events have affected the Iranian population in America and Europe much more, Iranians in Australia have not been unscathed.

In the Australian context, the sense of otherness has been heightened more recently with the large wave of asylum seekers who have been arriving on boats. The negative "refugee" lens through which many Iranians are viewed in Australia adds another layer of otherness and contains nuances that lead to objectification. As Aidani (2010) argues, those labeled as refugees, caught within a bureaucratic system, which is then reflected onto the society at large through the media, lose their sense of individual subjectivity. This kind of labeling "categorizes and objectifies people as being without an identity, a country or a history; it marginalizes and condenses their diverse cultural and historical backgrounds."[42] This categorization leads to homogenization and creates a grand narrative about a cultural group that overrides their individual and cultural identities.

One way to overcome the otherness and loss of subjectivity faced by Iranians and other immigrants is to gain and negotiate a space of human understanding and dialogue between the self and the other. As Oliver (2001) reminds us, a significant part in the process of regaining subjectivity and overcoming the patterns of objectification is reciprocal recognition through similarity of human experiences. As she argues, "Subjectivity is dialogic because the subject is a response to an address from the other."[43] It is in this dialogue that recognition, according to her, occurs, but only when a "subject recognizes . . . something familiar in that other, for example, when he can see that the other is a person too."[44] This means that for any immigrant group to integrate and regain their subjectivity, they must create a space that negotiates and allows for the construction of dialogue through the expression of shared human experiences. One way immigrants can negotiate their identities in their new setting is through drawing on and highlighting cultural elements of their home culture and sharing universal aspects of it with those in their host society (Hall 1997). As indicated by Hall (1996), there is a close relationship between our cultural past and identity as well, embracing the "so-called return to roots . . . [that also necessitates] a coming-to-terms-with our 'routes.'"[45] This means that engagement with roots/routes dynamics, which invokes an origin in cultural past, is not about a mere obsession about our identities as "who we are" or "where we came from." Rather it becomes about "using the resources of history, language and culture in the process of becoming or 'what we might become' rather than 'being.'"[46] Drawing on and engaging with our cultural past can lead to "transformed future" in the host community. This process also provides an opportunity for creating understanding and negotiating spaces of recognition or, as he puts it, understanding "how we have been represented and how that bears on how we might represent ourselves."[47] This means that drawing and engaging with cultural elements of a past left behind can also become a space for negotiation of the representation and recognition of shared human experiences.

While for the Iranian community in diaspora the universal elements of

Persian poetry is a potential tool for constructing a sense of recognition between self and other, those elements are not as easily accessible to members of the host community because of linguistic barriers. Alternatively, since early 1990, Iranian films have been an important platform for the expression and introduction of Iranian cultural experience and a primary medium through which a connection has been made between Iranians and the rest of the world.

During this time, Iranian films have provided a major negotiating space between the Iranian culture and other cultures. Given the seemingly restricted access to Iranian society for the general population of the Western world, both in terms of its traditionally gender-segregated setting and, more recently, the restrictions of access to the country by the Islamic government, Iranian society has usually been marred with a sense of mystery for the West. This is why, despite all sorts of restrictions and censorships, Iranian films have gained enormous popularity among Western audiences.[48] As Hamid Dabashi (2007) observes, Iranian films have "opened up the perils and promises of its secrets in full view of the whole world to see."[49] More important, they have managed to do this through the depiction of a range of universally acknowledged human feelings. Through connection with those feelings on screen, framed in an Iranian context, the gap between the viewer and the culture represented (which is the other) lessens. The viewer gains better cultural understanding through a topic that he or she personally recognizes and understands. There is an acknowledgment that the other also has similar human feelings, a step that is significant in recognizing the other as human. The resonances of this kind of recognition on screen can have cultural reverberations into the Australian society at large. Through an acknowledgment of culturally recognized and universally shared human feelings by those in the dominant host community, Iranians are no longer viewed as the refugee other but as "one of us." This recognition brings them one step closer to integration and negotiating, enabling them to create a space for defining a collectively acknowledged sense of Iranian Australian identity.

Although films, in and of themselves, can be seen as spaces for negotiating a sense of human understanding, a festival setting expands and takes this recognition to a different level. As Cindy Hing-Yuk Wong (2011) argues, film festivals are "vital nodes," spaces in which "multiple agents negotiate local, national, and supernational relations of culture, power and identity."[50] She adds, "Festivals constitute a dynamic system where a specific cultural artifact—cinema articulates and multiple actors continuously strive to redefine its meaning and place in its immediate environment, a wider film world, and larger socio-economic and political context."[51] Festivals, she believes, "provide a unique network through which all those involved . . . may view the past, explore the present, and create the future."[52]

This suggests that film festivals provide more room for negotiating and opening up spaces for mutual understanding and dialogue. Although watching a film, without the continued interaction, can be seen as a kind of passive acknowledgment, a festival, by contrast, provides an interactive, culturally charged, and active for cross-cultural negotiation and understanding. This is because, in a festival setting, specifically one revolving around one dominant yet subordinate immigrant culture, the audiences get to experience much more than a film. In a setting like the one offered by PFF and IFFA, Iranian and non-Iranian audiences mingle after the film in a casual environment. This interethnic social interaction not only provides a window where the Iranian immigrant community becomes accessible to non-Iranians; it also creates a social space for cultural dialogue beyond the film. Thus, the festival setting breaks down the barrier between what is usually the dominant culture and the other. In such a setting, which often extends to include other cultural elements such as food and music, non-Iranians also experience elements that constitute the cultural identity of the other, feel intrigued about Iranian history and culture, and experience similarity through human connections. Moreover, here the status of Iranian immigrants is shifted from being on the periphery to the center. Here, the festival becomes a space where Iranians see themselves overtly reflected, literally, on the big screen, with specific cultural reflections that highlight their true human experiences, something that is not often seen in Australian society. This experience is best captured in the following comment by a respondent in my survey:

> Movies can be an incredibly effective way to communicate how a community sees itself to an outsider. They can show how we interact with each other, what is important to us and what isn't, what are the cultural norms/status quo, and what are the things that people deal with in the socio political landscape of the country. It is also a wonderful mirror to ourselves that can provide great insight to what are parts of our culture that hold us back and what parts of our culture support growth in the various areas of our lives.

Drama Groups: Constructing a Stage for Belonging

The Iranian community in Melbourne has some active drama performance groups run by a number of prominent Iranian playwrights. Shahin Shafaei, a playwright, worked in Iran until one of his works got him into trouble with the authorities.[53] To escape persecution, he fled to Malaysia and came to Australia as a refugee in 2000. After months in a Curtin detention center, he collaborated in the production of the play *Through the Wire*, which was staged across Australia, including at the Opera House in 2004. This highly praised production, which recounts the experience of four refugees, returned to Shafaei an incentive to continue his career as an established and creative playwright. Since 2010, he has produced a number of other plays and has been helping refugee and migrant communities to express themselves through drama.

Mammad Aidani, a scholar and philosopher based at the University of Melbourne, is another notable Iranian playwright who migrated to Europe and then to Australia. Since 1988, as a theater director, he has produced a number of substantial plays[54] and worked with many theaters across Melbourne, including some with Iranian refugees. Unlike in Melbourne, Iranians in Sydney formed an active drama group, Ayla, in 2010, thanks to the young Iranian migrant Mehran Mortezaei and a few of his friends. Since its establishment through Kanoon Aknoon, Ayla has produced eleven shows. While their more recent plays were either adapted and translated from English to Persian or were original plays, the earlier shows were Iranian plays performed in Persian. The latest production was written by Freidoun Najai, an Iranian playwright based in Sydney, and directed by Mortezai, titled *Ship of Fools*[55] and performed in Persian. It reflects the experiences of Iranian refugee and asylum seekers in Australia and almost 500 people have seen this play. This suggests that nearly 3 percent of the Iranian population spread across New South Wales attended these shows.

Much like the film festivals, participation in drama performances and running stage production shows are activities that assist migrants to construct a sense of self and identity in their new host countries. As discussed earlier, migration destabilizes an individual's sense of self. Distanced from their familiar cultural surroundings, migrants, especially refugees and asylum seekers, lose their social and cultural agency. As Aidani (2010) observes, "The categorization of an individual as a refugee by the bureaucracy is a crude way of constructing collective narratives that are cross-cut by social, economic, gender, class, cultural, and religious differences."[56] Film festivals create a social space to create dialogue between migrants and members of the host community and space for recognition and negotiation for cultural, emotional, and human understanding. However, they do not provide an opportunity for migrants to regain their personal identities and voices lost in the process of migration. This is because our identity is fluid and needs construction and reconstruction according to the space in which we live and in relation to others. As Alison Jeffers suggests in *Refugees, Theatre and Crisis* (2011), "Identities, and concepts of identity, change throughout the individual's life and this does not happen in a vacuum but always in relation to the Other."[57] Therefore our sense of identity is always about "becoming as opposed to reaching any totalizing identity destination."[58] As Hall (1996) also believes, "Identity emerges as a kind of unsettled space . . . or an unresolved question within that space, between a number of intersecting discourses."[59] It is thus "important to re-conceptualize the very idea of identity which has to be forged in a newly diverse or pluralized society."[60] This becomes specifically important for migrants, as they must redefine and reconstruct themselves and their sense of identity in relation to the new setting in which they have now arrived. But as Jeffers (2011) puts in relation to the way this identity is redefined, the question to ask is: "In whose hands does this re-definition take place and according to whose vision?"[61]

This is where performance and theater, particularly if it is self-reflective and autobiographical, can be seen as a space for identity construction. While a film festival's setting can be space that *reflects* some cultural and historical truths about a culture, it is a constructed mirror that is reflected out there. It is not an activity that is personally and physically embodied. To put it in another way, it is not a *participatory* kind of activity where people are actively engaged in showing or acting out or participating in the making of their own personal and current narratives. This is why a play that is created and performed by migrants can be seen as the total engagement of the body, which reflects specific, lived, and current realities of immigrants and their dilemma. It thus allows for the embodiment, embracement, and projection of certain realities that now make up their sense of self as migrants, refugees, or asylum seekers. As Lorna Marshall (2001) argues, the engagement of the body and the physical senses in performing these new identities is extremely important because "we begin with the body, since this is, and has always been, the mediator between who we are and the world."[62] Marshall continues: "The enhancement of experience and the constitution of identity in personal narrative depend upon our bodies as our access to and means of expression."[63] Performance on stage, especially if it is a self-reflective role of a new sense of identity that needs to be embraced, can provide a platform, literally a stage, for the way migrants come to terms with and construct their new identity. It gives them voice and an active audience that recognizes and acknowledges their experience. This is important, as we know that the combination of having a voice and being recognized is the first step in regaining agency and constructing or reconstructing our self.

The Iranian playwright community in Australia is aware of the significance of this space. Aidani acknowledges the importance of play, performance, and narrativity in the way Iranians in Australia embrace and construct their new identity. During Aidani's fieldwork in Melbourne, some Iranians asked him to help them write a play that reflected their experiences. Although at first reluctant, he gradually agreed to this "unforeseen methodology." He realized that it was in the process of remembering, narrating, and embodying the part for a performance that many of the participants recounted and came to terms with their past. According to Aidani, in this process the participants embraced and constructed their own sense of self that made up their new realities. "In their acting I saw the physicality of their displacement, their anger, their cries, their laughter, and of course their hope."[64] He goes on to say about how the outcome, a show that was performed in front of some 300 people, was effective: "The stage that they created for their performance was riveting. . . . The performance gave a deeper meaning to their narratives and I understood the meaning of the 'lived body,' which is an important element in how we perceive the world. Their performance also underscored the idea that our experiences always come from an embodied perspective."[65]

The importance of theater for the Iranian community in Australia is best examined through tracing Ayla's development and history. Ayla began with a young man's vision to reflect his own existence on stage in a foreign country where he felt unrepresented. It began staging Iranian plays, something that the Iranian participants felt, at that time, could best reflect their sense of identity and connection to Iran. Their transition to adapting and translating English plays into Persian represents the group's desire to integrate and reflect their engagement with the community in which they live. Finally, the writing and production of a play such as *Ship of Fools*, which is an original and direct response to the Iranian migratory experience to Australia, in Persian is a reflection of the way this community has used the theater space to embrace, reflect, and construct aspects of their social and cultural identity in Australia.

Conclusion

The Iranian community in Australia has been changing and expanding continuously. As Aidani (2010) observes about the shifting nature of the Iranian community and how it sees itself: "The question for many Iranians is no longer just about 'who are we?' and 'what have we become?' . . . but rather how to represent the Iranian experience."[66] Regardless of their representation, Iranians, like many other diasporic communities in Australia, will continue to struggle in the process of integration and resettlement and will "employ tactics to resist . . . alienation and exclusion,"[67] both among themselves and within the larger Australian society.

In this chapter I examined some of the social and cultural activities that Iranians use to integrate and resettle in Australia. These are also attempts to maintain, negotiate, and reconstruct a sense of Iranian identity, helping them to overcome their homogenous and stereotypical representations in Australia. As Aidani (2010) observes, "The simplistic notions about their identity expressed in the popular imagination of Western culture ignore how their narratives of home (Iran) are connected with the host (Australian) context."[68] These activities have "a lugubrious [resonance] which tries to express the effects of the cultural, social and political ruptures they have experienced."[69] They have become a means to connect their two alienated worlds together and to make sense of the new kind of identity they must now claim, represent, and embody.

Although challenging, this process is hopeful. As Hossein Adibi has found in a study of Iranian youth in 2003, despite the sense of difficulty and isolation some Iranians (and second generations) felt, "they constantly expressed the pride they have in their own Iranian heritage. They also expressed their frustration that the value of their Iranian culture and civilization were not understood by many people in Australia."[70] At the same time, "they were aware of their multiple identities, and they took pride of being partly Iranian and partly Australian."[71] What can be concluded here is that, despite the frustration that exists among the Iranian community in Australia, there is still a sense of hope for constructing a better future, for integration and for settlement. Perhaps Aidani sums up this situation well when he says "the Iranian voices [we hear] express the complexity of their stories which is not linear or fixed and to which a conclusion has yet to be written."[72] As he goes on to say, "their status in Australia is an ongoing negotiation,"[73] and surely in this process, as this analysis has demonstrated, the activities and events described here play an integral role.

Notes

1. This is according to the 2011 census found on the Australian government's Department of Immigration and Citizenship. Specific factsheet about the Iranian community ("Iranian-Born") can be found at www.dss.gov.au/sites/default/files /documents/02_2014/iran.pdf.
2. Laetitia Nanquette, "Refugee Life Writing in Australia: Testimonios by Iranians," *Postcolonial Text* 9(2): (2014).

3. Stuart Hall, "The Question of Cultural Identity," in *Modernity: An Introduction to Modern Societies*, ed. Stuart Hall et al. (New York: Blackwell Publishers, 1996), 596.

4. What needs to be noted is that there are numerous researchers working across Australia on different aspects of Iran and Iranian studies, though not necessarily related to an Australian context. Across Australia, there are dozens of PhD candidates working on a range of topics about Iran on issues of human rights, feminism, film studies, literature, linguistics, and cinema. There are also a number of established scholars such as Michelle Langford, who work on Iranian cinema, Laetitia Nanquette, who is studying Iranian literature in diaspora, as well as Gillian Whitlock, who explores Iranian women's memoirs in English. Yet, most of these studies are not specific to an Australian context.

5. "Origins: History of Migration from Iran" (last modified 2013), museumvictoria.com.au/origins/history.aspx?pid=28.

6. See the Australian census record factsheet "Iranian-Born" and "Origins: History of Migration from Iran."

7. Aidani, *Welcoming the Stranger*, 14.

8. Aidani, *Welcoming the Stranger*, 14.

9. "Origins: History of Migration from Iran."

10. "Iranian-Born."

11. For detailed information, see the Australian Bureau of Statistic's census results: "People Born in the Middle East" (last modified May 12, 2009), www.abs.gov.au/AUSSTATS/abs@.nsf/Lookup/3416.0Main+Features42008.

12. Aidani, *Welcoming the Stranger*, 14.

13. Farsight, an independent research group, has conducted research, in progress, about the Iranian patterns of migration to Australia. They have so far presented their findings on the estimated number of Iranian refugees who came by boat to Australia in "Iranian Refugees: Irregular Migration to Australia," seefar.org/iranian-refugees-irregular-migration-to-australia.

14. "Iranian-Born."

15. Iranian Australian Community Organization, www.aic.org.au/index.php.

16. aknoon.com.au.

17. www.iranian-vic.org.au.

18. www.iranian-vic.org.au/index.php/en/house-of-persia.

19. www.airys.org.au.

20. www.apacentre.com.au.

21. This information is found only in the Persian section of AICO's website, www.aic.org.au/index.php/fa/about/aico-history.

22. Hamid Dabashi, *The World Is My Home: A Hamid Dabashi Reader*, ed. Andrew Davison and Himadeep Muppidi (New York: Palgrave, 2011), 122.

23. For a more in-depth discussion of the significance of Persian poetry for the way the sense of Iranian identity is maintained and constructed both in Iran and abroad, see "Sufi Poetry—Universal and Profound" in my book *The Literature of the Iranian Diaspora: Meaning and Identity since the Islamic Revolution* (London: I. B. Tauris, 2015).

24. Seyyed Hussein Nasr, *Islamic Spirituality: Manifestations*, vol. 2 (New York: Crossroad, 1991), 328.

25. Nasr, *Islamic Spirituality*, 328.

26. Seyyed Hussein Nasr, "Persian Sufi Literature: Its Spiritual and Cultural Significance," in *Heritage of Sufism*, vol. 2, ed. L. Lewishon (London: OneWorld), 5.

27. Jahanshah Rashidian, "Our Iranian Identity," jahanshahrashidian-rashidian -blog.blogspot.com/2010/10/our-iranianidentity.html.

28. Hall, "Who Needs Identity?," 223.

29. Hall, "Who Needs Identity?," 223.

30. A. Davidson and Eng Kuah, eds., *At Home in the Chinese Diaspora: Memories, Identities and Belongings* (New York: Palgrave Macmillan, 2007), 3.

31. Davidson and Kuah, *At Home*, 3.

32. Stuart Hall, "Cultural Identity and Diaspora," in *Theorizing Diaspora: a Reader*, ed. J. E. Braziel and A. Mannur (Oxford: Blackwell, 2003), 224.

33. For specific examples, and his findings on how he observes this sense of connection is created, see "Poetics of Displacement" in *Welcoming the Stranger*, 27–38.

34. Aidani, *Welcoming the Stranger*, 22.

35. Aidani, *Welcoming the Stranger*, 36.

36. Aidani, *Welcoming the Stranger*, 37

37. www.persianfilmfestival.com.

38. Aidani, *Welcoming the Stranger*, 15.

39. Kelly Oliver, *Witnessing: Beyond Recognition* (London: University of Minnesota Press, 2001), 4.

40. Oliver, *Witnessing*, 23.

41. Oliver, *Witnessing*, 7.

42. Aidani, *Welcoming the Stranger*, 17.

43. Oliver, *Witnessing*, 9.

44. Oliver, *Witnessing*, 9.

45. Hall, "The Question of Cultural Identity," 4.

46. Hall, "The Question of Cultural Identity," 4.

47. Hall, "The Question of Cultural Identity," 4.

48. For a social history of the reasons for the popularity of Iranian cinema in the West, see Dabashi's introduction in *Masters and Masterpieces of Iranian Cinema*. For a more chronological analysis, see the introduction to Richard Tapper's *The New Iranian Cinema*.

49. Dabashi, *Masters and Masterpieces of Iranian Cinema*, 14.

50. Cindy Hing-Yuk Wong, *Film Festivals: Culture, People, and Power on the Global Screen* (New York: Rutgers University Press, 2011), 1.

51. Wong, *Film Festivals*, 2.

52. Wong, *Film Festivals*, 2.

53. Based on the data found on his website, www.shahinshafaei.com.

54. Because of the nuances of his plays, Aidani's dramas have also been the subject of studies in Iran. For example, in her article in Persian, "Adabiyat Namayeshi Mohajerat Iranian Saken dar Australia: Tahlil pasa estemari namayesh nameyeh Dar Ayehen, Asar Mohammad Aidani" (Dramatic Literature of Iranian Migrants in Australia: A Post-colonial Examination of Mammad Aidani's *In the Mirror*), the Iranian scholar Zardhost Afshari Behbani, from an Iranian university, provides a brief background to Aidani's work and examines his work in an Australian context from a postcolonial perspective.

55. See aylatheatre.com/index.php?id=ship-of-fools (in Persian) about the production.

56. Aidani, *Welcoming the Stranger*, 18.

57. Alison Jeffers, *Refugees, Theatre and Crisis: Performing Global Identities* (New York: Palgrave McMillan, 2011), 10.

58. Jeffers, *Refugees*, 9.

59. Hall, quoted in Jeffers, *Refugees*, 10.

60. Jeffers, *Refugees*, 10.

61. Jeffers, *Refugees*, 10.

62. Lorna Marshall, *The Body Speaks: Performance and Expression* (New York: St. Martin's Press, 2001), 8.

63. Marshall, *The Body*, 461.

64. Aidani, *Welcoming the Stranger*, 9.

65. Aidani, *Welcoming the Stranger*, 8–9.

66. Aidani, *Welcoming the Stranger*, 75.

67. Aidani, *Welcoming the Stranger*, 75.

68. Aidani, *Welcoming the Stranger*, 1.

69. Aidani, *Welcoming the Stranger*, 1.

70. Hossein Adibi, "Identity and Cultural Change: The Case of Iranian Youth in Australia," paper presented at Social Change in the Century Conference, Centre for Social Change Research, Queensland University of Technology, November 21, 2003.

71. Adibi, "Identity and Cultural Change."

72. Aidani, *Welcoming the Stranger*, 78.

73. Aidani, *Welcoming the Stranger*, 78.

CHAPTER 7

Diaspora and Literary Production: Iranians in France

LAETITIA NANQUETTE

Although the size of Iranian population in France is relatively smaller than other countries with a substantial number of Iranians, they have played a major role in the cultural, political, and intellectual landscape of the Iranian diaspora. This chapter examines the literary production of Iranians in France and the important cultural role it has played in Iranian diaspora. France has been a crucial place for the production of Iranian texts outside Iran since the 1979 Iranian Revolution, written predominantly by secular intellectual writers. During the first thirty years after the revolution, literary texts by Iranians in France were dominated by works in Persian narrating the anxieties of exile. After around 2009, literary production in the French and Persian languages increased, and a new generation of Iranian intellectuals gradually transformed and diversified the production of their texts and changed its distribution through their work for literary institutions such as bookstores and publishing houses. The new literary generation of Iranians in France, perhaps paradoxically, has more connection to Iran than the postrevolutionary migrants of the first generation, whose strong political engagement meant that they could not return home and lost many of their connections to Iran.

The data for this chapter was partly collected through my personal involvement with the Iranian community in France between 2006 and 2016. During this time, I interviewed dozens of Iranians working largely in the field of culture in France and Iran, as well as in the United Kingdom, the United States, and Australia. They were primarily writers, translators, and bookstore owners. I was also a participant observer at cultural events and an active participant in some projects, such as the Persian Publishers Network (PPN), through the International Alliance of Independent Publishers.

In this chapter, I will first sketch the history of Iranian migration to France and describe its demographic profile and its diasporic characteristics. I will then present a classification of the literary production of Iranians in France, whether written in French or Persian. I will make frequent comparisons between the Iranian literary field in France and the United States and explain the difference between the two. Finally, I will discuss the cultural connections to Iran and to the other diasporic literary communities maintained by Iranian writers in France, looking specifically at literary institutions.

In the section below, I analyze the Iranian diaspora according to the characteristics proposed by Robin Cohen (1997: 180). Although Cohen's definitions in his seminal book do not apply to the Iranian diaspora perfectly, they have been used in diaspora studies by many scholars and thus allow comparing the Iranian diaspora with other diasporas, which is critical in a field that often tends to insist on specificities. This is particularly important because the social and political characteristics of the Iranian diaspora have an influence on the way Iranian culture, and particularly literature, circulates in France. It provides clues to help in understanding texts, especially when put into the broader context of Iranian migration. Indeed, why do Iranian French texts differ so much from texts by Iranian Americans?

Migration History and Demographic Characteristics of Iranians in France

Despite a strong desire to maintain an Iranian identity—however it is defined—there is a high level of assimilation into the host country among Iranians across diasporic sites. As Ali Akbar Mahdi argues: "The record of Iranian immigrants in developing a sense of ethnic identity and community is mixed. While they often express a strong desire for the preservation of their cultural heritage, they show no significant resistance to the assimilating forces of the host society" (Mahdi 1998, 94). Mahdi's observation appropriately applies to the case of Iranians in France and explains why the links between the Iranian diasporic communities are not always strong. In fact, the links that are created tend to be to the homeland and to the host country, not to other diasporic communities. Although one can speak about an Iranian diaspora throughout the world, there is not a cohesive Iranian "community" in France. This is partly because of the diverse political affiliations and activities of Iranian members of the diaspora, which hindered people from coming to terms on other matters. Consequently, there has not been a strong sense of community built over the thirty-five years of postrevolution migration. As Nader Vahabi suggests:

Generally, Iranians living in France constitute a population presenting a considerable diversity, so much so that one can say there is no "Iranian community" but culturally and politically very diversified Iranian groups. The attachment to France is less that of a new community of belonging than the expression of values where the individual is prioritized over the group (Vahabi 2015: 38–39).

Political affiliation, more than class or religion, seems to be a dividing force, with Iranians divided between leftist parties, such as the Tudeh (Communist Party), the Fedayan-e khalq, and the Mujahedin-e khalq (both left-leaning political organizations), and the monarchists, who support the Shah's son, Reza Pahlavi, exiled in the United States.

The history of Iranian migration to France can partly be explained by the important role France played in the Iranian imaginary in the nineteenth and twentieth centuries. Unlike the imperialist ambitions of the United States, Great Britain, and Russia, France's involvement in Iran was based on cultural cooperation, with French the most widely spoken foreign language in Iran until World War II, when it began to be replaced by English. French was the language spoken by the elite, as well as the language through which Iran came to learn about Europe, especially its literature, with French works and translations introducing Iranians to new genres such as the novel (Balaÿ 1998) and unrhymed poetry (Ahmed 2012; Hadidi and Carnoy 1994). The Iranian education system comprised many French Catholic missions and their schools: before the revolution, in Tehran alone one could find the Lazarist schools of St. Louis and Jeanne d'Arc, the Franco-Persane school, the Alliance Française, the Lycee Razi, and the Alliance Israélite schools (Nateq 1994). The system was largely modeled on the French, especially in the institutions that formed the elite, such as the Dar al-Fonun, which was inspired by the Ecole Polytechnique (Nateq 1994).

After Mohammad Ali Shah's coup against the constitutional government in 1908, some intellectuals and politicians opposed to his regime fled to Paris, including the prominent man of letters Mohammad Qazvini (Nassehy-Behnam 2000). Many members of the Qajar dynasty, which ruled Iran from 1785 to 1925, including Ahmad Shah, also settled in Paris after forced exile. In the first half of the twentieth century, Iranian elites sent their children to France to pursue their studies, and it is from this time on that one can trace the formation of an Iranian community in France. As Reza Arasteh notes: "In 1918 there was a total of 500 Iranians studying in Europe, of whom 200 were in France, 34 in England, 9 in Germany and the rest in Switzerland and other countries" (Arasteh 1962, 444). By midcentury, more

Iranians were choosing to migrate to Germany and the United States instead: in 1958–1959 there were 4,000 Iranian students in Germany and 3,700 in the United States, with only 800 in France and 600 in England (Arasteh 1962, 448).

One can distinguish several periods in the history of Iranian migration to France: the Qajar period, including the Iranian constitutional revolution; the Pahlavi period; and the postrevolutionary period. During the Qajar and Pahlavi periods, Iranians primarily moved to gain an education in France, and sometimes they decided to stay. Students formed the main population of Iranians in France until the 1970s, like in other countries of Iranian migration. Some of them were part of the Confederation of Iranian Students, opposed to the Shah (Matin-Asgari 1991), which was strongly represented in France, Germany, and the United States. Iran's modernization process after World War I and the lack of political freedom during the Shah's rule shaped the political activities of Iranian dissidents during this period. Before the revolution, "what was published outside Iran was mainly in the form of opposition literature consisting of political tracts and pamphlets" (Sepehri 1988, 6).

Large-scale migration of Iranians in the twentieth century began in 1978–1979 at the onset of the Islamic Revolution, increased after the revolution and the establishment of censorship in Iran (Sepehri 1988), and continued during the Iran-Iraq War between 1980 and 1988. Many Iranians who left the country migrated to North America and Europe. Much like the prerevolutionary period, many Iranians who migrated to France were intellectuals and political leaders. Even Ayatollah Khomeini, the leader of the Islamic Revolution, moved to France to spread his revolutionary message to Iranians inside the country. Unlike the prerevolutionary period, however, the postrevolutionary Iranians who migrated to France were more diverse and divided and included political asylees, refugees, and political activists with different political affiliations, some of whom stayed in France temporarily before they moved on to other countries.

The postrevolutionary period also witnessed multiple waves of migration. The first wave primarily formed a victim diaspora, as defined by Cohen. These were people who fled the nascent Islamic regime, which was in the process of establishing itself, as well as the war with Iraq. The second wave formed more of a cultural diaspora, combined with a labor diaspora, as economic conditions became more difficult in Iran. The third and most recent wave involved political migrants and started after the political repression following the 2009 Iranian presidential election. Thus, it can be said that today the Iranian diaspora consists of a combination of several different Iranian groups who left their country for social, cultural, economic, and political reasons.

In 2006, the number of Iranians in France was estimated to be between 24,000 and 26,000 (Vahabi 2015: 38).[1] This is much lower than the estimated population in Germany, which numbers around 160,000. However, the significance of the Iranian diaspora in France is not captured in these numbers, primarily because France has traditionally hosted a higher proportion of intellectuals and prominent political figures including, for example, the first Iranian president, Abolhassan Bani Sadr, Massoud and Maryam Rajavi, the leaders of the Mujahedin-e khalq, and Farah Pahlavi, the former Iranian empress. Nader Vahabi (2015) notes that, while migration of Iranians to France in the 1980s was mainly promoted by political forces, since the 1990s Iranians who have settled in France are more diverse and have migrated for social and cultural reasons. In contrast to the first wave of Iranians who were mainly political migrants and intellectuals, Iranians who have been migrating to France since 1990 represent a broader Iranian demographic, including rural and uneducated individuals (Vahabi 2015).

An outstanding characteristic of the Iranian community in France, as in some other Western countries, is "the high level of education of its members. According to Nassehy-Behnam (2000) 78.5 percent of Iranian immigrants in France have at least a university degree. Despite this impressive figure, close to half (46 percent) of Iranians in France are unemployed and many highly qualified Iranians are unable to find suitable jobs" (Nassehy-Behnam 2000). Iranians in France are no exception when it comes to this characteristic associated with migration from developing countries to Western countries, whereby many well-qualified people have to work in jobs for which they are overqualified or are not able to find work at all. Despite these numbers, the main discourse among members of the Iranian community in France and elsewhere is to insist on how well they are adapting to the new country and how much they contribute to it. In unison with the general view of the French and other Western governments on integration and assimilation of immigrants, Iranians tirelessly claim that they are "good migrants" who have assimilated and contribute to the country.

This discourse of the Iranian community was present, for example, in recent debates over the new US visa waiver program that was announced by the US State Department in January 2016.[2] Nadereh Chamlou of the National Iranian American Council, a nonprofit organization with the stated mission of "advancing the interests of the Iranian American community," said: "We feel we are being singled out. Iraq and Syria are warzones and I cannot comment on Sudan. Everywhere we have gone as Iranians, we have been exemplary citizens" (Smith, January 16, 2016). At times when integration and assimilation are keywords associated with migration, this claim concerning the assimilation of Iranians into host societies can be positively valued by the receiving country, whether France or the United States, and answers the criteria for "successful migration."

In the following sections I will trace the evolution of literary production by Iranians in France. After providing the background information on cultural production in general, I then move on to conceptualizing the evolution of the Iranian literary production with an emphasis on the dramatic changes since the arrival of the third wave of postrevolutionary migrants in 2009.

Background to Franco-Iranian Cultural Production

Different periods in the history of Franco-Iranian relations have been studied—for example, during 1807–1808 (Amini 1995) and between 1907 and 1938 (Habibi 2004)—and there is also a comprehensive study of their 400 years of dialogue (Hellot-Bellier 2007). There are also some accounts of the general image of Persia and Iran found in Western literature (Ansari 2005). Moreover, the reception of Persian literature in France from 1600 to 1982 has been thoroughly studied (Hadidi and Carnoy 1994). More recently, an edited collection has analyzed Franco-Iranian relations across a variety of disciplines, including literature (Delfani 2009). However, until recently, there have not been any comprehensive studies of Iranian cultural production in France since the 1979 revolution. My recent book, titled *Orientalism versus Occidentalism: Literary and Cultural Imaging between France and Iran since the Islamic Revolution*, was an attempt to remedy this lack by studying the mutual representations of France and Iran in their contemporary literatures (Nanquette 2013). This chapter continues in the same direction, integrating the most recent developments. It follows in the footsteps of scholars who have worked on other Iranian diasporic literatures, particularly on Iranian American works (Fotouhi 2015; Karim and Rahimieh 2008; Grassian 2013; Karim March/April 2015). Among these works, there has been a focus on the genre of the memoir (Malek 2006), especially after the publication of Azar Nafisi's memoir (Nafisi 2003), which was strongly criticized for being simplistic in its portrayal of Iran and playing the game of neoconservative American politicians wanting to invade Iran (Dabashi 2006).

Inspired by these studies, and focusing on a diasporic space that has not been studied, it became apparent that there is a need to look at the broader cultural landscape of Iranians in France to better understand the literary texts being produced there. There are dozens of Iranian associations in France scattered across the country. Some of them are professional (such as associations of dentists or lawyers), and others are devoted to promoting Persian culture and Persian language through language classes (Idjadi 2012). They work as cultural institutions devoted to maintaining and perpetuating Iranian culture, and they primarily serve Iranians. They often function as community centers, although occasionally events cater to a wider audience and are purposefully intended to attract the French and demonstrate the richness of Persian culture. These include Aftab and the Pouya cultural center, as well as the Cultural Centre of the Islamic Republic, which represents the Islamic regime's cultural viewpoint. However, unlike in the United Kingdom, there is no Iranian school and no religious or faith-based groups. One reason for this might be that France has mainly attracted secular people—although it has been claimed that some Iranians in France have recently become interested in Sufi brotherhoods (Nassehy-Behnam 2000).[3]

In terms of cultural production, there are several ethnic journals and newspapers published by Iranians in France. One should, however, be cautious when counting such texts, as some publishers do not observe the requirement for an ISBN, and this makes the publication untraceable. In addition, Persian publications are not consistently listed in Western bibliographical databases because of the Persian alphabet. It is more likely that works that have both a Persian and a European-language title will be found there. Between 1979 and 1989, the Centre for Iranian Documentation and Research recorded more than forty Persian or Iranian periodicals published in France, ranging from political to cultural to general interest (Centre for Iranian Documentation and Research 1989). These formed the basis of a healthy Iranian newspaper production on French soil. However, most of these publications were short-lived, printing just a few issues before closing down, mainly due to the lack of sufficient resources or low readership.

There were fewer journals and magazines published in the 2000s than previously. One of the longest on the market was *Arash: A Persian Monthly of Culture and Social Affairs*, which started in 1991, with Parviz Qelichkhani as editor-in-chief and Najmeh Mussavi Peimabari as editor, and closed down in 2014. The cultural and political journals of the first three decades after the revolution have not been replaced by other print journals. However, there are new initiatives, such as Naakojaa (Placeless), an online bookstore and publisher based in Paris, which fills the gap. I will come back to Naakojaa below. With this background in mind, I continue by analyzing some texts produced by Iranian writers living in France, using literary production as a practice of diaspora. In so doing, I will use the term "Iranian" to describe texts published in French by writers of Iranian origin, although these texts may also be considered as elements of French literature. However, Iran remains a referent for Iranian writers, and although many hold French citizenship they would define themselves as Iranian or Franco-Iranian.

Iranian Texts in France since the 1979 Iranian Revolution: Evolution of the Field and Emerging Categories

For the first three decades after the Iranian Revolution, orientalism and occidentalism were essential intertextual references in Iranian texts published in France as the basis for images of the Other that come into play (Nanquette 2013). While some texts overcome these references and complicate the image by resisting such discourses, they are exceptions. As I have suggested elsewhere, in contemporary French and Persian texts "literature happens only when images are deliberately complicated" when the simple opposition between Self and Other fails (Nanquette 2013, 10). Since the arrival of the post-2009 generation, there has been a change in the nature of Iranian literature production in France. Although it took a couple of years before the new wave of Iranian immigrants began producing more substantial work—due to their adaptation to the country and to the typical time lag when it comes to migrant cultural production—around 2010–2011 there was a noticeable increase in Iranian literary production in France. For example, between 2012 and 2015, a series edited by Ata Ayati at L'Harmattan, called *L'Iran en transition*, published around twenty literary and scholarly books on Iranian topics. The texts that were published also became more diverse and are thus less easily categorized.

Overall, one could say that the first decades of literary production by Iranians in France were represented by books such as Esmaeil Fassih's *Sorraya in a Coma* (Fassih 1985), describing the war with Iraq, the beginning of exile, and the difficulties of migration. More recently, new literary texts in which the agony of exile has been replaced by an acceptance of one's diasporic identity, especially among those who write in French, has appeared. One can also see the emergence of entirely new genres such as crime novels in the field. However, for those who continue to write in Persian, exile remains the main topic.

Given the small size of Iranian literary production in France since 1979 (around 150 works), it is possible to classify the literary texts by Iranian writers in France. Although any classification scheme undermines the specificities of texts, the Iranian literary field can be organized into six broad categories.[4] These categories are based on the common themes and genres of the books. They help the reader who has not had access to this corpus to see the commonalities and differences between these books. The first three categories (new orientalist narratives, counternarratives on Iran, autobiographies of suffering) are related to autobiographical themes and are dominated by women writers. However, despite their significance, unlike the Iranian texts in the United States (where Iranian autobiographies and memoirs swept the market), these themes and the genre of the autobiography don't occupy an important and central place in France. This is true for both the first wave of Iranians who came to France after the revolution and the more recent arrivals. The other three categories (the Persian novel in French, Persian literature of exile in French, and Persian literature of exile in Persian) are more fluid. They are useful for readers who might not have read the books by Franco-Iranian writers, and their categorization help us think through commonalities in the literary production of Iranian writers in France.

1. *New orientalist narratives* comprise texts such as *The Tears of Exile* (Azernour 2004) or *How Can Anybody Be French?* (Djavann 2006). They are autobiographies or autobiographical thesis novels (*romans à thèse*) aimed at a general French readership, were published by a variety of publishers, and are usually well received by readers. They systematically oppose France and Iran. Interestingly, compared to classical orientalist texts written by European writers, they use the native voice of Iranian writers. These new orientalist narratives are characterized by three discursive elements, including a simplified version of Islam, a representation of the world as a bipolar system, and a preference for France (Nanquette 2013). These texts are counterparts to Iranian American stories such as *Reading Lolita in Tehran* by Azar Nafisi (2003).

2. *Counternarratives on Iran* comprise texts such as *Persian Gaze* (Yalda 2007), *Passport Iranian-Style* (Tajadod 2007), the graphic novel *Persepolis* (Satrapi 2000–2003), and *I Am Writing to You from Tehran* (Minoui 2015). They offer an alternative image of Iran to a general French readership. This genre tends toward autobiography, with the writers using their dual identity to demonstrate the human reality of Iranians to the French reader. They are often critical of the Islamic regime and stand in direct contrast to new orientalist narratives. They are published by recognized publishers and are well received by French readers, who are interested in a different understanding of Iran. This is also a category that can easily

be compared to literary texts in other Iranian diasporic locations. Some Iranian American "return narratives" like *Lipstick Jihad* (Moaveni 2005) follow a similar endeavor.

3. *Autobiographies of suffering* consist of texts such as *The Valley of Eagles* (Kasmaï 2006), *The Life of an Iranian Woman in the 20th Century* (Mahindokht 2004), and *Child of the Wheat* (Djavani 2005). Published by well-known publishers, they are testimonies that recount experiences of difficult times, either a single event (such as illegally escaping from Iran) or events spanning a lifetime. As they are focused on misfortune, they cater to a particular kind of reader, and do not reach a large French audience. They also target second-generation Iranians who might not read Persian but would like to know more about life in Iran at a particular time or for particular people (women, political activists, etc.). An American counterpart is *Journey from the Land of No: A Girlhood Caught in Revolutionary Iran* (Hakkakian 2004), which recounts the revolution as both a complex and intense and thus endearing event for a girl.

4. *Persian novels in French* comprise texts such as *Land of Mirages* (Shayegan 2004), *The Glass Cemetery* (Kasmaï 2002), *One Day before the End of the World* (Kasmaï 2015), *Farewell Ménilmontant* (Erfan 2005), *The Sigh of the Angel* (Javaheri 2003), and *Ask the Mirror* (Chafiq 2015). The genre of the novel is particularly important here, as it allows an author to emphasize his/her hybrid identity. These works are polyphonic novels that can be interpreted in multiple ways, contrary to the previous three categories, which have a didactic aspect (Nanquette 2011). Published by well-known but sometimes small French publishers, they do not sell many copies, and they target a French or Iranian intellectual readership. A similar Iranian American book, written in English, would be *Moonlight on the Avenue of Faith* (Nahai 1999), which uses magical realism to tell stories about the Jewish ghetto of Tehran.

5. *Persian literature of exile in French* consists of texts such as *The Last Poet of the World* (Erfan 1990) and *All My Days Are Farewells* (Adle 1998). I do not distinguish between exile and migration literature, as the categories often change over time for the same writer. The Persian literature of exile is defined primarily in terms of content, as it focuses on themes of alienation from the host country, trajectories of migration, and the desire to return to the homeland. The category covers a variety of narrators, readerships, and images. The French language helps the writer gain more exposure in France. These works are published by recognized French publishers. Many more texts of exile have been written in Persian, as we will see in the final category below; however, they do not sell many copies.

There are many Iranian American texts that deal with the same topic of loss, like *Against Gravity* (Moshiri 2005).

6. *Persian literature of exile in Persian* is a category defined by the use of exile thematically, generically, and stylistically. This is an important trend, with around forty texts published since 1979. The Persian language appears here as a space of memory, and here one can think of authors such as Reza Ghassemi (Ghassemi 1991; Qassemi 2001) and Mahshid Amirshahi (Amirshahi 1995; Amirshahi 1998–2010). Many of these texts are published by small Persian publishers abroad, with an example being Reza Ghassemi's *Nocturnal Harmony of Wood Orchestra* (1991), which has been translated into French and received positive reviews from the press. It is one of those rare texts published abroad that has also been well received in Iran, where it won the Hooshang Golshiri prize for best first novel. While there are a few others that have succeeded in Iran, such as *Funny in Farsi* by Firoozeh Dumas, a writer based in the United States writing in English (Dumas 2003), as a rule, until very recently, texts published abroad did not succeed in Iran and did not have a strong Iranian readership. This is primarily due to censorship issues, as well as some disconnection between the Iranian readership and writers in the diaspora. Goli Taraghi, who lives partly in Paris and partly in Tehran, publishes in Persian in Tehran. Her books have been translated to many languages. Taraghi is on the fringe of this category of Persian literature of exile, and while the themes of her stories and novels deal with exile, she also has a connection to Iran and to Iranian readers that few foreign-based writers have because she spends time in both Paris and Tehran. Unlike many Iranian writers who live in exile, Taraghi's dual residence has pushed her to the fringe of this category of Persian literature in diaspora and has enabled her to publish in Persian in Tehran and to obtain a global readership. Writers such as Taraghi are best-sellers in Iran and abroad, but in general the reception of Persian literature of exile written in Persian varies greatly. Some texts published abroad only have print runs of 100 copies, mainly distributed within the writer's network.

The categories defined above primarily apply to texts published before 2009, although I have included some post-2009 texts that fit those categories. In the next section, I focus on the most recent changes in the Iranian literary field in France, mainly after 2009, when the third wave of Iranian migrants to France led a dramatic change in cultural production. In the 2010s, some new genres have appeared that make the categories presented above a little more difficult to sustain. It appears that the field of Franco-

Iranian writing is becoming more diverse and that the authors are moving beyond the few clearly defined topics and genres. For example, in recent years in France, Naïri Nahapétian has published a number of crime novels (Nahapétian 2009, 2012, 2015, 2016) that delve into the problems of Iranian society and engage with political and social issues such as drug trafficking. These novels often focus on large cities, particularly Tehran and Isfahan, as an essential landscape. This is unusual because the crime novel genre is not prominent in Iran or in the diaspora. Even in the United States—where the genre is so popular that it might be expected that Iranian writers would use it more than in France—it is only a very recent addition to the field of Persian literature, along with noir novels and short stories, such as those by Abdoh Salar (Abdoh 2000, 2014a, 2014b). In France, collections of short stories have also begun to appear, such as "Eclats de vie, histoires persanes" (Musavi 2013), which provides nostalgic glimpses of the life of an Iranian woman in French exile. Apart from Ali Erfan, who has always used the genre of short stories, such collections are usually favored by Iranians writing in Persian only, and it is rare to read them in French (or in any other European languages, for that matter). Indeed, writers of Iranian origin who write in French have preferred genres that are more accessible to a French readership, such as novels and autobiographies. There has thus been a radical reshaping of the Franco-Iranian literary field in recent years, testified not only in literary texts but also in cultural institutions.

The Death of a Certain Kind of Iranian Literary Diaspora and the Birth of a New One

The evolution of Iranian bookstores and publishers in Paris since the revolution is telling evidence of the major changes that have taken place among Iranian literary scholars and institutions (especially publishers and bookstores) in France. For example, traditional bookstores such as Khavaran have closed down in recent years due to financial problems and have been replaced with modern digital outlets. This evolution reflects not only an evolving book economy, less focused on print, but also changes in the Iranian population structure in France, as the older, leftist generation is replaced by younger intellectuals. Generally speaking, bookstores with a national/ethnic orientation usually function as diasporic political spaces for the perpetuation of political activism. Moreover, they create links between literary production and the maintenance of cultural identity. In France, the managers (and some consumers) of these spaces, be they digital or brick-

and-mortar spaces, use the Iranian ethnic identity as a "commodity" to compete with non-Iranian businesses.

The bookstore Khavaran was established in 1983 in Vincennes, a suburb close to the center of Paris. It was managed by Bahman Amini, who worked as a writer for an Iranian magazine before he moved to France in 1981. As Farid Moradi (2015) explains:

> As the publication business was not profitable, he started a printing business to help him run his publications. The business started by printing 500 to 1000 copies per book. This has now been reduced to 200 to 300. . . . He claims that only 5 percent of Iranian books published abroad succeed in having a second edition. Since the start of his business only three books have had this experience.

Amini did not receive help from French institutions and relied solely on his Iranian network to promote his books. Khavaran primarily published prison memoirs and books that were banned in Iran. In addition to books in Persian, Khavaran published a few French books in collaboration with a French publisher and commissioned a few works.

Khavaran was a meeting place for Iranian intellectuals in the 1980s, especially for leftist intellectuals who composed the majority of readers; Amini himself was politically active and had been a political prisoner in the 1970s in Iran. Thus, Khavaran provided a solid platform that connected literary texts and political engagement together. In the early 2000s, Khavaran became a specialist Persian bookstore and a patron for book readings and talks for Iranians in Paris. Khavaran then moved to a different location in Paris and scaled down its activities. The bookstore discontinued its Persian specialty, and the Persian books were stored (or displayed) in the back of the store, invisible to most customers. Ultimately, Khavaran was closed down permanently in 2015 due to a huge financial loss and lack of clientele.

Exile bookstores like Khavaran that functioned as cultural centers did not disappear altogether but have been replaced by others. Naakojaa, to be discussed below, is one example. Its form differs quite dramatically from Khavaran, reflecting a change in reading habits of book lovers. A major characteristic that differentiates the new Iranian bookstores from the old ones is a less marked political engagement and party affiliation as well as the potential to attract a larger spectrum of Iranian and non-Iranian readers.

Before Khavaran closed, initiatives such as the Persian Publishers Network were set up with the help of the International Alliance of Independent Publishers. The network was organized by Sonbol Regnault Bahmanyar and managed by Bahman Amini. Since 2016, it has been managed by Tinouche Nazmjou, the director of Naakojaa, thus reinforcing the change from one generation of publisher to another. My personal involvement in this initiative enabled me to witness its development. The main goals of PPN were to coordinate and support the efforts and activities of Iranian publishers abroad, promote collaboration and partnership among them, and help them with copyright and other legal issues. The publishers involved were: Hamid Mehdipour of Forough in Cologne; Farhad Shirzad of Ibex in Maryland; Bahman Amini of Khavaran in Paris; Reza Chavoshi of Dena in the Netherlands; Naser Zera'ti of Bokartus in Sweden; Masoud Mafan of Baran in Sweden; Abbas Maroufi of Gardoon in Berlin; and Tinouche Nazmjou of Naakojaa in Paris. After meetings in Paris, PPN published an ebook in Persian and English about Iranian publishers abroad (Moradi et al. 2013). While this initiative was innovative, PPN's activities have been limited to a few copublications.

I will now look more closely at Naakojaa, arguing that its online format and international orientation is changing the Franco-Iranian literary scene in general and the Iranian texts written in the diaspora in particular. Writers abroad are often disconnected from readers in Iran. In reference to Naakojaa, I will ask whether the digital era is bridging this gap in cultural exchange. The cultural, political, and social support networks linking France and Iran are generally weak, and the Iranian community in France is fragmented. However, perhaps paradoxically, the post-2009 generation of Iranians in France, of which Naakojaa is representative, is more connected to Iran than the previous generations because its members travel to Iran more often. This is something that was mostly forbidden to the first generation of migrants, who, because of their strong political activities and the inflexibility of the Islamic regime, could not return. This is not to say that the post-2009 generation is not politically active, but it appears to be able to negotiate around issues more readily, as it is generally not affiliated to one party and has a subtle understanding of the political struggle thanks to its daily interaction with the complex Iranian system.

Naakojaa is a publishing house based in France founded by Tinouche Nazmjou in 2012. It also runs a bookstore based in Paris, the Librarie Utopiran. After the second term of President Mahmoud Ahmadinejad, when censorship in Iran grew stronger, Nazmjou, who had extensive publishing experience, decided to open his publishing house in Paris. He focused on digital distribution in order to reach Iranians globally. Contrary to most publishers in Iran, Naakojaa respects the Universal Copyright Convention. It offers a contract and copyright protection to writers, which provides an interesting option for writers in Iran who usually do not have such opportunities. Naakojaa receives around a hundred manuscripts per month from Iranians around the world and publishes three or four works each month (Nazmjou 2016). Naakojaa's goals are to publish quality texts from lesser-known writers based in Iran and abroad or on subjects that are less commonly treated, and to promote reading throughout Iran and France. E-publishing makes a difference in Iran, insofar as it replaces the many poor-quality scans that circulate illegally. Furthermore, considering that Iranians are scattered around the world and are often highly educated, it makes sense to create electronic publications that are easily accessible. In a personal communication in 2015, Nazmjou also insisted on the fact that the texts must have a universal appeal so that they are potentially translatable and might be read by a Western audience.

Naakojaa offers a rich website with notes, articles, videos, discussions, and the collected works of most of its authors, and it plays the role of a cultural platform (Nanquette 2017, 163). It also introduces books published by other Iranian publishers, giving a wide view of the Iranian literary scene. Naakojaa also uses Twitter, Telegram, and Facebook to promote its publications. In addition, Naakojaa's bookstore, Utopiran, offers printed Persian books and texts in French about Iran and organizes cultural events linked to Iran. Other activities of Utopiran include readings of texts, talks by writers, and biweekly book club discussions in Persian and in French. These events are well attended and draw a diverse audience depending on the topic discussed. As such, Naakojaa aims to be a place of literary dialogue, as reiterated by its manager:

> *Naakojaa* is not just a bookstore; it's a place for reviewing books and, more importantly, it's a place for dialogue and exchanging ideas and comments about world literature and its impact on life and our society (Mehtari March 7, 2012).

Organizing book discussions with the hope of impacting both French and Iranian societies is a form of politics. This venture shows how a bookstore need not simply be a place where books are sold but also a place where ideas and ideals are formed and circulate.

Unlike the previous generation of Iranian publishers, Naakojaa is not as clearly linked to a political party. Naakojaa can be described as a committed publisher with an obvious policy of publishing books that have been censored or banned in Iran, those that writers think will probably be banned, and those that have been published and then banned by the government.

Such books are cataloged under a category entitled *Safar be digar-e soo* (Travel to the Other Side). For example, Naakojaa has published the poems and short stories of the Iranian writer, translator, and journalist Sepideh Jadiri, whose poems are banned in Iran and who founded the first Iranian Women Poets award (*Khorshid*). She lived in Italy for some time as a guest writer of PEN, and her poems have been translated into English, Dutch, Swedish, Kurdish, Turkish, and French. She also translated *Blue is the Warmest Colour*, a graphic novel about female homosexuality that has been banned in Iran (Nanquette 2017: 163).

Three types of books are available through Naakojaa's website: printed books, e-books in PDF, and ePub. Some of them have a Digital Rights Management lock. E-books can be read on a personal computer, reader device, iPod, or iPhone; there are also audio books that are read by one or several actors. The sales model of Naakojaa is broadly based and usually offers several purchasing options, including directly from Naakojaa or from other providers such as Google, Lulu (a US-based independent print-on-demand and self-publishing bookstore), and Amazon in Germany, Spain, the United Kingdom, Italy, and France. For those in Iran, it is possible to buy books without using a credit card if you do not want to be traced.

Naakojaa's revenues come only from the sale of books, as it does not receive financial help from French institutions, although this might change in the future if it produces French translations, as institutions such as the Centre National du Livre are devoted to promoting such translations. As Nazmjou points out, the e-publication of books is what allowed Naakojaa to reach the readership based in Iran, but because of its limited spending power the sales from e-books were low. Nevertheless, this is still the main source of revenue

Naakojaa is the largest global Iranian ethnic institution that caters to Iranians across the world. Others, like the self-publishing house H&S Media and Nogaam, a crowd-funded publisher, both based in the United Kingdom, are innovative but do not have as much institutional power. Naakojaa is an example of how electronic media create a bridge between the Iranian diaspora in France and Iranian diasporic communities in other countries, as well as Iran. Naakojaa's success is due to the fact it includes Iranians from around the world and has very close ties to Iran. The shift in production and circulation of Iranian literary texts from a print modality to a digital modality has had an impact on Iranian social and political networks in the diaspora. This shift has expanded the cultural and literary activities of Iranians outside France and has created a global network with a new global consciousness, especially oriented toward political processes in Iran.

With this shift, local practices and diasporic spaces such as the Khavaran bookstore, where intellectuals met regularly and organized literary meetings for members of the community, have today been replaced with a diasporic space that is partially virtual. In addition to its role as an electronic space for promotion dialogue and networking among Iranian intellectuals in diaspora, Naakojaa also functions as a local physical space and a bookstore that hosts readings. Indeed, the capability of digital spaces should not be inflated. Crucial studies about the Iranian digital space, whether the website Iranian.com (Alexanian 2008) or weblogs (Akhavan 2013), insist on caution when speaking of an Iranian digital space "as a kind of virtual community" (Alexanian 2008, 129). It is important to remind us that expressions of identity online have "consequences in the offline world" (Alexanian 2008, 133). The virtual and the local are linked, and the virtual does not replace the local but is closely intertwined with it (Nanquette 2017: 164). Naakojaa is a good example of the articulation of physical space and the virtual space that reaches readers both in the diaspora and in Iran.

Conclusion

The analysis of the literary production of Iranians in France presented in this chapter reveals that there is a strong connection between the nature, evolution, and cultural role of Iranian literary production in exile and the challenges faced by Iranian migrants. It also suggests a link between production of literary texts and the specific immigrant generation and migration wave since the Iranian Revolution. Finally, the analysis also shows that there has been a radical reshaping of the Franco-Iranian literary field in recent years, testified not only in production of literary texts (which are more diverse and more difficult to categorize) but also in its global distribution and circulation through modern digital channels and the creation of new online cultural institutions. The online bookstore platform Naakojaa is an example of one such modern cultural institution that has transformed the diasporic flow and function of Iranian literary production.

In addition to its successive transformation in form and content, literary production by Iranians in France has unique characteristics that make it considerably different from the other Iranian diasporic literary productions. This difference is particularly salient in comparison with the United States, where a relatively large volume of Iranian literary texts has been produced since the revolution. The most important difference is that Iranian autobiographies produced in France do not have the same important place as they have in the Iranian American literary field.

The case of Iranians in France demonstrates that evolution in the literary production of an immigrant group in diaspora may partly be a response to political conditions in its home society. As I outlined in this chapter, the circulation and use of literary production as a political tool to resist the Iranian government has taken different forms and contexts in different periods since the Iranian Revolution, ranging from reading gatherings in a local bookstore in Paris to electronic publication and circulation of books banned in Iran at the global level. As discussed at the beginning of this chapter, Iranian literary production in exile is not new, and Iranian writers have been published abroad since the 1908 Iranian constitutional revolution. What is new, however, is the local and global implications of these texts for the Iranian diaspora, as well as the extent to which it enables diasporic Iranians to stay connected to Iran in a manner that was not possible before. In this chapter, I have argued that the increasing literary and cultural linkages between the Iranian diaspora and Iran, as well as the technological revolution in the digital media and frequent travel between Iran and France, have significantly affected the nature, function, and dissemination of Iranian literary production in diaspora.

Notes

1. Nader Vahabi uses figures from INSEE (National Institute of Statistics and Economic Studies) and OFPRA (French Office for the Protection of Refugees and Stateless People).

2. The US State Department announced in 2016 a change to its Visa Waiver Program, which allowed visitors from thirty-seven countries to enter the United States without a visa. From January 2016, those who traveled to Iran, Iraq, Sudan, or Syria on or after March 1, 2011, were not able to enter the United States without a visa. They had to apply for a visa through the regular process. This change came under the Visa Waiver Program Improvement and Terrorist Travel Prevention Act 2015. It applied to binationals of those countries during 2016. In 2017, rules around visas tightened again.

3. In the context of postrevolutionary youths within Iran, Roxanne Varzi has studied the appearance of "Sufi cool," mixing New Age and Islamic elements (Varzi 2006: 10). As Varzi argues, their practice of spirituality is different from religious practice. There is a similarity with the Sufi brotherhoods developing in the West, to which many people who describe themselves as "secular" belong. Thanks to Michelle Langford for pointing out this reference.

4. I use classifications defined in my book and make comparison to other literary fields of Iranian production: (Nanquette 2013).

CHAPTER 8

Diaspora and Ethnic Identity Construction and Negotiation through Literary Production: Iranians in Italy

ALICE MIGGIANO

The Iranian Italian political ties were never broken completely after the 1979 Iranian Revolution, and there has never been major political tension between the two governments. Italy has substantial economic interests in Iran and has recently became Iran's first European trading partner.[1] Due to economic sanctions, trade between the two countries, which was about $7 billion a year, has dropped $800,000 in US dollars. With the recent easing of some of the sanctions imposed on Iran, Italy will benefit from a significant recovery in the volume of trade with Iran. When considering the reopening (or enhancement) of trade, it is significant to consider the fact that the Iranian president, Hassan Rouhani, in his first trip to Europe after the end of the sanctions, chose Italy as the first European country to visit. Although it will take time to return to the same levels of export before the sanctions, reliable estimates indicate the possibility to recover about 3 billion Euros by the end of 2018.[2] Even air travel by the Italian national airline company increased as a result of the end of sanctions. Since March 2016, the Rome-Tehran route operated by Alitalia increased from four weekly flights to daily flights. The increase in flights to Iran represents a greater commitment to the resumption of trade between the two countries and to better support the activities of Italian entrepreneurs in Iran and in tourism.[3] The strong relationship between Italy and Iran is not only commercial; the two countries have in fact a long tradition of cultural and diplomatic exchanges, which have never been interrupted despite the international economic sanctions in the past. As for the cultural relationship between the two countries, it is important to point out that Italy has been chosen as the guest of honor at the annual 2017 Tehran International Book Fair. Italy is the first European country to have had this honor, thus reaffirming its primacy for being the first country that has been visited by Rouhani after the sanctions were lifted.

Despite the positive diplomatic, commercial, and cultural ties between Iran and Italy as well as the extensive publications on Persian literature and history in Italy, very little research has been carried out on Iranian immigrants and their diasporic experience since the Islamic Revolution of 1979. One of the main reasons for this dearth of research on Iranian immigrants in Italy is that, unlike in other European countries, the Italian census does not regularly provide separate statistical data by nationality.[4] Another reason for the lack of systematic research on Iranians in Italy is their small population in this country. Given their smaller size in comparison to those in the other European countries, most studies on the Iranian diaspora carried out by social scientists in other countries overlook Iranians in Italy.

The primary aim of this chapter is to provide information about the demographic and socioeconomic characteristics of Iranians in Italy. After discussing some of the main features of the Iranian community, I will briefly describe the ways in which the national political context, as well as the immigration policies and prejudicial public opinion in Italy, have impacted the experiences of Iranians in this country. Most of the information for this chapter was collected between 2011 and 2015, when I was studying the characteristics of the Iranian community and conducting research for my doctoral dissertation on the literature of exile produced by Iranian writers in Italy. In addition to data collected during my PhD dissertation research, I obtained other valuable information about Iranians in Italy from the consular archives during my employment at the Iranian embassy in Rome between 2007 and 2013. Moreover, to have a better understanding about the migration experience of Iranians in Italy, I became acquainted with several members of the Iranian community in Italy, in particular those living in Rome, and I conducted forty face-to-face interviews in Italian and in Persian.

Literature Review and the Migration History of Iranians to Italy

Two of the major studies on Iranian immigrants in Italy were conducted by Chantal Saint-Blancat (1988, 1989, 1990) and Mario Casari (2006). The first systematic sociological study on the Iranian community in Italy was conducted in 1988 by the sociologist Chantal Saint-Blancat, and her findings were published in a monograph titled *Nazione e religione fra gli Iraniani in Italia* (Nation and Religion among Iranians in Italy). She also published two articles, "L'immigrazione iraniana in Italia: vera o falsa parentesi?" (The Iranian Immigration in Italy: A True or False Interlude?) (1989) and "La presenza iraniana in Italia" (The Iranian Presence in Italy) (1990), in which she described the migration experience of Iranians in Italy. According to Saint-Blancat, in 1986 as many as 13,536 Iranians were residing in Italy. Among them, 2,009 individuals had come to Italy for family reasons, 748 for business reasons, 27 for health reasons, 19 for religious reasons, 409 for elective residence, 15 for judicial reasons, 452 for self-employment, 25 for unspecified reasons, 7 for political asylum, and 737 for tourism. Students represented 65 percent (8,798 students) of the Iranian population in Italy in 1986. The large volume of the student population in 1986 in Italy was primarily due to less government restriction for individuals who left Iran for educational reasons. The largest concentrations of Iranians in Italy in 1988, according to Saint-Blancat, were in the regions of Lazio (20 percent), Umbria (18 percent), and Lombardy (13 percent). The concentration of Iranians in these areas, she continues, was largely due to the strong presence of university students who mainly concentrated around college campuses and major urban centers where support networks were more easily found.[5]

When considering the relationship between religion and national identity, the researcher claims that, among all the different Muslim communities, the Iranian Shiites are particularly a significant group because of the close relationship between Shiism and national identity in the Iranian historical memory. The events of the 1979 Islamic Revolution in Iran confirmed not only the strength of the dual force between religious identity/national identity but also the powerful role that religion played in shaping national identification and opposition to Westernization.[6] Iranian immigrants raised and educated in this sociocultural context have lived a concrete historical situation that has somehow forced them to take a position within the relationship between religious, national, and social identity.[7] In general, according to Saint-Blancat, Iranian immigrants face a very ambiguous situation, reinforced by the complexity and the hypocrisy of the postrevolutionary Iranian laws and by the current Iranian reality. In her opinion, the myth of the return, which is always present among immigrants, appears to be a particularly intense feeling in the case of the recent and young Iranian immigrants. In most cases, in fact, Iranian immigrants tend to take refuge in the utopia of the return while having mixed feelings between the nostalgia for a country that limits individual freedom and an unknown foreign country and culture from which they feel disconnected.[8]

Chantal Saint-Blancat has also observed the impact that Islam has on Iranian Immigrants' behavioral norms and on their choices of life strategies. Her analysis suggests that, for both practicing and nonpracticing Iranian Muslims, religion affects not only individual decisions regarding their daily life, social integration, and community organization but also the construction of national identity in diaspora. Despite the importance of belonging to a national group, Iranian national identity appears to be particularly controversial because it is built around and rooted in more diverse ethnoreligious groups, including pre-Islamic Zoroastrian, Armenian, Jewish, and Shiite Islam adherents. According to Saint-Blancat, in the constitution of their identity structures Iranians are faced with the absence of a united ethnic or national community. Therefore, Iranians find themselves in a precarious context, and they generally respond to this situation by refusing to give a partial and mutable picture of themselves. They turn to three alternative ways to search for security by: maintaining primary bonds within their kinship network, belonging to an ideological group, and seeking refuge in the myth of the past.[9]

A second interesting work on the Iranian immigrants and their community in Italy is published in the *Encyclopaedia Iranica* (2006) by Mario Casari, a scholar of Iranian studies. According to Casari, it has always been difficult to speak about a real community of Iranians in Italy. Over the centuries, there have been successive waves of emigration from Iran, but few Iranians ever ended up staying for a long period or forming a cohesive social group in Italy. In the past, notably before and during the eighteenth century, there were considerable waves of Iranian migration to countries such as India and France. Later, and especially after World War II and the Islamic Revolution of 1979, Sweden, Canada, and the United States became the primary destinations for Iranians. Furthermore, the Italian bureaucracy and laws regarding immigration, refugee status, and employment have created further disincentives to Iranians seeking a new host country in which to live.[10] Casari's analysis of Iranian immigration to Italy reveals that, starting from the 1950s until today, there has been a large influx of students followed by Persian carpet merchants during the time of the boom in rug sales in the 1970s and the resulting increase in trade. The trade in Persian carpets reached new heights in the twenty-five years following the Islamic Revolution. As a direct result of the Persian rug stores, trading houses, repair, and cleaning services were introduced. All this provided the main source of income and work for a new generation of postrevolutionary Iranian immigrants in Italy.

The goal of the first wave of students who emigrated from Iran to Italy was essentially to acquire the necessary skills for the technical and scientific progress of their country.[11] With the onset of industrialization in Iran, promoted by the Pahlavi monarchy in the 1960s, Iranian universities faced limited opportunity for training all those who were to function as the future leaders in their fields. However, as has been the case with many other immigrant groups, with the advent of the Islamic Revolution most of the students who had arrived in Italy under the Pahlavi dynasty stayed in Italy after the completion of their studies and never returned to Iran. Furthermore, following the outbreak of the Iran-Iraq War in the early 1980s, a new wave of emigrants left Iran and settled in Europe and North America.[12] Since the 1979 Islamic Revolution, a number of different groups of Iranians, including members of religious minorities and of the Pahlavi regime, political refugees, intellectuals, women, and entire families who had difficulty in accepting the new rules imposed by the new government, began to arrive in Italy as well as other European countries and the United States. However, the majority of the new arrivals in Italy were university students,[13] which is still the case today.

As for the years before the Islamic Revolution, no literature on the Iranian presence has been produced in Italian, apart from a few references provided by Casari (2006). But we can get an idea about the number of Iranian students resident in Italy in those years by consulting research papers that have been conducted internationally. A study published in 1962, for example, reveals that, in the 1958/1959 academic year, among the total number of 10,183 students enrolled in foreign universities abroad, a hundred resided in Italy.[14] A survey conducted in Tehran during the summer of 1960, and published in 1963, shows that, out of a sample of 414 Iranians who returned to Iran after studying abroad for a period of time, less than five had studied at universities in Italy.[15]

The findings of the interviews that I personally conducted with some members of the Iranian community who came to Rome before the Islamic Revolution to enroll at university indicate that in the capital city in the late 1950s there were about eight or nine students and one or two Iranian traders, while in the 1970s the number of university students in the city had grown to about forty to fifty people, most of them enrolled in the faculties of architecture or fine arts. During the same time, almost all Iranian students were active against the Shah's regime. Although the active core of the student movement in Europe was in Germany and France, even in Italy there was strong political activism, especially at the faculty of architecture in Venice and Florence, and in Rome in almost all the faculties attended by Iranian students.

The student confederation in Rome, coordinated by the architect Rahmat Khosravi, had close political contacts with Iranian communities active in France and in West Germany. The members of the group's executives of the three countries often met. In spite of the great difficulties, there were also contacts with the Tudeh Party, which sent directions from Iran. Very little economic help came from Iran, mainly due to the difficulty they had in sending money abroad; sporadic funding was provided by the Italian Communist Party. One of the major economic aids, for example, followed an encounter between a group of politically active Iranian students in Rome with Palmiro Togliatti, the leader of the Italian Communist Party, in the 1960s. The student confederation used these funds to rent basements, where they would meet almost every evening to discuss politics. Iranian students had limited funds, and in those years in Italy there was a ban on hiring foreigners who were in the country on a student visa. Therefore, many Iranian students in the 1960s went to work in Germany during the summer months to earn money to pay for their studies.

In general, members of the student confederation lived in a climate of fear and mistrust because there was the risk of being reported to SAVAK (Sāzemān-e Eṭṭelāʿāt va Amniyat-e Keshvar [National Security and Intelligence Organization], the Iranian imperial secret services that operated between 1957 and 1979 under the Pahlavi dynasty) and having their passports confiscated or even being arrested upon their return to Iran. There were attempts to occupy the Iranian embassy, but the Italian police have always intervened to suppress this type of initiative. The political movement lasted until the 1990s, some students left Italy soon after graduating, and many of those who have remained did not get the opportunity to work in their field and started a variety of businesses, including the trade of Persian rugs. Others have established themselves as doctors, architects, engineers, artists, and so on.

Demographic Characteristics of Iranians in Italy

Due to lack of particular attention to immigrant groups in Italy, there are no major financed research studies on foreign communities, including Iranians. The data for this chapter was collected from a variety of sources. Unfortunately, the available data regarding the total number of Iranians is very inconsistent. It is reported that in 1986 there were 13,536 Iranians living in Italy;[16] another report suggests that in 1999, thirteen years later, the number of Iranians in Italy was 8,371.[17] According to the census provided by the annual statistical dossier on immigration in 2006, 5,910 Iranians resided in Italy.[18] The number of Iranians increased to 7,444 in 2010 and to 11,530 in 2014 (ISTAT for 2010[19] and Caritas for 2014[20]). According to the archives of the Iranian consulate in Rome, there are about 25,000 Iranians in Italy, between 8,000 and 10,000 of whom are students.[21]

The difference between these figures is due to differences in data collection procedures. For example, data collected by scholars and the Italian government consider only the Iranians in possession of a valid residence permit—for study, for work, or for family reasons—while the consular archives produce a different dossier for every Iranian who gets in touch with the Iranian embassy. In addition to the Iranians with residence permits, this archive includes Iranians who have obtained Italian citizenship (or the citizenship of another country of the European Community) and therefore do not need residence permits; temporary residents in possession of a visa; undocumented immigrants, political refugees, and asylum seekers; members of the diplomatic corps and their families; detainees without documents; minors who are noted in the residence permit of their parents; and also children of Iranians with Italian citizenship at birth.[22] Data provided by the Iranian embassy are to be regarded as the most reliable, and the real number of Iranians in Italy is likely higher. To gain a better understanding about the rapid increase in the number of Iranians in Italy, it is best to look at the data provided by the Italian Ministry of the Interior, according to which the number of Iranians increased by approximately 2,000 individuals from 2006 to 2013. During this period, there was also an increase in the number of municipalities of residence from 823 to 881.[23]

In 2011, the Italian government subdivided the Iranian population living in Italy based on age cohort. The groups with the highest number of Iranians correspond to the age group ranging from twenty-five to twenty-nine years old and to the one ranging from thirty to thirty-four years old. Out of a total of 8,437 Iranians, these two groups represented, respectively, 1,252 and 1,144 Iranians in 2011. The least represented age group was the one between sixty and sixty-four years old, with a total of only 270 Iranians among 8,000.[24] This analysis provided further evidence for the large proportion of young Iranians who come to Italy requiring a residence permit to pursue further education. With regard to the sex ratio in 1999, men constituted 71 percent of total Iranian residents,[25] in 2011 they accounted for 54 percent,[26] and in 2014 53 percent.[27]

As for the districts of residence of Iranians over the whole Italian territory, we can compare two different figures for the year 2014. According to the Italian government, the distribution of the Iranian population shows that in 2014 in just four Italian regions[28] there were over 1,001 Iranians; two regions had between 501 and 1,000 Iranians; and in the remaining fourteen regions up to 500 Iranians were resident.[29] By contrast, according to the Iranian government, in 2014 the distribution of the Iranian population in Italian areas was the following: approximately 10,000 Iranians lived in the north of Italy (the regions under the territorial jurisdiction of the Consulate General of the Islamic Republic of Iran in Milan), and more than 14,000 Iranians lived in central and southern Italy (the regions under the territorial jurisdiction of the Consular Section of the Embassy of Islamic Republic of Iran in Rome).[30]

Regarding the geographic distribution of Iranians in Italian cities, the five largest Iranian populations in 2013 were in Rome with 1,393 Iranians, Milan with 1,102, Turin with 675, Florence with 464, and Bologna with 383.[31] On the website "Roma Multietnica," managed by the municipality of Rome, there is a page that provides some interesting data on the Iranian community, but only as related to the capital city. Based on the information provided in this website, according to the statistics office of the city of Rome, in 2012 the Iranian community in Rome numbered 2,059 residents, mostly located in the northern part of the city. This constitutes the largest concentration of Iranians in Italy, followed by Milan and Florence.[32]

Since the Italian government does not collect data on the employment and educational qualifications of immigrants, the only available statistical data is that relating to small groups such as the number of college students, detainees, and asylum seekers, as we can see below. As mentioned above, much like in the past, a very large portion of Iranians who arrive in Italy are students who immigrated for educational reasons. Most students come to Italy primarily because of the relatively easy university admission process and the availability of scholarships. A large number of Iranian students intended to move to other European countries or to the United States as soon as possible. According to the data found in the archives of the Iranian embassy in Rome, between 600 and 1,000 new Iranian students arrived annually in Italy between 2007 and 2013. However, many of them stayed in Italy for a short time before moving to other countries. Given that many Italian universities offer courses that place no limit on the number of students enrolled and provide scholarships to low-income foreign students, many young Iranian students are eager to apply to Italian universities. Once established, many of these students request for a visa from another country and relocate. In addition to a scholarship fund offered by universities, many Iranian students in Italy can also benefit from scholarships offered by the Iranian government, which finances college students (the ones who are legally resident and in compliance with the university exams) who agree to register with the closest Iranian consulate to their residence[33] and provide appropriate school documents. This process is mandated by the Iranian government as is designed to check on the number and the identities of young Iranians living abroad. If qualified, students who register with the Iranian consular offices in Italy receive a scholarship equal to about a thousand Euros per semester. In addition to the Iranian university students, the data from the Italian Ministry of Education, Universities, and Research suggests that in the 2013/2014 school year there were 716 Iranian students attending Italian public schools.[34] The comparable number for 2012/2013 school year was 690.[35]

According to a *nota verbale* (official letter) sent in September 2013 by the Italian Ministry of Foreign Affairs to the Iranian embassy in Rome, in the 2013 academic year there were as many as 2,667 Iranian students registered (1,418 women and 1,249 men) in Italian public universities. Iranian students represented 9.79 percent of the total population of 27,246 foreign universities students attending Italian universities.[36] While this data considered only the students who were registered in public universities, and only those with a residence permit to study, it excluded Iranians with dual citizenship, those enrolled in private universities, and those with residence permits for family reasons or for work. Another recent report published by Centro Studi e Ricerche IDOS in 2016 reveals that, out of a total of 10,719 international students in 2014, Iranian students, with 378 graduates (3.5 percent of international graduates), came in at the fifth position after Albanian, Chinese, Romanian, and Cameroonese students.[37]

According to the Italian Ministry of Justice, in 2015 there were thirty Iranian male detainees in Italian prisons. Iranians detainees constituted only 0.2 percent of the total of 17,403 foreign detainees.[38] The negligible number of Iranian detainees suggests that Iranians in Italy are generally law abiding and are not involved in criminal behavior. In terms of asylum seekers, it is worth noting that Italy extended the right of asylum to non-European citizens only in 1990 and that the data provided by the government on the number of refugees refers exclusively to the five nationalities with the largest number of requests. Since 1990, Iran has been continually among the five nations with the largest number of asylum seekers, with 102 applications in 1994, 134 in 1995, 46 in 1996, 75 in 1997, and 239 in 1999.[39] Compared to other European countries, the number of Iranian refugees and asylum seekers in Italy is much smaller. For example, in 2009 8,565 Iranians in Europe applied for political asylum. This number increased to 10,340 in 2010 and to 11,890 in 2011. In 2012 and 2013, a little more than 26,000 political asylum applications were filed by Iranians in Europe.[40] Despite the gradual increase in the number of political asylum applications filed by Iranians in Europe, there was a drastic reduction of application numbers in Italy. This suggests that Iranian asylum seekers choose other nations as their destination.

As for religious affiliation, Vartanian (2013) claims that the majority of Iranians residing in Italy are Shiite from different ethnic groups and that, among the non-Muslims, there are many Jews (about 1,400, mainly residents in northern Italy), a few Orthodox Christians and Catholics, and only a dozen people claiming to be Baha'is or Zoroastrians. It is important to mention that, unlike other Muslim immigrants who rely on the Islamic faith as a central force in group cohesion, ethnic identity, and group boundary maintenance, among Iranian immigrants the religious dimension is almost completely absent. For Iranians, ethnic and cultural identity is best preserved and promoted through cultural celebrations.

The only available data about the general socioeconomic characteristics of Iranians in Italy reveals that in 1989 98.3 percent of Iranians in Italy belonged to the middle class and had a good level of education,[41] and in 1999 the majority of Iranians in Italy came from middle-class backgrounds in the capital city of Tehran. Moreover, close to 80 percent of Iranian immigrants in 1999 were under thirty years old, and slightly over 70 percent were men, more than half of whom were single.[42] Despite the absence of more recent studies, it is safe to suggest that these demographic characteristics remain more or less true today.

Immigration Policies, Islamophobia, and the Social Status of Iranians in Italy

There is a marked difference between migration patterns in Italy and other industrialized countries. Above all this is because Italy, before becoming a destination for migrants in the current period, was typically a migrant-sending country from which many emigrated in the late nineteenth and twentieth centuries to countries such as the United States, Argentina, and Brazil in search of better economic opportunities.[43] Furthermore, compared to other European colonial powers, Italy spent a far briefer period as a colonizer. Therefore, Italy had a far more limited colonial experience, and as a result the cultural reflections of former colonies on Italy have been quite different in comparison to those in other European contexts such as France.

Even though immigration to Europe accelerated at the end of World War II as a response to labor shortages in the workforce during postwar reconstruction, Italy became a destination of massive immigration only after 1975, when northern European countries began to enforce restrictive policies on immigration and Italy became the country of second choice for millions of immigrants who were denied entry by other nations.[44]

Currently, the majority of overall immigration to Italy is for economic reasons, with a very high number of immigrants coming from developing countries. Many of these immigrants usually take the low-wage jobs that have little prestige and are disdained by Italians.[45] Moreover, they are often employed in the underground sector, labeled as "black labour."[46] Immigration to Italy, particularly since the 1980s and 1990s, has coincided with economic and productive stagnation as well as high unemployment. Therefore, the availability of such a pool of low-cost labor coming from the third world appears to be something that could be potentially very helpful in restructuring the economic base of Italian companies.[47]

Furthermore, since becoming an immigrant-receiving rather than an immigrant-sending country, Italy has attempted, for the most part, to implement migrant policies aimed at the protection of immigrants. These policies include regulating the status of illegal immigrants involved in the "black economy" and providing means by which immigrants are integrated into Italian society and culture.[48]

In general, Italian migration policies are not discriminatory toward any particular immigrant group and community. Nevertheless, they are limited and inadequate in addressing the current immigration crisis in Italy. This limitation, as indicated earlier, is caused by a delay in developing a comprehensive social response to the immigration dilemma in Italy since the beginning of 1990s. Since large-scale immigration to Italy is a relatively new phenomenon, the Italian immigration policies are nascent and lack thorough and prudent objectives and principles, and they are developed primarily as an urgent reaction to the emerging immigration crisis in Europe. The real limitation in immigration policies adopted since the 1990s in Italy has been related to a cultural delay, which has hindered the maturation of a structural approach (as opposed to an emergency one) toward the management of the phenomenon of present-day migration.

The first immigration law in Italy (formulated as an emergency law) was passed in 1990, and the first actual law on the regulation of immigration and the status of foreigners ("Disciplina dell'immigrazione e norme sulla condizione dello straniero") was enacted in 1998.[49]

Despite their intention to solve immigration problems, Italian government officials have neither developed a comprehensive immigration policy nor promoted the integration of immigrants. The existing immigration policies of the Italian government refrain from addressing and recognizing foreign nationals and their identities and do not provide any financial or social support for immigrants and their families. In fact, to this day, there are no official ethnic unions or professional associations for immigrants.

According to the statistics provided by the *Dossier statistico immigrazione 2016* (Statistical Dossier on Immigration 2016), by the end of 2015 the population of foreigners in Italy remained practically the same as in the previous year. The official number of immigrants on Italian soil at the end of 2015 was 5,026,153, which amounts to just 12,000 more than the previous year. In 2015, 250,000 foreigners arrived in Italy; 72,000 children (about one-seventh of total births) born to foreign parents were registered in Italy. At the same time, 178,000 foreigners with resident status in the country obtained citizenship, raising the number of foreign-born Italian citizens to about 1,150,000 individuals.[50] In the meantime, huge numbers of migrants land on Italian soil on a daily basis. In 2015, a total of 154,000 political asylees, refugees fleeing war and persecution, and migrants were embarked to Italy.[51]

Despite the efforts by the Italian government to combat discrimination and prejudice against immigrants, particularly Muslims, anti-Muslim and anti-immigrant sentiments in Italy have increased since the eruption of the refugee crisis in 2015 and the terrorist attacks since then in Europe.[52] Islamophobic behaviors escapes exact definition[53] and risks being confused with a general tendency to criticize the normal habits of Muslims in general.[54]

In Italy, Islamophobia is on the rise and is accelerated by the climate of insecurity and threat that is to be found in society in general.[55] Statistics show a very different picture and suggest that in 2010 the number of Muslims resident in Italy was 2,200,000, or 3.7 percent of the total population.[56] The contexts in which Islamophobia is frequently observed in Italy include the workplace (in particular in the cases where practicing Muslim women wear the veil),[57] educational institutions, political institutions, the media, and social networks (which can be the vehicle for "hate speech" directed against Muslims).[58] Despite the legal ban against all forms of discrimination in Italy, numerous incidents of discrimination against Muslims were recorded in 2015. Discrimination against Muslims is exacerbated due to the lack of any law that guarantees religious freedom in Italy and the absence of any ad hoc agreement between the state and the Muslim community. As such, the Islamic community in Italy has no civil rights protection in the religious sphere and has no legal power to effectively combat the rise of Islamophobia.[59]

Under the current pervasive Islamophobic context, Iranians in Italy avoid being recognized as immigrants and disassociate themselves from being identified as Muslims. To avoid discrimination and prejudice, they isolate themselves even more from Italian society and either take refuge in the myth of return or in the idea that their time in Italy is just a transitory period and a stepping-stone to move to another Western country. Therefore, notwithstanding that Iranians in Italy are considered a successful professional group with a high cultural standing, after the Islamic Revolution of 1979 they have not been recognized as a real immigrant community[60] or been able to move into the mainstream of Italian society. Moreover, as indicated by Casari (2006), Iranians generally neither have, nor prefer to have, their own ethnic neighborhood and enclave. This is predominantly because they avoid building social networks and relationships with other Iranians unless they are family or kin members. They also tend to avoid relations with Italians, mainly because of the strong prejudice against immigrants in general and Muslims in particular.

As indicated above, despite the positive economic, political, and cultural ties between Iran and Italy, many Iranian immigrants in Italy feel socially isolated from Italian society. Many more either conceal their ethnic and religious identity or deny their social status as an immigrant. Furthermore, most Iranian nationals in Italy deliberately refuse to be identified as immigrants. Iranians' self-disassociation with immigrant populations in Italy is mainly a protective measure against the pejorative connotation associated with immigrants as individuals with low sociocultural backgrounds who come to Italy mainly for employment opportunities, as well as an overall ignorance of many Italians about Iran and Iranians. Since Iranians in Italy generally come from middle-class and upper middle-class families for education, they feel insulted and disrespected to be viewed and labeled as an immigrant in the eyes of Italians and consider themselves to be temporary migrants who have voluntarily chosen to live, work, or study in another country.

Iranian Community, Ethnic Associations, and the Preservation of Iranian Ethnic and Cultural Identity in Italy

Iranian immigration to Italy seems to be mostly considered as temporary, especially because legislation regarding residence and employment for foreigners has already been far from perfect for anyone considering a long-term stay and eventual integration into Italian society. In general, as cited above, the majority of Iranians come to Italy with the intention of going to college, although they may neglect this in order to take some form of temporary work. The fact that employment of this type may last for many years does not detract from the fact that the ultimate goal for Iranians in Italy is to return to Iran or move to another Western country once there is a genuine possibility.[61]

In general, it is difficult to identify Iranians in Italy as a distinguished ethnic group because they either live alone or in family units and are not clustered in an ethnic enclave. They are primarily concentrated in medium- to high-level professions, carry limited personal relations with other members of the Iranian community, and maintain strong links with Iran.[62] While it is difficult to find visible religious, social, political, and demographic markers to identify the Iranian communities abroad, Iranians in Italy can generally be recognized for their high cultural and social status and good socioeconomic position, as seems to happen in other Western countries.[63]

According to Mario Casari (2006), Iranians who have arrived in Italy more recently have established a variety of ethnic associations through which they express their ethnic identity and maintain the Iranian cultural heritage. He cites, among others, Entešārāt-e Bābak (Babak Press), which was a small publishing house in existence for a number of years. In Rome, the bookstore Nimā has been selling books in Farsi as well as books about Iran and Iranian culture in other languages since 1994.[64] Perhaps the most active and long-standing cultural association, the Associazione Culturale Italia-Iran, was based in Florence. Other important Iranian ethnic associations in Italy include, for example, the Iranian-Italian cultural association AlefBa[65] in Rome, the Casa della Cultura Iraniana (House of Iranian Culture) in Venice, ASI (Association of Iranian Students in Florence), ADDI (Association of Democratic Iranian Women Living in Italy), and AID (Democratic Iran Agency), whose internet site is also the official page of the Association of Iranian Political Refugees Living in Italy. Almost every major Italian city usually has at least one Iranian association of this kind.

In addition to establishing ethnic associations and institutions, Iranians in Italy maintain their ethnic identity and cultural heritage through participation in ethnic celebrations, Iranian cultural festivals, concerts, traditional Persian music, Persian language courses, Iranian art exhibitions, plays, thematic conferences, lecture series, and thematic fairs run by the annual Asiatica Film Festival and the Casa del Cinema (House of Cinema). The few and the most important traditional festivals that Iranians celebrate are Noruz (Iranian New Year), Chaharshanbesurì (the last Wednesday of the Iranian year), Shab-e Yalda (the longest night of the year, generally corresponding to December 21), and the nature festival (which is celebrated on the thirteenth day from the start of Noruz). Some of these cultural events are organized by ordinary Iranians and business owners, and others are organized by the Cultural Institute of the Iranian embassy in Rome. The Iranian embassy in Rome is very active and plays an important role in the cultural, educational, religious, and political lives of Iranians in Italy. For example, the embassy organizes an annual Persian language course and administers the only Iranian private school from elementary to high school exclusively for the children of Iranian diplomats. Other ethnic activities and cultural festivities organized by the embassy include the celebration of national political events such as the anniversary of the Islamic Revolution (Ruz-e melli), during which over a thousand guests, including leading figures in Italian politics, entrepreneurs, journalists, intellectuals, famous people who have relations with Iran, as well as the most influential Iranians residing in Italy, are received by the ambassador.

In addition to Iranian ethnic associations and cultural events sponsored by the Iranian embassy, there are several non-Iranian associations that promote Iranian culture and language in Italy. For example, these include the Gemellaggio dei Tre Ponti (Three-Bridge Twinning, involving Italy, Iran, and Armenia) promoted by the Associazione di Amicizia Italo-Armena Zatik[66] (Armenian-Italian Friendship Association Zatik) and publishing houses such as Ponte 33 specializing in the work of Iranian authors with the intention to spread contemporary Persian literature written in Iran, Afghanistan, Tajikistan, and other countries (mostly in the United States and in Europe),[67] where many diaspora writers live and work.

One of the most recent initiatives aimed at providing a framework for understanding the Iranian community in Italy was the photo exhibition "Persia Mon Amour" by Jacopo Storni with photos by Edoardo Delille for the fifth edition of the Middle East Now festival held in Florence in 2014. The report consists of twenty portraits of Iranians accompanied by their stories. This exhibition explored the Iranian community in Florence, where—according to the organizers of the exhibition—there are about 2,000 Iranian citizens who are doctors, students, merchants, dissenters, upholsterers, musicians, beauticians, butchers, and bartenders.[68]

Diaspora and the Literary Production of Iranian Authors in Italy

To cope with social isolation, prejudice, discrimination, cultural disconnection, and uprootedness, some Iranians in Italy, much like other Iranian intellectuals and writers in exile, have turned their attention to writing and literary production. To analyze the Italian literary production of Iranian authors, it is necessary to refer to other studies about the theoretical reflections of Iranian literature that has been produced in other European languages since the 1990s.[69] Most of these studies indicate that the themes of nostalgia and longing, as well as a distinct feeling related to the sense of distance and separation caused by exile, are the central elements of literary works of Iranian writers in diaspora. Regardless of the works' form and genre, one can notice a unified view among most Iranian authors in exile in perceiving this feeling of nostalgia in a very emotionally intense way. However, these feelings are best expressed and captured through writing novels, short stories, and poems. For a great number of Iranian intellectuals in exile, writing not only represents an activity that provides an immediate remedy and response to the "shock of events"; it also is one of the most common reactions (Beard and Javadi 1986).[70] For other Iranian intellectuals and writers outside Iran, writing consists of an attempt to re-create the facts and details related to the life left behind in Iran through the written narration of events that preceded exile. Still others find writing as a powerful channel for maintaining links with their origins and cultural roots.

Much like other immigrant writers, writing about feelings of exile and life in diaspora is not easy for Iranian authors. The main writing challenges that Iranian writers in exile confront are expressing their feelings and ideas in a foreign language, identity negotiation and reconstruction, and overcoming alienation. Writing in the language of the host country to express conditions of exile and feelings of displacement[71] puts authors in exile in a continuous negotiation with their identity.[72] So, in addition to identity negotiation and the feeling of strangeness, writers who choose to tell their own experiences of exile and displacement also face the difficulty of expressing themselves in a different language.[73]

In Italy, as well as in other countries, the feeling and the experience of exile and separation are expressed mainly through the production of a vast amount of literature by Iranian authors. (See chapter 7 in this volume.) Much like Iranian writers in other countries, Iranian writers in Italy use different artistic forms and produce work in which they express feelings of nostalgia for their country of birth, abandonment and loss of their former identity in exile, and social and cultural uprootedness and displacement. As indicated by Bijan Zarmandili, an Iranian journalist and author of six novels and two short stories in Italian, among the few possibilities for one who is in exile, has lost his or her birthplace, and is at risk of losing identity and perhaps life, the ability to transform this nostalgia into a creative work is redeeming.[74]

To understand the diasporic experience of Iranian writers and intellectuals in Italy, I reviewed the literary production of thirty-six Iranian writers that were published between 1992 and 2017.[75] The quantitative analysis of the data I collected shows some interesting demographic information about gender, generation, and length of residence, as well as the preferred genre of the published work by Iranians in Italy. More than half (19) of the Iranian writers are women. One out of every three (12) authors has published at least one novel. Moreover, half (18) of the writers published at least one short story, and nearly half (17) published at least one poem. Finally, one out of every six (6) has a publication related to children's literature. Among the total number of publications reviewed, thirteen authors published only one work, fourteen published between two and five works, four published between six and nine works, and five published more than ten works. Regarding the immigration generation of Iranian authors based on their age upon arrival in Italy,[76] nearly four out of five (29) are first-generation immigrants and immigrated after the age of eighteen, and five are second-generation Iranians who were born and raised in Italy. One other Iranian writer in the group immigrated to Italy between age thirteen and seventeen, and another one attended primary school in Iran before immigrating to Italy.

A more detailed analysis of the data suggests that writers of the first generation are more concerned with politics and articulate a stronger link with Iran's history and culture. The literary production of the first-generation authors, who started writing in Italian for the first time in the 1990s, has evolved and transformed stylisticly in recent years. In general, compared to their earliest narrative works, in which writers followed the conventional and traditional theme of exile literature that contained at least one character who was forced to live away from the motherland, the more recent narratives show a progressive detachment from these features and a search for a more personal style, which naturally differs for each author.

Unlike the first-generation writers, the second-generation writers who were either born in Italy (such as Mehdi Mahdloo) or migrated to Italy at a very young age (such as Nader Ghazvinizadeh), present their narratives either in a predominantly Italian context or express the difficulty of integration into Italian society and culture for a non-Italian subject in their narrations (such as Nima Sharmahd).

In general, the literary production of Iranian authors in Italian can be classified into four major genres: novels, short stories, poetry, and children's literature. Most of the novels published by Iranian authors in Italy contain some autobiographical elements in which some past real life history is transferred into the story and is infused with the main character's role. This is particularly the case for novels written by the first-generation writers. In these novels, the main character is situated in a period of Iranian history that the author has personally lived. They also sometimes highlight characters representing an extended family member or a friend they personally know. Short stories are usually written either by the same novel authors or by Iranian poets. Some of the short stories are set in Italy or in another place outside Iran with no reference to Iran, Iranian culture, or its history. Most Iranian poetry in exile is published either as single poems in online magazines or in anthologies. There are also few poets who have collected and published their poems in a single edited volume (such as Nina Sadeghi,

Maryam Fatemifar, and Sashinka Gorguinpour). In some of the short poems, it is usually very difficult to recognize any element that is directly connected to Iran. In others, however, one can find some themes and topics that are borrowed from traditional Persian literature and poetry. Finally, most the literary production for children, unlike the other categories, is produced by professional Iranian artists and photographers in Italy who have successfully blended their artworks—mainly in painting—with drawing and illustration books for children (such as Elham Asadi or Behnam Ali Farhazad).

My content analysis of the published literary work by Iranians in Italy reveals some common elements and patterns. The Persian landscape is a powerful feature found in the many of the novels. Furthermore, most of the narratives are set in Iran, and their protagonists are Iranians whose actions take place at a crucial time in the history of their mother country. Finally, there are constant references to Persian traditions, habits, food, culture, and literature in these novels and short stories.[77]

Of all the Iranian writers in Italy, Bijan Zarmandili and Hamid Ziarati are considered most representative from the Italian panorama. These two Iranian writers are not only the best known to Italian readers but also have published the largest number of novels by major Italian publishers. Bijan Zarmandili was born in Tehran in 1941 and moved to Rome in 1960 to complete his university studies in architecture and political science. Zarmandili is a professional journalist and is famous for his articles on politics, particularly Middle East politics, published in well-known Italian newspapers and political journals. Between 2004 and 2016, he published six novels and two short stories in Italian[78] and is currently completing his seventh novel. Zarmandili's second novel, published in Italy in 2007, has recently been translated into Persian and was published in 2015[79] by Forough Publications, an Iranian publisher based in Germany, because there were no Iranian publishers in Italy. Hamid Ziarati was born in Tehran in 1966 and moved to Turin in 1981 both for medical reasons and for family reunification with his two older brothers, who had moved to Italy a few years earlier to study medicine. He obtained a doctoral degree in applied mechanics, and he currently works as a project manager. He published his first short story in 1995, and between 2006 and 2013 he published three novels and four short stories in Italian.[80] Given the large volume of their works in different genres since the 2000s, as well as their popularity in Italy, I focus next on a textual analysis of their work.

Textual analysis of works by Zarmandili and Ziarati reveals the constant presence of some recurrent themes, including the feeling of nostalgia that follows the main characters of the narratives and the presence of at least one other character forced to live abroad. The narrative typologies of both authors present a number of similarities. For example, almost all of their narratives can be classified within the Bildungsroman genre. This is mainly because the events in the life of the main characters in these narratives occur over time and involve a path of growth and self-discovery. Another recurrent theme in their writings is reference to Iranian historical, social, and political events. In almost all of their novels and short stories, the main character is portrayed as a person who is directly involved in crucial moments in Iranian history. In their works, one can also trace passionate references to specific cultural elements of Iran, including Persian literature and traditional Persian cuisine.

Despite the common themes found in the work of these two Italian Iranian writers, each has his own unique and peculiar orientation and narration style. For example, in all the novels and short stories written by Zarmandili, there is at least one character who lives in exile or far from his loved ones and suffers from nostalgia. Nevertheless, once the feeling of nostalgia is fought and overcome, if directed properly it can become positive and evolve among other things into a stimulus for creativity. Another unique element of Zarmandili's work is the presence of a protagonist who echoes Iranian historical events with a sort of pedagogical intent, aiming to teach the Western reader about Iranian social and political events.

Unlike Zarmandili, Ziarati grapples with exile and its psychological consequences only in his novels, choosing to focus on different themes in his short stories. Similar to Zarmandili's work, the main characters in Ziarati's novels suddenly find themselves in exile and consequently suffer from longing. What distinguishes Ziarati from other diaspora authors is his deliberate modification of the "classical" character of the exiled. For example, in his first novel, feelings of exile and separation are not experienced by a person who is separated from his family and lives outside of Iran. To the contrary, separation and longing are experienced by someone who remains in Iran and lives in his family house but experiences nostalgic feelings for family members who have been forced to live outside of Iran.

Conclusion

As for Iranian authors in recent years in Italy who explore the social implications of diasporic literary production and the transnational practices of Iranian writers, one can detect a major change from a low profile with no visibility to a more self-confident sense with more publicity. This shift is partly due to the improved political and cultural ties between the two countries, and partly a consequence of relative political improvements and less censorship in Iran. The Persian translation of Bijan Zarmandili's second novel symbolized the change that has been taking place. Besides its importance as the first work of fiction published in Italian by an Iranian author and its translation into Persian, this novel also represents the transnational link between two diasporic Iranian communities in two different European countries, because it was published by an Iranian publisher in Germany. Given the political changes in Iran in recent years and the availability of Zarmandili's novel in Persian, it is very likely that the novel may reach the Iranian market, an option that was never available before. In fact, until a few years ago Zarmandili had not considered the possibility of having his novels translated and circulated abroad, particularly in Iran. This shift reflects the change that has been taking place in recent years in terms of the relationship between Iranians and Iran, both in Iran and abroad.

Today, Iranians in diaspora can return and visit Iran more freely. They also have the opportunity to stay connected to Iranian communities in other countries and to create multitude of new cultural, political, social, and economic linkages with Iran. For example, in recent years some of the most famous Iranian authors have been more active in the public presentation of their literary works. These presentations have been organized by Iranian cultural associations as well as Italian organizations in various location inside and outside of Italy. As a result of greater political openness in Iran since 2013 (the first election of the Iranian president Hassan Rouhani), there is now more approval and recognition for the artistic and literary production of Iranian writers by the diplomatic components of both governments. Despite the recent political and social changes, and the ease of connecting to Iranian communities in diaspora through modern global technology, most Iranian authors in Italy prefer to establish relationships with the Italian community. Still today, the literary production of Iranians in Italy does not promote social solidarity among Iranians or strengthen the Iranian community in exile; nor does it aim to reconstruct the Iranian community in exile. It is rather a medium to either (re)construct and maintain the Iranian ethnic and national identity in exile or to give voice to a political rhetoric and ideology to educate ordinary Italian readers about the social and political situations in Iran.

Notes

1. Abbasi, Davood (2017), "Italia-Iran, ripresa interscambio, Roma torna primo partner UE," *Agenzia Giornalistica Italia* (AGI), www.agi.it/rubriche/asia/2017/05/23/news/iran-iran_ripresa_interscambio_roma_torna_primo_partner_ue-1804274.

2. (2016), "Italia-Iran, rilancio 'made in Italy', si punta +3 miliardi di export,"

Agenzia Giornalistica Italia (AGI), www.agi.it/economia/2016/01/23/news/italia-iran _rilancio_made_in_italy_si_punta_3_miliardi_di_export-444365.

3. (2016), "Italia-Iran: Alitalia, da 27/3 tutti i giorni Roma-Teheran," *La Repubblica.it*, www.repubblica.it/ultimora/24ore/italia-iran-alitalia-da-273-tutti-i -giorni-roma-teheran/news-dettaglio/4619748.

4. Saint-Blancat (1988: 58).

5. Ibid., 60.

6. Ibid., 3–4.

7. Ibid., 4.

8. Ibid., 61.

9. Ibid., 140–142.

10. Casari (2006: 290).

11. See also: Bozorgmehr (1996).

12. About the subdivision into different waves of the recent phenomenon of Iranian immigration and the Iranian diaspora worldwide, see also: Bozorgmehr (1996), Modarresi (2001), and Sieberny-Mohammadi and Mohammadi (1987).

13. Casari (2006: 291).

14. Arasteh (1962: 448).

15. Baldwin (1963: 270).

16. Saint-Blancat (1989).

17. Casari (2006).

18. Caritas Italiana–Fondazione Migrantes (2006).

19. Data from the Italian Ministry of Interior (2010), www.interno.gov.it/it.

20. Centro Studi e Ricerche IDOS (2014).

21. Archives of the Consular Section of the Embassy of Islamic Republic of Iran in Rome.

22. Miggiano (2015b: 3).

23. (2013), "Iraniani in Italia," *Comuni-italiani.it*, www.comuni-italiani.it/sta tistiche/stranieri/ir.html.

24. (2011), "Demografia in cifre," *Istat.it*, demo.istat.it/altridati/noncomunitari /index.html.

25. Casari (2006).

26. (2011), "Demografia in cifre," *Istat.it*, demo.istat.it/altridati/noncomunitari /index.html.

27. Data from the Italian Ministry of Interior (2010), www.interno.gov.it/it.

28. The four regions are: Lombardy (the region with Milan as its chief city, with 2,409 Iranians); Lazio (the region with Rome as its chief city, with 1,948 Iranians); Emilia-Romagna (the region with Bologna as its chief city, with 1,098 Iranians); and Piemonte (the region with Turin as its chief city, with 1,009 Iranians).

29. (2014), "Iraniani in Italia," *Comuni-italiani.it*, www.comuni-italiani.it/sta tistiche/stranieri.html.

30. Archives of the Consular Section of the Embassy of Islamic Republic of Iran in Rome.

31. (2013), "Demografia in cifre," *Istat.it*, demo.istat.it/altridati/noncomunitari /index.html.

32. Djalali, Leila (2012), "La comunità iraniana a Roma," *Roma Multietnica. La guida all'intercultura delle Biblioteche di Roma*, www.romamultietnica.it/iran.html, currently updated to 2017.

33. There is an Iranian consular section in Rome for Iranians resident in central and southern Italy, and a General Consulate in Milan for the Iranians resident in the northern regions of Italy.

34. Ministero dell'Istruzione, dell'Università e della Ricerca. Servizio Statistico (2014), "Gli alunni stranieri nel sistema scolastico italiano. A.S. 2013/2014," ed. Carla Borrini, www.istruzione.it/allegati/2014/Notiziario_Stranieri_13_14.pdf.

35. Ministero dell'Istruzione, dell'Università e della Ricerca. Servizio Statistico (2013), "Gli alunni stranieri nel sistema scolastico italiano. A.S. 2012/2013," ed. Carla Borrini and Laura Boi, www.istruzione.it/allegati/Notiziario_Stranieri_12_13.pdf.

36. Archives of the Consular Section of the Embassy of Islamic Republic of Iran in Rome.

37. Centro Studi e Ricerche IDOS (2016: 210).

38. Data from the Italian Ministry of Justice (2015), www.giustizia.it/giustizia/it/homepage.page.

39. Centro Studi e Ricerche IDOS (2014).

40. Ibid.

41. Saint-Blancat (1989).

42. Casari (2006).

43. Bevilacqua et al. (2001).

44. Calavita (1995: 305). For a detailed analysis of the various Italian laws and legislative decrees on immigration up to the mid-1990s, see Calavita (1995).

45. Ibid., 308.

46. Ibid., 310.

47. Ibid., 313.

48. Centro Studi e Ricerche IDOS (2016).

49. "Legge 6 marzo 1998, n. 40 Disciplina dell'immigrazione e norme sulla condizione dello straniero," *Gazzetta Ufficiale n. 59*, 12/03/1998, Supplemento Ordinario n. 40, www.camera.it/parlam/leggi/98040l.htm.

50. Centro Studi e Ricerche IDOS (2016: 7).

51. Ibid., 9.

52. Ibid., 57.

53. For a possible definition of the term "Islamophobia," see Bayrakli and Hafez (2016: 7).

54. Centro Studi e Ricerche IDOS (2016: 58).

55. Siino and Levantino (2016: 269).

56. Ibid., 60.

57. Regarding the first Italian legal ruling on the question of the Islamic veil, see Centro Studi e Ricerche IDOS (2016: 175).

58. Centro Studi e Ricerche IDOS (2016: 58). About single discriminatory events and incidents that occurred in Italy in 2015, see Siino and Levantino (2016: 276–286).

59. Siino and Levantino (2016: 269).

60. Casari (2006: 291).

61. Ibid.

62. Ibid.

63. Regarding the high cultural and social level of the Iranians in the United States, see, for example: Ansari (1977), Bozorgmehr (1996), Hakimzadeh (2006), Modarresi (2001), and Sreberny-Mohammadi and Mohammadi (1987).

64. The bookshop has been recently close.

65. AlefBa is a cultural association whose main aim is to promote and preserve Iranian culture in Italy, organizing, for example, Persian-language courses for Italians, Italian-language courses for Iranian students, book presentations, and a lot of other cultural activities.

66. The three bridges are Ponte Milvio in Rome, Allah Verdi Khan Bridge in Isfahan, and Sanain Bridge of Allaverdi in Armenia. The twinning ceremony was held on May 4, 2006, in Rome. Zatik primarily promotes Armenian culture, mainly in relation to Iranian and Italian culture. They also sponsor political initiatives.

67. (2017), "Chi siamo," Ponte33, www.ponte33.it/chi-siamo-2.

68. (2014), "Persia mon amour," Internazionale, www.internazionale.it/portfolio/persia-mon-amour.

69. Such as the studies carried out by Naficy (1993) and Malek (2006).

70. Beard and Javadi (1986).

71. See: Naficy (1993) and Malek (2006).

72. The negotiation of a new identity in the context of exile is described by Naficy as "a process of perpetual becoming, involving a separation from home, a period of liminality and an in-betweenness that can be temporary or permanent, and incorporation into the dominant host society that can be partial or complete" (Naficy 1993: 8–9).

73. One example of an analysis of the process of adopting a new language and of the resulting translingualism is provided by Nasrin Rahimieh. In terms of the narratives of Iranian immigrants in exile, while investigating the question of cultural identity in the authors of the Iranian diaspora and referring to her own experience, she states: "Especially when they have adopted a second language, I recognize a shared community free of borders and boundaries. Persian immigrant writers may agonize over their apparent loss of language, memory, and identity, but they also write, in a newly discovered language, about their arrival into a community of transcultural writers" (Rahimieh 1993: 167).

74. Zarmandili (2011: 426–427).

75. Miggiano (2015a).

76. According to sociological criteria explained, for example, in Visconti et al. (2007).

77. Another common feature found in most literary production of Iranians in Italy is insertion of terms from Iranian language into Italian narratives, using what in sociolinguistics is known as "code-mixing" or "intrasentential code-switching." Authors often insert terms commonly known to Western readers, but in some cases they also use words or expressions without any explanation, which can be difficult to understand for the common Italian-speaking reader. This happens especially when the authors believe that the Persian term corresponds better with the concept they want to express or when they believe that there is not an Italian term that exactly matches.

78. For the complete bio-bibliography and textual analysis of Bijan Zarmandili's narratives, see Miggiano (2015a: 123–269) and Miggiano (2016: 1–13).

79. The translation was made by Abolhassan Hatami, an Iranian architect residing in Rome since 1969 and president of the Iranian-Italian cultural association Alefba.

80. For the complete bio-bibliography and textual analysis of Hamid Ziarati's narratives, see Miggiano (2015a: 270–381).

CONCLUSION

Prospect for Integration of Iranians and Questions for Future Research

MOHSEN MOSTAFAVI MOBASHER

No one knows exactly how many Iranians have left the country since the 1979 revolution or the exact number of Iranians who live outside Iran. This is partly because of the illegal flight of so many Iranians after the revolution and during the war with Iraq, and partly because neither the Iranian government nor the governments of host countries where Iranians have settled provide systematic and reliable records of outflows and inflows of Iranian nationals. Although the number may be disputed, the Iranian government estimates that between 2 and 4 million Iranians live and work outside of Iran. Other reports by international organizations such as the United Nations and independent scholars estimate the number of modern Iranians in diaspora to be between 3.5 million and 4 million (Aidani 2010; Sheffer 2003).

It is hard, if not impossible, to find reliable statistics about the size and de-mographic composition of Iranians in each country in the West. The most reliable and accurate information comes from government sources where the majority of Iranian immigrants live: Europe, Canada, the United States, and Australia. The data collected by the Federal Statistical Office of Germany, Sweden Statistics, and Statistics Canada between 1980 and 2005 suggests that the number of Iranian immigrants who were admitted to Germany, Sweden, and Canada were 97,177, 61,057, and 87,379, respectively. Similarly, the UK Home Office reports indicate that between 1991 and 2005 as many as 21,305 Iranian immigrants were admitted to the United Kingdom (Hakimzadeh 2006). The Australian Bureau of Statistics reveals that by 2005 the number of individuals with Iranian ancestry in Australia had reached 24,588 (Aidani 2007).

As indicated in the introduction, except for the United Arab Emirates, all the countries examined in the book face two major immigration challenges. The first challenge is controlling or managing migration, and the second is integrating Muslim immigrants, including Iranians, without undermining their full social, political, and civil rights. These challenges have not only pressured Western governments to adopt more restrictive policies but also provoked great public hostility toward immigrants, particularly Muslim immigrants. As noted by many social scientists, these challenges are inevitable reactions to the changing demographic, economic, and political changes in the West.

Despite tough immigration restrictions against Iranians, and the continuing perception and treatment of Iranians as a suspect group since the hostage crisis, Iranians have been entering countries in the West as students, refugees, entrepreneurs, and professionals in surprising numbers since the mid-1990s. According to statistics compiled by the US Department of Homeland Security, between 2013 and 2015 nearly 36,592 Iranians obtained legal permanent resident status, and another 94,713 nonimmigrant residents entered the United States from Iran. As in previous decades, most Iranians who entered the United States during this time were either immediate relatives of US citizens or students and tourists. Students represented 23 percent (21,838) of the total nonimmigrants who arrived in the United States. In addition to immigrants and nonimmigrants, during the same period 8,534 refugees and another 1,824 individuals from Iran were granted political asylum. PEW's analysis of Eurostat data indicates the same growth in Europe and suggests that the number of asylum seekers in Europe increased from 11,000 in 2013 to 27,000 in 2015.[1] Given the high rate of unemployment, inflation, lack of job opportunities for educated Iranians, and lack of political freedom in Iran, the international migration of Iranians, particularly to the West, is likely to increase in coming years. The country cases in this volume provide ample evidence that Iranian immigrants have not integrated into their new host societies. Even in the United States, where Iranians have accomplished remarkable educational and economic success, the ongoing hostility of the American government toward Iran and Iranians thwarts the integration of immigrants.

Since the election of Donald Trump as US president, US-Iran relations have entered a new phase. Trump has threatened to impose a new set of sanctions on Iran's missile program.[2] Given the increased hostility between Iran and the United States and the possible implementation of more restrictive immigration sanctions, such as the president's executive order temporarily banning travel from seven Muslim-majority nations, including Iran, it is reasonable to believe that the number of Iranians entering the United States will decline substantially in coming years. Moreover, as long as Donald Trump and his administration condemn the Iranian government as a terrorist state and refuse to embrace bilateral diplomatic negotiations, it seems unlikely that the immigration policies and the overall prejudice and discrimination against Iranians in the United States will be altered in the foreseeable future.

In contrast to the ongoing political tension between Iran and the United States, the political and diplomatic ties between Iran and Europe have improved significantly since 2015. After prolonged talks between Iran, the United States, the United Kingdom, France, Germany, Russia, and China, world leaders in 2015 agreed to lift sanctions on Iran but place strict limits on its nuclear program for more than a decade. According to a report by the European External Action Services in 2016, relations between the European Union (EU) and Iran have been broadened since all nuclear-related economic and financial sanctions against Iran have been lifted. Following this historic agreement, a series of high-level dialogues and negotiations between the EU and Iran have resulted in more areas of engagement and cooperation in the future, including migration, human rights, economic relations, science, and culture.[3]

With the landslide victory of a reformist Iranian president in 2016, improved diplomatic relations between Iran and the European Union, and more cooperation and engagement after 2015, particularly on migration, it is very likely that the number of Iranians who will be admitted to Europe will increase significantly in the future. Nevertheless, in light of the recent terrorist attacks by first- and second-generation immigrants with Islamic backgrounds in Europe and the United States, we can expect to see a continuing increase in Islamophobic sentiments, backlash, discrimination, and hate crimes against Muslims, including Iranians in the Western world. Moreover, as the religious division between Muslims and non-Muslims in Western Europe becomes sharper, any integration of Iranians becomes more complex and intractable due to the fact that Muslim Iranians are doubly stigmatized.

Today, the Iranian diaspora remains internally differentiated by political ideology, ethnoreligious membership, gender, generational status, home orientation, class, and time of arrival. Regardless of the nature and the extent of their diversity, members of the Iranian diaspora as a whole continue to have a troubled relationship with their original homeland and their host societies. It is uncertain whether Iranians in diaspora continue to be demonized, discriminated against, excluded, and othered, or whether they will be accepted by the wider society and move closer to the center of their host society. As indicated before, what is certain is the fact that the nature and the extent of connections Iranians have with both Iran and their host society will change overtime depending largely on future diplomatic and political relations between Iran and the West, global politics, political and social developments in Iran, and attitudes toward the Iranian government within the international community. As long as political relations between Iran and Western powers, particularly the United States, remain conflictual, and as long as the distorted generalizations and stereotypes about Muslims, Iran, and Iranians persist in the West, Iranians in diaspora will be subjected to prejudice, discrimination, profiling, and strict immigration policies.

Similarities and Differences between Iranians in this Study

All eight case studies examined in this book reveal that Iranian immigration and its consequences have been largely shaped by the 1979 Iranian Revolution and its distinctive postrevolutionary domestic policies and diplomatic relations with other countries. As demonstrated in the preceding chapters, except for the case of working-class Iranians in the United Arab Emirates, the Iranian diasporas in Western Europe, Australia, and the United States are primarily a product of the Iranian Revolution and is predominantly composed of middle-class and upper middle-class educated professionals from big cities with relatively high human capital. This is particularly the case for Iranians in the United States. Moreover, unlike many other immigrants in the West who are concentrated in low-wage jobs and neighborhoods populated disproportionately by poor immigrant families, Iranians work predominantly in better paying professional jobs and live in middle-class neighborhoods. Nevertheless, despite their advanced degrees, professional skills, middle-class or upper middle-class origin, and proficiency in the host country's language, the majority of Iranians in the countries considered in this book face relatively similar sociopolitical barriers for integration and suffer from the same identity crisis, such as concealing their ethnonational or religious identity or inventing a new identity as "Persian" that deemphasizes Islamic heritage.

The striking similarities across Iranian communities in diaspora in terms of social isolation and detachment from their new host country, underemployment, discrimination and treatment as a suspect group, immigration restrictions, and spoiled ethnic and religious identities as Iranians and Muslims suggest that the integration problems of Iranians in diaspora lay not so much with human capital deficiencies as with the political nature of Iranian immigration as well as the global Islamophobia and the framing of Iran as a pariah state. It also points to the inadequacy of the assimilationist paradigm in migration studies and its limited application to the case of Iranians in diaspora. Contrary to the fundamental premises of assimilationist theories, Iranians' lack of assimilation in the United States, Europe, and Australia appears to be linked neither to the cultural collision and incompatibility between Iranian and Western cultures, nor to the transition of Iranian immigrants from one culture to another and the lack of such human capital as language proficiency and adequate educations. Rather, the real source of Iranians' lack of assimilation and retarded integration seems to be related to the simultaneous political transformation of Western Europe and North America regarding immigration control, as well as the emergence of Islamophobia and the global framing of Iran as a state sponsor of terrorism.

In emphasizing the powerful impact of global Islamophobia and Iranophobia on the lives of Iranians in diaspora, we should not ignore or deny the role of national contexts in contributing to their marginality, social isolation, and lack of integration in their new receiving societies. As demonstrated in the cases of Iranians in Germany, Netherlands, and Italy, the racialized national contexts combined with antiforeigner attitudes have created enormous integration barriers for first- and second-generation Iranians in these countries. As indicated by Portes and Rumbaut (2006), the policies of the receiving nation, labor conditions of the host market, and characteristics of the ethnic community, as well as the combination of positive or negative experiences at each of these levels, are the most relevant contexts of reception that can greatly shape the mode of incorporation for new immigrants. The cases of Iranians particularly in Germany and the Netherlands shed light on the powerful impact of national contexts and immigration policies in their receiving societies and demonstrate that even high-status immigrants such as Iranians can suffer from "integration paradox" and remain excluded and marginalized in host countries with an unfavorable context of reception. As described in chapters 2, 3, and 5, this integration paradox has generated similar psychological reactions, including social detachment, tension, cynicism, and a sense of in-betweenness for Iranians in countries where belonging and identity are racialized and dominated by the negative social discourse of othering. Another significant similarity is the strategy adopted by Iranians in coping with Iranophobia and Islamophobia, as well as prejudice and discrimination against Iranians. As indicated in most of the chapters in this book, to cope with discrimination, prejudice, feelings of foreignness, and the stigma attached to Muslim immigrants, Iranians not only keep a very low ethnic profile and mask their ethnoreligious identity but also adhere to the good foreigner trope and marry natives, or they redefine and negotiate their identity and reconstruct a less threatening secular identity based on a selective combination of Persian history, culture, literature, art, and poetry.

Notwithstanding the broad similarities in the diasporic experiences of Iranians, there are specific differences in the collective experience of Iranians in different countries in terms of income, occupation, social mobility, entrepreneurship, housing, education, citizenship, political participation, and community organization. These differences are embedded in the national economic, political, and social structures of the host societies where Iranians have settled. Take, for example, the first- and second-generation Iranians in the United States who seem to have integrated more successfully than Iranian immigrants in any other country economically, socially, and politically. As indicated in chapter 1, by Bozorgmehr and Ketcham, the extent of educational attainment, labor force participation in professional specialty occupations in high-skill sectors, self-employment, and income of Iranians in the United States is distinctive. Ironically, Iranians in the United States were victims of discrimination, prejudice, and the harshest immigration restrictions long before those in any other country due to the 1979 hostage crisis in Iran. The remarkable socioeconomic integration and financial success of Iranians in America, despite the pervasive backlash against them, in my view, result from the unique capitalist economic structure of the United States, where laissez-faire liberal market principles and minimum state intervention provide a great opportunity for a large number of immigrants with ethnic resources, capital, and the premigration entrepreneurial skills to become self-employed and gain economic success. Similarly, the political integration of Iranians and the appointment or election of Iranian descendants to various political positions, including US House of Representatives member, superior county judge, district attorney, mayor, city council member, and local board of supervisors member, result from the principles of inclusion, multiculturalism, and integration as well as the immigrant naturalization policies of the United States. As indicated by Alba and Foner (2015), states that are based on an ethnic integrative national model and are more likely to acknowledge immigrants as ethnic minorities with distinctive needs are more open to ethnically based political appeals.

What This Book Achieved and Questions for Future Research

As indicated in the introduction, the eight chapters in this book provide a compelling case to examine the triadic relations between an immigrant population, the home society, and the receiving host nation(s). Various theoretical models have been developed by migration scholars and social scientists to explain the nature of this triadic connection. Most of these theories give primacy to micro- and macroeconomic forces (Massey et al. 1993). Unlike the economic theories, the cases of Iranians highlighted in this book bring to light the powerful force of global politics and its impact on the resettlement and integration of politicized diasporic groups who are victims of political tensions between home and host societies in this triadic relation. The chapters in this book not only highlight the large-scale, objective political forces such as the Iranian Revolution and the ensuing political tensions between Iran and Western powers that have been shaping the Iranian diaspora; the chapters also reveal the small-scale, subjective consequences of these events on the day-to-day social and psychological lives of Iranian immigrants. Demonstrating the link between these two levels of social reality, and integrating the two together throughout this volume, are two of the major overall features and a strength of this book. As an anthropologist, I attribute this theoretical strength to the advantages of ethnographic research, which was another strength and the backbone of all the chapters in this book except for chapter 1. Despite the authors' differences in academic training, participant observation was the unifying methodology employed in all but one of the chapters. No other methodological approach could have captured such intricate and subjective aspects of the Iranian diaspora such as ethnic identity negotiation in Germany, secular practices in Great Britain, the lived experiences of the working class in Dubai, and film festivals as social sites for negotiating ethnic identity with natives in Australia, not to mention the insightful ethnographic research employed by contributors to this volume. As aptly noted by Nancy Foner, ethnographic studies "provide up-close, in-depth knowledge of the day-to-day lives of individuals and bring people-their perspectives, social relations, and problems-to life" (Foner 2008: 244).

Without this ethnographic approach, we would not have been able to demonstrate the novel strategies that Iranians utilize in combating the host hostility or challenging the postrevolutionary government in Iran. Likewise, it was only through ethnographic research that we were able to demonstrate that, despite the existing powerful racialized forces in receiving societies, Iranians are active social agents that not only resist and challenge the discriminatory political, social, and economic practices of their host institutions but also constantly seek individual and collective opportunities for reintroducing themselves and their heritage, renegotiating their social space, and initiating a dialogue with members of the host society for reciprocal understanding.

Since the Iranian Revolution, for various political, economic, and social reasons, between 4 and 6 million Iranian nationals from diverse socioeconomic origins, cultural backgrounds, ethnic and religious affiliations, political orientations, family situations, and age distributions have been dispersed globally. As demonstrated in this book, certain features of the contemporary Iranian diaspora fit the descriptions that were outlined by scholars and are very similar to those that typify diasporas that were established by other ethnonational groups. However, despite the large size of the Iranian diaspora and the immense contributions made by some researchers and scholars since the 1990s, the subject of Iranian diaspora studies is still in its intellectual infancy, and there are many questions about Iranians in diaspora that will remain unanswered until more comparative research projects are conducted. Many studies of Iranians abroad examine the challenges of the adjustment and integration of Iranians in their new host society. As indicated earlier, however, these studies do not situate the experience of Iranians in a comparative and international context. They are limited to a single case study within a single country.

The United States stands out as the ideal destination for Iranian immigrants and continues to attract a major share of Iranians who immigrate to the West. The striking point about Iranians in the United States is not only their size but also their financial, ethnic, and class resources as well as their impressive level of socioeconomic success and upward mobility. Given that Iranian immigrants in the United States represent the largest and the most successful Iranian population outside Iran, and despite the relatively large number of Iranian nationals with longer migration histories in some other Western countries, much of the empirical academic research on the Iranian diaspora has focused on this single country. Such an imbalanced focus has not only led to production of a disproportionate amount of publications on Iranians in the United States; such skewedness has also dominated intellectual circles, professional conferences, and political debates in Iran regarding the diaspora, undermined the visibility of Iranian immigrants and refugees in other countries and ignored their integration challenges, and impeded scholars of Iranian migration from collaborative cross-national comparative work. Consequently, despite the relatively large number of Iranian nationals in other countries, as well the persistence of a common set of concerns in diaspora, there is a significant lack of research that compares Iranian immigrants in multiple countries and examines the interconnectedness of Iranian communities in diaspora. Certainly, more comparative studies in other countries with sizable Iranian populations that were not included in this book will shed light on the extent of the uniformity and the divergence in integration of Iranians in diaspora in light of the same international pressures and sociopolitical problems in Iran. Moreover, more studies are needed to examine the extent to which Iranian communities in diaspora are interconnected and to answer an important question: What role can the American Iranian diaspora's social, political, and cultural processes play in relation to Iranian communities throughout the world?

Except for a handful of research studies on second-generation Iranians in the United States, including the one by Bozorgmehr and Ketcham in this volume (chapter 1), most research on the Iranian diaspora focuses primarily on the experience of first-generation immigrants. Because the 1979 Iranian Revolution and its sociopolitical consequences were a major impetus for the exodus of millions, Iranians in diaspora have always been interested and actively involved in the political life of Iran. As indicated in the introduction, the political and ideological divisions among Iranians in exile have divided and complicated their experiences and have minimized their political power and engagement as well as their unified demands for political, legal, and civil rights in their new host societies. This is particularly the case for first-generation Iranians who remain strongly concerned about postrevolutionary home politics. Unlike their parents, who have a different political socialization and consciousness, second-generation Iranians not only identify with both their new country and their ancestral land but also are more politically organized and active in the political processes of their new host country. They aspire to maintain and elevate the legal status of their parents in diaspora and lobby to improve the diplomatic relations between Iran and their host governments. This is particularly the case for second-generation Iranians in the United States. Whether second-generation Iranians in other countries are as politically active, and whether they continue their transnational political practices and citizenship, are subjects for future research.

Clearly, second-generation Iranians face unique problems and prospects. Given the rise in their number, an intriguing research area involves comparative ethnic identity formation in multiple Western countries. Other interesting research areas include political orientation, occupational outlook, social mobility, and ethnic/national identity formation and maintenance for second-generation Iranians. In light of the persistent tensions between Iran and the West, and the rapid rise of anti-Muslim attitudes in Europe and other continents since the 9/11 terrorist attacks in 2001, it will be interesting to see whether second-generation Iranians will be as politicized, victimized, marginalized, devalued, and discriminated against as their parents. Will they have better prospects and more opportunities for economic and political advancement than their first-generation parents? Will they remain loyal to their ancestral land and act as cultural entrepreneurs and political ambassadors to reduce the political tensions between Iran and the rest of the world? Will they continue veiling their ethnic and religious identities, or will they resist demonization of their ethnic heritage and adopt a more positive ethnoreligious identity? Answering these questions will have major policy implications in migration studies, including whether the incorporation and integration of second-generation Iranians are based on ethnic heritage and the racialized political process in host countries or whether they are grounded in skills, resources, and level of education.

In addition to focusing on second-generation Iranians, further research should examine how the diasporic experience of Iranian women differs from men and whether women encounter the same challenges in adjustment and integration. Despite the recognition of Iranian immigration as an important area of scholarship with a great deal of interdisciplinary research, gender as a topic of research has not yet become a high priority. The lives and the experiences of Iranian women in diaspora remain relatively unexplored. It is time for scholars concerned with the Iranian diaspora to bring gender into the mainstream of Iranian immigrant studies, pay more scholarly attention to the experiences of Iranian women in diaspora, and explore important questions. How has migration changed gender relations, gender norms, gender stereotyping, and gender ideologies among Iranians in diaspora? What has been the impact of migration on gender role socialization of second-generation Iranians in diaspora? How have Iranian immigrant women been influenced by forces of revolution, migration, and transnationalism? How do the experiences of Iranian women in diaspora differ, if at all, from those of men? And what are the major roles and social, cultural, economic, and political contributions of Iranian women in diaspora?

Despite the severe challenges of integration and the unwelcoming context of reception in host societies, the return rate for Iranian immigrants as a whole is extremely low. Except for occasional visits to Iran, most first-generation Iranian immigrants prefer living in diaspora and maintaining ties with their families and multi-stranded linkages with Iran over permanent return. However, the extent of formal transnational practices among Iranians is unknown. Therefore, another major focus for future research that is very timely must be the extent, nature, forms, and implications of cultural, economic, and political transnational flows, activities, and practices that connect Iranians in diaspora with their homeland. Equally important is to explore and describe the cultural, economic, and political linkages between Iranian immigrants within various countries across the globe and how they are maintained. The international sanctions against Iran not only imposed legal barriers for trade, financial transactions, and other economic relations with Iran; they also hindered and retarded the emergence of viable transnational financial, cultural, and economic ties between Iranian communities in diaspora and Iran. This was particularly the case for Iranian communities with extensive economic, cultural, financial, and entrepreneurial resources such as the one in the United States. Many Iranian entrepreneurs with sufficient financial and social capital in Iran and the United States were unable to develop formal transnational economic ties because of the severe penalties imposed by the US Office of Foreign Assets Control, or by the international community under US pressure through the United Nations Security Council. Now that the sanctions have been partially lifted, it will be interesting to see and examine what types of transnational ties Iranians will develop between Iran and their new host societies, if any. The volume and channels for transferring remittances to Iran, and how such remittances impact families and communities in Iran, are very fascinating areas to examine in future research.

Finally, given the massive social, economic, and political push factors in Iran, and the annual increases in the numbers of Iranian immigrants who become naturalized citizens, more Iranians continue to immigrate to the West to reunite with families, pursue academic goals, find jobs, or achieve political freedom. Unlike the first, postrevolutionary wave of "high status" middle-class and upper middle-class Iranian immigrants who left Iran with substantial resources and were preoccupied with themes of revolution, exile, dislocation, war, and forced migration, many new arrivals have much fewer resources and a very different view of Iran and the revolution. This demographic increase, coupled with abandoning any hope for returning to Iran for an overwhelming majority of Iranian immigrants who have been in exile for a long time, has had major transformative social, cultural, and political consequences for Iranian communities in diaspora. It is time for scholars to document the demographic as well as the structural transformations of Iranian communities through various methodologies, such as oral histories and archival research, and to describe the emerging diversity and the challenges that Iranian communities in diaspora are experiencing.

Conclusion

1. Connor Phillip (2016), "Number of Refugees to Europe Surges to Record 1.3 Million in 2015," Pew Research Center, www.pewglobal.org/2016/08/02/number -of-refugees-to-europe-surges-to-record-1-3-million-in-2015.

2. Wilkinson Tracy (2017), "Trump Administration Slaps new Sanctions on

Iran but Preserves Nuclear Deal," *Los Angeles Times*, www.latimes.com/politics/washington/la-na-essential-washington-updates-trump-administration-slaps-new-1495049254-htmlstory.html.

3. Iran and the EU (2016), "European Union External Action," eeas.europa.eu/headquarters/headquarters-homepage/2281/iran-and-eu_en.

Bibliography

Abdoh, Salar. 2000. *The Poet Game*. New York: Picador USA.
——. 2014a. *Tehran at Twilight*. Brooklyn, NY: Akashic Books.
——. 2014b. *Tehran Noir*. Brooklyn, NY: Akashic Books.
Abdullah, Muhammad M. 2007. *The United Arab Emirates: A Modern History*. Dubai: Makarem.
Abrahamian, Ervand. 1982. *Iran between Two Revolutions*. Princeton: Princeton University Press.
Absal, Rayeesa. 2007. "No Place for Illegal Immigrants after Amnesty." *Gulf News*, October 29.
Adibi, Hossein. 2003. "Identity and Cultural Change: The Case of Iranian Youth in Australia." Paper presented at Social Change in the Century Conference, Centre for Social Change Research, Queensland University of Technology, Brisbane, AUS.
Adle, Maria. 1998. *Tous mes jours sont des adieux*. Paris: J. C. Lattès.
Afshari Behbahanizadeh, Zardosht, and Farrindokht Zadehi. 2013. "Adabiyat Namayeshi Mohajerat Iranian saken dar Australia: Tahlil Pasa Estemari Namayeshnameh Dar Ayeneh, Asar Mohammad Aidani" *Jame'e Shenasi Honar va Adabiyat* 5.1: 147–164.
Ahmad, Anwar. 2013. "UAE Amnesty Woos More Than 61,000 Illegals." *The National*, February 7.
Ahmed, Amr Taher. 2012. *La 'Révolution littéraire': étude de l'influence de la poésie française sur la modernisation des formes poétiques persanes au début du XXe siècle*. Wien: Verlag der Österreichischen Akademie der Wissenschaften, ÖAW.
Aidani, Mammad. 2010. *Welcoming the Stranger: Narratives of Identity and Belonging in an Iranian Diaspora*. Altona, VIC: Common Ground.
Akhavan, Niki. 2013. *Electronic Iran: The Cultural Politics of an Online Evolution*. New Brunswick, NJ: Rutgers University Press.
Al Arabiya News. 2010. "Sanctions Squeeze Iranians in Trade Hub Dubai." April 2.
Alba, Richard. 2005. "Bright vs. Blurred Boundaries: Second Generation Assimilation and Exclusion in France, Germany, and the United States." *Ethnic and Racial Studies*, 28: 20–49.
Alba, Richard, and Nancy Foner. 2015. *Stranger No More: Immigration and the Chal-*

lenges of Integration in North America and Western Europe. New Jersey: Princeton University Press.

Alba, Richard, and Victor Nee. 2003. *Remaking the American Mainstream: Assimilation and Contemporary Immigration.* Cambridge, MA: Harvard University Press.

Al Jandaly, Bassma. 2012. "Thousands Expected at Centres as UAE Visa Amnesty Begins." *Gulf News*, December 3.

———. 2013. "UAE Labour Bans Still Enforced." *Gulf News*, June 10.

Al-Sayegh, Fatma. 1998. "Merchant's Role in a Changing Society: The Case of Dubai, 1900–90." *Middle Eastern Studies* 34: 87–102.

Ali, Seyed. 2010. *Dubai: Gilded Cage.* London: Yale University Press.

Al-Ali, N., and K. Koser. 2002. *New Approaches to Migration: Transnational Communities and the Transformation of Home.* London and New York: Routledge.

Alinejad, Donya. 2017. *The Internet and Formations of Iranian American-ness: Next Generation Diaspora.* New York: Springer.

Alexanian, Janet. 2008. "Poetry and Polemics: Iranian Literary Expression in the Digital Age." *MELUS* 33(2).

Amini, Iradj. 1995. *Napoléon et la Perse. Les relations franco-persanes sous le Premier Empire dans le contexte des rivalités entre la France, l'Angleterre et la Russie.* Paris: Editions de la Fondation Napoléon.

Amirrezvani, Anita, and Persis M. Karim. 2013. *Tremors: New Fiction by Iranian American Writers.* Fayetteville: University of Arkansas Press.

Amirshahi, Mahshid. 1995. *Dar safar.* Los Angeles: Ketab Corporation.

———. 1998–2010. *Madaran va dokhtaran* (4 volumes). Spanga, Sweden/Stockholm: Baran/Ferdowsi.

Ansari, Abdoulmaboud. 1977. "A Community in Process: The First Generation of the Iranian professional Middle-class Immigrants in the United States." *International Review of Modern Sociology* 7(1): 85–101.

———. 1998. *Iranian Immigrants in the United States: A Case Study of Dual Marginality.* New York: Associated Faculty Press.

Ansari, Ali. 2005. "'Persia' in the Western Imagination." In *Anglo-Iranian Relations Since 1800*, ed. Vanessa Martin. London: Routledge.

Anthias, F. 2006. "Belongings in a Globalising and Unequal World: Rethinking Translocations." In *The situated politics of belonging*, ed. N. Yuval-Davis, K. Kannabiran, and U. M. Vieten, 17–31. London: Sage.

Arasteh, Reza. 1962. "The Education of Iranian Leaders in Europe and America." *International Review of Education* 8(3): 444–450.

Archives of the Consular Section of the Embassy of Islamic Republic of Iran in Rome (years 2007–2013). Rome: Embassy of Islamic Republic of Iran.

Australian Bureau of Statistics. n.d. "People Born in the Middle East." www.abs.gov.au/AUSSTATS/abs@.nsf/Lookup/3416.0Main+Features42008.

Australian-Iranian Youth Society of Victoria. n.d. www.airys.org.au.

Azernour, Ladane. 2004. *Les larmes de l'exil. L'Iran confisqué.* Paris: Les Quatre Chemins.

Bakalian, Anny, and Mehdi Bozorgmehr. 2009. *Backlash 9/11: Middle Eastern and Muslim Americans Respond.* Berkeley: University of California Press.

Balaÿ, Christophe. 1998. *La genèse du roman persan moderne.* Téhéran: Institut français de recherche en Iran.

Baldwin, George B. 1963. "The Foreign-Educated Iranian: A Profile." *Middle East Journal* 17(3): 264–278.

Barth, Fredrick. 1969. *Ethnic Groups and Boundaries.* Boston: Little, Brown.

Bayrakli, Enes, and Farid Hafez. 2016. *European Islamophobia Report 2015.* Istanbul: SETA.

Basch, L., G. Schiller, and S. Blanc. 1995. "From Immigrant to Transmigrant: Theorizing Transnational Migration." *Anthropological Quarterly* 68(1): 48–63.

Basch, Linda, Nina Glick Schiller, and Cristina Szanton Blanc. 1994. *Nations Unbound: Transnational Projects, Postcolonial Predicaments, and Deterritorialized Nation-States.* Amsterdam: Gordon and Breach.

Beard, Michael, and Hasan Javadi. 1986. "Iranian Writers Abroad: Survey and Elegy." *World Literature Today* 60(2): 257–261.

Bhabha, H. K. 1990. "The Third Space: Interview with Homi K. Bhabha." In *Identity: Community, Culture, Difference,* ed. J. Rutherford, 207–221. London: Lawrence & Wishart.

Bjornson, M. 2007. "Speaking of Citizenship: Language Ideologies in Dutch Citizenship Regimes." *Focaal—European Journal of Anthropology* 49: 65–80.

Blair, Betty. 1991. "Personal Name Changes among Iranian Immigrants in the USA." In *Iranian Refugees and Exiles since Khomeini,* ed. Asghar Fathi, 145–160. Costa Mesa, CA: Mazda.

Boal, Augusto. 1998. *Legislative Theatre.* New York: Routledge.

Bonilla-Silva, Eduardo. 2000. "This Is a White Country: The Racial Ideology of the Western Nations of the World System." *Sociological Inquiry* 70: 2.

Bonilla-Silva, Eduardo, and Sarah Mayorga. 2011. "In (Not) Belonging: Why Citizenship Does Not Remedy Racial Inequality." In *State of White Supremacy: Racism Governance, and the United States,* ed. M. Jung, J. Costa Vargas, and E. Bonilla-Silva, 77–87. Redwood City, CA: Stanford University Press.

Bos, Matthijs van den, and Wahideh Achbari. 2007. "Cultural Migration: Networks of Iranian Organizations in the Netherlands." *Migration Letters* 4(2): 171–181.

Bosma, Ulbe. 2012. "Post-colonial Immigrants and Identity Formations in the Netherlands." In *Post-Colonial Immigrants and Identity Formations in the Netherlands,* ed. U. Bosma, 7–27. Amsterdam: Amsterdam University Press.

Bourdieu, Pierre. 1990. *The Logic of Practice.* Stanford: Stanford University Press.

Bozorgmehr, M., G. Sabagh, and C. Der-Martirosian. 1993. "Beyond Nationality: Religio-Ethnic Diversity." In *Irangeles: Iranians in Los Angeles,* ed. R. Kelley and J. Friedlander, 59–80. Berkeley: University of California Press.

Bozorgmehr, Mehdi. 1996. "Diaspora. viii. Diaspora in the Postrevolutionary Period." *Encyclopaedia Iranica,* vol. 7, 380–383. Costa Mesa, CA: Mazda.

———. 1997. "Internal Ethnicity: Iranians in Los Angeles." *Sociological Perspectives* 40: 387–408.

———. 2000. "Does Host Hostility Create Ethnic Solidarity? The Experience of Iranians in the U.S." *Bulletin of the Royal Institute for Inter-Faith Studies* 2: 1.

———. 2007. "Iran." In *The New Americans: A Guide to Immigration since 1965,* ed. Mary C. Waters and Reed Ueda. Cambridge, MA: Harvard University Press.

Bozorgmehr, Mehdi, and Georges Sabagh. 1988. "High Status Immigrants: A Statistical Profile of Iranians in the United States." *Iranian Studies* 21: 5–36.

Brah, A. 1996. *Cartographies of Diasporas.* London: Routledge.

Brettell, Caroline. 2003. *Anthropology and Migration: Essays on Transnationalism, Ethnicity, and Identity*. New York: Altamira Press.

———. 2006. "Introduction: Global Spaces/Local Places: Transnationalism, Diaspora, and the Meaning of Home." *Identities: Global Studies in Culture and Power* 13(3): 327–334.

Brubaker, Rogers. 1992. *Citizenship and Nationhood in France and Germany*. Cambridge, MA: Harvard University Press.

———. 2004. *Ethnicity without Borders*. Cambridge, MA: Harvard University Press.

———. 2005. "The 'Diaspora' Diaspora." *Ethnic and Racial Studies* 28(1): 1–19.

Bruneau, Michel. 2010. "Diasporas, Transnational Spaces and Communities." In *Diaspora and Transnationalism: Concepts, Theories and Methods*, ed. Rainer Bauböck and Thomas Faist, 35–50. Basel: Amsterdam University Press.

Buijs, F. J., F. Demant, & A. Hamdy. 2006. *Strijders van eigen bodem: Radicale en democratische moslims in Nederland*. Amsterdam: Amsterdam University Press.

Buitelaar, Marjo, and Femke Stock. 2010. "Making Homes in Turbulent Times: Moroccan-Dutch Muslims Contesting Dominant Discourses of Belonging." In *Muslim Diaspora in the West: Negotiating Gender, Home and Belonging*, ed. H. Moghissi and H. Ghorashi, 163–181. Surrey, UK: Ashgate.

Calavita, Kitty. 1995. "Italy and the New Immigration." In *Controlling Immigration: A Global Perspective*, ed. Wayne A. Cornelius, Philip L. Martin, and James F. Hollifield, 303–326. Stanford: Stanford University Press.

Caritas Italiana–Fondazione Migrantes. 2006. *Immigrazione. Dossier statistic. XVI Rapporto sull'immigrazione*. Rome: Nuova Anterem.

Carment, David, and David Bercuson. 2008. "Introduction." In *The World in Canada: Diaspora, Demography, and Domestic Politics*, ed. David Carment and David Bercuson, 3–15. Montreal and Kingston: McGill-Queen's University Press.

Casari, Mario. 2006. "Italy xiii. Iranians in Italy." *Encyclopaedia Iranica*, vol. 14(3): 290–292. New York: Encyclopaedia Iranica Foundation.

Central Bureau of Statistics (CBS). 2012. *Jaarrapport Integratie*. Den Haag/Heerlen: CBS.

Centro Studi e Ricerche IDOS. 2014. *Dossier statistico immigrazione—Elaborazioni su dati ISTAT forniti dal Ministero dell'Interno*. Rome: Edizioni Idos.

———. 2016. *Dossier statistico immigrazione 2016 in partenariato con la rivista Confronti*. Rome: Edizioni Idos.

Chafiq, Chahla. 2015. *Demande au miroir*. Paris: L'âge d'homme.

Chaichian, Mohammad A. 1997. "First Generation Iranian Immigrants and the Question of Cultural Identity: The Case of Iowa." *International Migration Review* 31: 612–627.

Clifford, James. 1994. "Diasporas." *Cultural Anthropology*. 9(3): 302–338.

———. 1997. *Routes: Travel and Translation in the Late Twentieth Century*. Cambridge, MA: Harvard University Press.

Cohen, Robin. 1997. *Global Diasporas: An Introduction*. Seattle: University of Washington Press.

Crul, Maurice, and Jeroen Doomernik. 2003. "The Turkish and Moroccan Second Generation in the Netherlands: Divergent Trends between and Polarization within the Two Groups." *International Migration Review* 37(4): 1039–1064.

Dabashi, Hamid. 2006. "Native Informers and the Making of the American Empire." *Al-Ahram Weekly*, June 1–7, 797.

————. 2007. *Masters & Masterpieces of Iranian Cinema*. New York: Mage.

————. 2011. *The World Is My Home: A Hamid Dabashi Reader*, ed. Andrew Davison and Himadeep Muppidi. New York: Palgrave.

Daha, Maryam. 2011. "Contextual Factors Contributing to Ethnic Identity Development of Second-Generation Iranian American Adolescents." *Journal of Adolescent Research* 26: 543–569.

Darvishpour, Mehrdad. 2002. "Immigrant Women Challenge the Role of Men: How the Changing Power Relationship within Iranian Families in Sweden Intensifies Family Conflicts after Immigration." *Journal of Comparative Family Studies* 33: 271–296.

Davaran, A. 1996. "Iranian Diaspora Literature since 1980: Contexts and Currents." *Literary Review* 40(1): 5–13.

Davaran, F. 2010. *Continuity in Iranian Identity: Resilience of a Cultural Heritage*. London and New York: Routledge.

Davidson, Andrew, and Eng Kuah, eds. 2007. *At Home in the Chinese Diaspora: Memories, Identities and Belongings*. New York: Palgrave Macmillan.

Davidson, Christopher M. 2005. *The United Arab Emirates: A Study in Survival*. Boulder: Lynne Rienner.

Delfani, Mahmoud, ed. 2009. *L'Iran et la France malgré les apparences*. Paris: Europerse.

De Genova, Nicholas, and Nathalie Puetz. 2010. *The Deportation Regime: Sovereignty, Space, and the Freedom of Movement*. Durham, NC: Duke University Press.

Der-Martirosian, Claudia. 2008. *Iranian Immigrants in Los Angeles: The Role of Networks and Economic Integration*. New York: LFB Scholarly Publications.

DeStatis Statistisches Bundesamt. 2011. *Zensus: Population with a Migrant Background*. www.destatis.de/EN/FactsFigures/SocietyState/Population/Migration Integration/PersonsMigrationBackground/PersonsMigrationBackground.html.

————. 2015. *Persons of a Migrant Background, Methodological Notes*. www.destatis .de/EN/FactsFigures/SocietyState/Population/MigrationIntegration/Persons MigrationBackground/MigrationBackgroundMethods.html.

Dijk, Teun van. 1993. *Elite Discourse and Racism*. Newbury Park, CA: SAGE.

Djavani, Raphaël. 2005. *L'enfant du blé*. Paris: Flammarion.

Djavann, Chahdortt 2006. *Comment peut-on être français?* Paris: Flammarion.

Dokter, Ditty. 1998. *Arts Therapists, Refugees, and Migrants*. London: Jessica Kingsley.

Dubai Land Department. 2013. "Arab and Foreign Investors Put in AED 58 Billion in Dubai Property Sector in 2012." Government of Dubai, www.dubailand.gov.ae /English/Pages/news-viewer.aspx?nid=123.

Dufoix, Stephane. 2003. *Diasporas*. Berkeley: University of California Press.

Dumas, Firoozeh. 2003. *Funny in Farsi: A Memoir of Growing up Iranian in America*. New York: Villard.

Duyvendak, J. W., E. Engelen, and I. de Haan. 2008. *Het bange Nederland*. Amsterdam: Bert Bakker.

Eijberts, M. 2013. *Migrant Women Shout It out Loud: The Integration/Participation Strategies and Sense of Home of First- and Second-generation Women of Moroccan and Turkish Descent*. Amsterdam: VU University Press.

Eijberts, M., and H. Ghorashi. 2016. "Biographies and the Doubleness of Inclusion and Exclusion." *Social Identities: Journal for the Study of Race, Nation, and Culture* 23: 163–78.

Elyachar, Julie. 2010. "Phatic Labor, Infrastructure, and the Question of Empowerment in Cairo." *American Ethnologist* 37: 452–464.

Entzinger, Han. 1998. "Het voorportaal van Nederland; inburgeringsbeleid in een multi-culturele Samenleving." In *Multiculturalisme*, ed. C. H. M. Geuijen, 67–81. Utrecht: Lemma.

Erfan, Ali. 1990. *Le dernier poète du monde*. La Tour-d'Aigues, FRA: Editions de l'Aube.

———. 2005. *Adieu Ménilmontant*. La Tour-d'Aigues, FRA: Editions de l'Aube.

Erfani, Farhang. 2012. *Iranian Cinema and Philosophy*. New York: Palgrave McMillan.

Essed, Philomena. 1991. *Understanding Everyday Racism: An Interdisciplinary Theory*. Newbury Park, CA: SAGE.

———. 1995. "Gender, Migration and Cross-Ethnic Coalition Building." In *Crossfires: Nationalism, Racism and Gender in Europe*, ed. H. Lutz, A. Phoenix, and N. Yuval-Davis, 48–64. London: Pluto Press.

Faillie, Robert. 2008. *Estimating the Contribution of Immigrant Business Owners to the US Economy*. Washington, DC: SBA.

Faist, Thomas. 2010. *Diaspora and Transnationalism: Concepts, Theories and Methods*. Amsterdam: Amsterdam University Press.

Farr, Grant. 1999. *Modern Iran*. Boston: McGraw-Hill.

Fassih, Esmail. 1985. *Sorraya in a Coma*. Translated from the Persian. London: Zed Books.

Fathi, Asghar. Ed. 1991. *Iranian Refugees and Exiles since Khomeini*. Costa Mesa, CA: Mazda.

Fereidouni, Hassan G., Tajul A. Masron, Anahita Malekmohammadi, and Ai-Yee Ooi. 2010. "The Interaction between Foreign Real Estate Investment and Tourism: The Iranian Case in Dubai." *World Applied Sciences Journal* 10: 40–44.

Foner, Nancy. 2005. *In a New Land: A Comparative View of Immigrants*. New York: New York University Press.

———. 2008. "Afterword: Some Concluding Reflections." In *Citizenship, Political Engagement, and Belonging: Immigrants in Europe and the United States*, ed. Deborah Reed-Danahay and Caroline B. Brettell, 244–251. New Brunswick, NJ: Rutgers University Press.

Fotouhi, Sanaz. 2015. *The Literature of the Iranian Diaspora: Meaning and Identity since the Islamic Revolution*. London: I. B. Tauris.

FutureBrand. February 2, 2010. "Gulf Real Estate Study: 2009." In William Shintani and Jae Hwang, "Gulf Real Estate Study: 2009." Dubai, UAE: Futurebrand.

Geroe, Anne Demy. 2015. "Pomegranates and Cinema: Some Observations on a Decade or so of Selecting and Screening Iranian Films." In *Iranian Cinema in a Global Context: Policy, Politics, and Form*, ed. Peter Decherney and Blake Atwood, 192–203. London: Routledge.

Ghassemi, Reza. 1991. *Hamnavaee shaban-ye orkestr-e choub-ha*. Los Angeles: Nashr-e ketab.

Gholami, R. 2014. "'Is This Islamic Enough?' Intra-Diasporic Secularism and Religious Experience in the Shi'a Iranian Diaspora in London." *Journal of Ethnic and Migration Studies* 40(1): 60–79.

———. 2015. *Secularism and Identity: Non-Islamiosity in the Iranian Diaspora.* London and New York: Routledge.

Ghorashi, Halleh. 1997. "Shifting and Conflicting Identities: Iranian Women Political Activists in Exile." *European Journal of Women's Studies* 4: 283–303.

———. 2003a. *Ways to Survive, Battles to Win: Iranian Women Exiles in the Netherlands and the United States.* New York: Nova Science.

———. 2003b. "From Marxist Organizations to Feminism: Iranian Women's Experiences of Revolution and Exile." *Journal of the Study of Religions and Ideologies* 6: 89–107.

———. 2004. "How Dual Is Transnational Identity? A Debate on Dual Positioning of Diaspora Organizations." *Culture and Organization* 10: 329–340.

———. 2005. "Refugees: Agents of Change or Passive Victims: The Impact of Welfare States (The Case of The Netherlands) on Refugees." *Journal of Refugee Studies* 18: 182–198.

———. 2008. "Giving Silence a Chance: The Importance of Life Stories for Research on Refugees." *Journal of Refugee Studies* 21: 117–133.

———. 2014. "Racism and 'the Ungrateful Other' in the Netherlands." In *Dutch Racism*, ed. Philomena Essed and Isabel Hoving, 101–116. New York: Rodopi.

Ghorashi, H., and M. van Tilburg. 2006. "When is my Dutch good enough?" *Journal of International Migration and Integration.* 7(1): 51–70.

Giddens, Anthony. 1991. *Modernity and Self-Identity: Self and Society in the Late Modern Age.* Cambridge: Polity Press.

Gilroy, P. 1994. "Diaspora." *Paragraph* 17(1): 207–212.

Gilroy, Paul. 1992. "The End of Anti-Racism." In *Race, Culture, and Difference*, ed. James Donald and Ali Rattansi. London: SAGE Publications.

Giroux, Henry A. 1995. "National Identity and the Politics of Multiculturalism." *College Literature* 22: 2.

Glass, Amy. 2007. "Who Would Be a Bachelor Boy?" *Arabian Business*, August 17.

Glastra, F. 1999. *Organisaties en Diversiteit: Naar een contextuele benadering van intercultureel management.* Utrecht: Lemma.

Glick Schiller, Nina. 1999. "Transmigrants and Nation-States: Something Old and Something New in the U.S. Immigrant Experience." In *The Handbook of International Migration*, ed. Charles Hirschmann, Philip Kasinitz, and Josh DeWind, 94–119. New York: Russell Sage Foundation.

Gordon, Milton. 1964. *Assimilation in American Life: The Role of Race, Religion, and National Origins.* New York: Oxford University Press.

Graham, Mark, and Shahram Khosravi. 1997. "Home Is Where You Make It: Repatriation and Diaspora Culture among Iranians in Sweden." *Journal of Refugee Studies* 10: 115–133.

———. 2002. "Reordering Public and Private in Iranian Cyberspace: Identity, Politics, and Mobilization." *Identities* 9(2): 219–246.

Grassian, Daniel. 2013. *Iranian and Diasporic Literature in the 21st Century: A Critical Study.* Jefferson, NC: McFarland.

Green, Simon. 2000. "Beyond Ethnoculturalism? German Citizenship in the New Millennium." *German Politics* 9: 3.

Grever, Maria. 2006. "Nationale identiteit en historisch besef: de risico's van een canon in de postmoderne samenleving." *Tijdschrift voor Geschiedenis* 119(2): 160–177.

Habibi, Mariam. 2004. *L'interface France-Iran, 1907–1938: une diplomatie voilée*. Paris: L'Harmattan.

Habibi, Nader. 2010. "The Impact of Sanctions on Iran-GCC Economic Relations." *Middle East Brief* no. 45. Crown Center for Middle East Studies, Brandeis University, Waltham, MA.

Haddad, Yvonne Yazbeck, and Jane I. Smith. 2002. "Introduction." In *Muslim Minorities in the West: Visible and Invisible*, ed. Yvonne Haddad and Jane Smith, v–xviii. Walnut Creek, CA: AltaMira Press.

Hadidi, Javad, and Dominique Carnoy. 1994. *De Sa'di à Aragon: l'accueil fait en France à la littérature persane (1600–1982)*. Téhéran: Éditions internationales Alhoda.

Haghighat, S. S. 2012. "Iranian Identity in the West: A Discursive Approach." In *Shi'i Islam and Identity*, ed. L. Ridgeon, 40–63. New York: I. B. Tauris.

Hakimzadeh, Shirin. September 1, 2006. "Iran: A Vast Diaspora Abroad and Millions of Refugees at Home." Migration Policy Institute. www.migrationpolicy .org/article/iran-vast-diaspora-abroad-and-millions-refugees-home.

Hakkakian, Roya. 2004. *Journey from the Land of No: A Girlhood Caught in Revolutionary Iran*. New York. Crown.

Hall, Stuart. 1991. "Ethnicity: Identity and Difference." *Radical America* 23(4): 9–20.

———. 1996. "Introduction: Who Needs Identity?" In *Questions of Cultural Identity*, ed. S. Hall and P. Du Gay, 1–17. London: SAGE Publications.

———. 2002. "Cultural Identity and Diaspora." In *Theorising Diaspora: A Reader*, ed. J. Braziel and A. Mannur, 233–246. Oxford: Blackwell.

Hankir, Zahra, and Haneen Dajani. 2009. "Expats in 57 Occupations Banned from Bringing Families with Them." *The National*, January 1.

Hassan, Hassan. 2009. "Police Conduct Random Visa Checks." *The National*, November 27.

Heard-Bey, Frauke. 1982. *From Trucial States to United Arab Emirates*. London: Longham.

Hellot-Bellier, Florence. 2007. *France-Iran, quatre cent ans de dialogue*. Leuven, Belgique: Peeters Press.

Hesse-Lehmann, K. 1993. *Iraner in Hamburg: Verhaltensmuster im Kulturkontakt*. Berlin and Hamburg: Dietrich Reimer Verlag.

Hessels, T. 2002. *Iraniërs in Nederland, een profiel*. The Hague: Ministerie van Binnenlandse Zaken en Koninkrijkrelaties.

Higgins, Patricia. 1977. "Intergenerational Stress: Parents and Adolescents in Iranian Immigrant Families." In *Beyond Boundaries: Selected Papers on Refugees and Immigrants*, vol. 5, ed. Diane Baxter and Ruth Krulfeld. Arlington, VA: American Anthropological Association.

———. 2004. "Interviewing Iranian Immigrant Parents and Adolescents." *Iranian Studies* 37(4): 695–706.

Hoath, Nissar. 2003. "Amnesty Begins on a Dull Note." *Gulf News*, January 2.

Hoffman, Diane M. 1988. "Cross-cultural Adaptation and Learning: Iranians and Americans at School." In *School and Society: Learning Content through Culture*, ed. Henry T. Trueba and Concha Delgado-Gaitan, 163–180. New York: Praeger.

Holdsworth, Nadine. 2015. *Theatre and National Identity: Re-Imagining Concept of Nation*. London: Routledge.

Hollifield James, Philip Martin, and Pia M. Orrenius. 2014. "The Dilemmas of Immigration Control." In *Controlling Immigration: A Global Persective*, ed. Hollifield, Martin, and Orrenius, 1–35. Stanford: Standford University Press.

Hosseini-Kaladjahi, Hassan. 1997. *Iranians in Sweden: Economic, Cultural and Social Integration*. Stockholm: Almqvist and Wiksell International.

Idjadi, S. 2012–. iranienfr.com. Iranian Australian Community Organization.

Iranian Center for Documentation and Research. 1989. *Listing of Persian Periodicals Outside Iran (1978–1989)*. Paris: Iranian Center for Documentation and Research.

Javaheri, Javad. 2003. *Le soupir de l'ange*. La Tour-d'Aigues, FRA: Editions de l'Aube.

Jeffers, Alison. 2011. *Refugees, Theatre and Crisis: Performing Global Identities*. New York: Palgrave McMillan.

Jones, Guno. 2012. "Dutch Politicians, the Dutch Nation and the Dynamics of Post-Colonial Citizenship." In *Post-Colonial Immigrants and Identity Formations in the Netherlands*, ed. U. Bosma, 27–49. Amsterdam: Amsterdam University Press.

Joppke, C. 2004. "The Retreat of Multiculturalism in the Liberal State." *British Journal of Sociology* 55: 237–257.

Kanna, Ahmed. 2011. *Dubai: The City as Corporation*. Minneapolis: University of Minnesota Press.

Kanook Aknoon. aknoon.com.au.

Karim, Persis. 2015. "Writing Beyond Iran: Reinvention and the Exilic Iranian Writer." *World Literature Today*. worldliteraturetoday.org.

Karim, Persis M., and Babak Elahi. 2011. "Iranian Diaspora." *Comparative Studies of South Asia, Africa, and the Middle East* 31: 381–387.

Karim, Persis, and Nasrin Rahimieh. 2008. Special Issue: Iranian American Literature. *Journal of the Society for the Study of the Multi-Ethnic Literature of the United States* 33(2).

Kasinitz, P., et al. 2009. *Inheriting the City: The Children of Immigrants Come of Age*. Cambridge, MA: Harvard University Press.

Kasmaï, Sorour. 2002. *Le cimetière de verre*. Arles: Actes Sud.

———. 2006. *La vallée des aigles. Autobiographie d'une fuite*. Arles: Actes Sud.

———. 2015. *Un jour avant la fin du monde*. Paris: Robert Laffont.

Kaya Ayhan. 2012. *Islam, Migration, and Integration: The Age of Securitization*. New York: Palgrave Macmillan.

Keddie, Nikki R. 2006. *Modern Iran: Roots and Results of Revolution*. New Haven: Yale University Press.

Kelley, Ron, Jonathan Friedlander, and Anita Y. Colby. 1993. *Irangeles: Iranians in Los Angeles*. Berkeley: University of California Press.

Kennedy, J. 2005. *De deugden van een gidsland: burgerschap en democratie in Nederland*. Amsterdam: Bakker.

Khanlou, N., J. Koh, and C. Mill. 2008. "Cultural Identity and Experiences of Prejudice and Discrimination of Afghan and Iranian Immigrant Youth." *International Journal of Mental Health Addiction* 6: 494–513.

Khoei, Effat, Anna Whelan, and Jeffery Cohen. 2008. "Sharing Beliefs: What Sexuality Means to Muslim Iranian Women Living in Australia," *Culture, Health & Sexuality* 20(3): 237–248.

Khosravi, Shahram. 1999. "Displacement and Entrepreneurship: Iranian Small Businesses in Stockholm." *Journal of Ethnic and Migration Studies* 25(3): 493–508.

Komaie, Golnaz. 2009. "The Persian Veil: Ethnic and Racial Self-identification among the Adult Children of Iranian Immigrants in Southern California." PhD diss., University of California, Irvine.

Krane, Jim. 2009. *City of Gold: Dubai and the Dream of Capitalism*. New York: St. Martin's Press.

Lambek, Michael. 2010. "An Ethics of the Act." In *Ordinary Ethics*, ed. Michael Lambek, 39–63. New York: Fordham University Press.

Leise, Eric. 2007. "Germany Strives to Integrate Immigrants with New Policies." *Migration Policy Institute*, July 9.

Levitt, Peggy. 2009. "Roots and Routes: Understanding the Lives of the Second Generation Transnationally." *Journal of Ethnic and Migration Studies* 35(7): 1225–1242.

Levitt, Peggy, and N. G. Schiller. 2004. "Conceptualizing Simultaneity: A Transnational Social Field Perspective on Society." *International Migration Review* 38: 3.

Lewin-Ahmadi, Fereshteh. 2001. "Identity Crisis and Integration: The Divergent Attitudes of Iranian Immigrant Men and Women Towards Integration into Swedish Society." *International Migration* 39: 121–135.

Ley, Graham, and Sarah Dadswell. 2015. *Critical Essays on British South Asian Theatre*. Chicago: University of Chicago Press.

Light, Ivan, and Steven Gold. 2000. *Ethnic Economies*. San Diego: Emerald Group.

Lindert, Annet, et al. 2008. "Perceived Discrimination and Acculturation among Iranian Refugees in the Netherlands." *International Journal of Intercultural Relations* 32: 578–588.

Longva, Anh. 1999. "Keeping Migrant Workers in Check: The Kafala System in the Gulf." *Middle East Report* 211: 20–22.

———. 2005. "Neither Autocracy nor Democracy but Ethnocracy: Citizens, Expatriates and the Socio-Political System in Kuwait." In *Monarchies and Nations: Globalization and Identity in the Arab States of the Gulf*, ed. Paul Dresch and James Piscatori, 114–135. London: I. B. Tauris.

Lutz, Helma. 1991. "Migrant Women of 'Islamic Background': Images and Self-Images." *MERA Occasional Paper* no. 11. Amsterdam: Middle East Research Associates.

———. 1997. "The Limits of European-ness: Immigrant Women in Fortress Europe." *Feminist Review* 57: 93–111.

Lutz, Helma, and Annelies Moors. 1989. "De mythe van de ander: Beeldvorming over Turkse migrantes in Nederland." *Lover* 16(1): 4–7.

Mackey, Sandra. 1996. *The Iranians: Persia, Islam, and the Soul of a Nation*. New York: Plume.

Maghbouleh, Neda. 2013. "The *Ta'arof* Tournaments: Cultural Performances of Ethno-National Identity at a Diasporic Summer Camp." *Ethnic and Racial Studies* 36: 5.

———. 2014. "Emerging Scholarship: Neda Maghbouleh on 'The Limits of Whiteness, Iranian-Americans and the Everyday Politics of Race.'" *Ajam Media Collective*, August 19.

———. 2017. *The Limits of Whiteness: Iranian-Americans and the Everyday Politics of Race*. Stanford: Stanford University Press.

Mahdi, Ali Akbar. 1998. "Ethnic identity among Second-Generation Iranians in the United States." *Iranian Studies* 31(1): 77–95.

Mahindokht (pseudonym). 2004. *La vie d'une Iranienne au vingtième siècle*. Paris: L'Harmattan.

Maira, Sunaina Marr. 2009. *Missing: Youth, Citizenship, and Empire after 9/11*. Durham, NC: Duke University Press.

Malek, Amy. 2006. "Memoir as Iranian Exile Cultural Production: A Case Study of Marjane Satrapi's Persepolis." *Iranian Studies* 39(3): 353–380.

———. 2011. "Public Performances of Identity Negotiation in the Iranian Diaspora: The New York Persian Day Parade." *Comparative Studies of South Asia, Africa, and the Middle East* 31(2): 388–410.

———. 2015a. "Displaced, Re-rooted, Transnational: Considerations in Theory and Practice of Being an Iranian outside Iran." Edited by the Heinrich Böll Foundation in cooperation with Transparency for Iran. Idea and editing: Resa Mohabbat-Kar. In *Identity and Exile: The Iranian Diaspora Between Solidarity and Difference*, 24–31. Berlin: Heinrich Böll Foundation.

———. 2015b. *Producing Culture, Producing Practice: Iranians in Sweden and Canada*. PhD diss., University of California, Los Angeles.

Marchant, James. 2015. *Writer's Block: The Story of Censorship in Iran*. Small Media Publication. smallmedia.org.uk/work/writers-block-the-story-of-censorship-in -iran.

Marshall, Lorna. 2001. *The Body Speaks: Performance and Expression*. New York: St. Martin's Press.

Matin-Asgari, Afshin. 1991. "The Iranian Student Movement abroad: The Confederation of Iranian Students, National Union." In *Iranian Refugees and Exiles Since Khomeini*, ed. Asghar Fathi, 55–74. Costa Mesa, CA: Mazda.

Marashi, A. 2008. *Nationalizing Iran: Culture, Power and the State, 1870–1940*. Seattle: University of Washington Press.

Martin, V. 2005. *Anglo-Iranian Relations since 1800*. London and New York: Routledge.

Marvasti, Amir, and Karyn McKinney. 2004. *Middle Eastern Lives in America*. Oxford, UK: Rowman & Littlefield.

Massey, Douglas S., et al. 1993. "Theories of International Migration: A Review and Appraisal." *Population and Development Review* 19(3): 431–466.

McAuliffe, Cameron. 2007a. "A Home Far Away? Religious Identity and Transnational Relations in the Iranian Diaspora" *Global Networks* 7(3): 307–327.

———. 2007b. "Visible Minorities: Constructing and Deconstructing the 'Muslim Iranian' Diaspora." In *Geographies of Muslim Identities: Diaspora, Gender and Belonging*, ed. C. Aitchison, P. Hopkins, and M. Kwan, 29–56. Aldershot, UK, and Burlington, VT: Ashgate.

———. 2008. "Transnationalism Within: Internal Diversity in the Iranian Diaspora." *Australian Geographer* 39: 63–80.

Mehtari, Ebrahim 07/03/2012. "Interview with Tinoush Nazmjou, manager of Naakojaa publisher." www.roozonline.com/persian/news/newsitem/article/-cb82957 990.html.

Miggiano, Alice. 2015a. *La letteratura della lontananza. Gli autori iraniani in Italia*. Università degli Studi di Napoli L'Orientale. Dottorato di Ricerca in Turchia, Iran, Asia Centrale, XI Ciclo, Nuova Serie.

———. 2015b. "The Iranian Diaspora in Italy," *Research in Iran and Iranian Dias-*

poras: Findings, Experiences, and Challenges. Proceedings of a Conference Sponsored by D\ANESH Institute, Inc., 2–9. Bloomington: Indiana University.

———. 2016. "La 'Storia di Sima' nella narrativa di Bijan Zarmandili, autore italo-iraniano." *Quaderni di MEYKHANE*. Rivista di studi iranici VII: 1–14.

Miller, D. A. 2014. "Living among the Breakage: Contextual Theology-making and ex-Muslim Christians." Unpublished doctoral thesis, PhD in Divinity [concentration on World Christianity], University of Edinburgh.

Mills, Charles. 1999. *The Racial Contract*. Ithaca: Cornell University Press.

Min, Pyong Gap. 2006. "Major Issues Related to Asian American Experiences." In *Asian Americans: Contemporary Trends and Issues*, ed. Pyong Gap Min, 80–107. Thousand Oaks, CA: SAGE.

Minoui, Delphine. 2015. *Je vous écris de Téhéran*. Paris: Seui.

Ministry of Labor. 2007. *The Protection of the Rights of Workers in the United Arab Emirates Annual Report*. Abu Dhabi: UAE Government.

Moallem, Minoo. 2003. "Transnationalism and Immigrant Entrepreneurship: Iranian Diasporic Narratives from the United States, France, England, and Germany." In *The Social Construction of Diversity*, ed. Christiane Harzig and Danielle Juteau, 84–104. New York: Berghahn Books.

Moaveni, Azadeh. 2005. *Lipstick Jihad: A Memoir of Growing up Iranian in America and American in Iran*. New York: PublicAffairs.

Mobasher, Mohsen M. 2004. "Ethnic Resources and Ethnic Economy: The Case of Iranian Entrepreneurs inn Dallas." In *Migration, Globalization, and Ethnic Relations: An Interdisciplinary Approach*, ed. Mohsen M. Mobaher and Mahmoud Sadri, 297–306. Upper Saddle River, NJ: Pearson Prentice Hall.

———. 2006. "Cultural Trauma and Ethnic Identity Formation among Iranian Immigrants in the United States." *American Behavioural Sociologist* 50: 100–117.

———. 2012. *Iranians in Texas: Migration, Politics, and Ethnic Identity*. Austin: University of Texas Press.

———. 2013. "Iranians and Iranian-Americans, 1945-Present." In *Immigrants in American History: Arrival, Adaptation, and Integration*, vol. 3, ed. Elliott Robert Barkan. Santa Barbara, CA: ABC-CLIO.

———. 2016a. "Shift in U.S.-Iran Political Relations, and Status of Iranian Immigrants in the United States." In *Inside the Islamic Republic: Social Change in Post-Khomeini Iran*, ed. Mahmood Monshipouri. London: Hurst/Oxford University Press.

———. 2016b. "Immigration Restrictions, and Political Mobilization among the Second-Generation Iranian Immigrants in the United States." In *Immigration in the Era of Restriction*, ed. Nestor Rodriguez and David Springer, 147–164. Switzerland: Springer International Publishing.

Modarresi, Yahya. 2001. "The Iranian Community in the United States and the Maintenance of Persian." *International Journal of the Sociology of Language* 148(1): 93–115.

Moradi, Farid. 2015. "Publishing Persian Books in Europe." In *Book title Publishing in Persian language in Iran, Afghanistan, Tajikistan, Uzbekistan, Europe and the United States*, ed. Farid Moradi.

———, ed. 2015. *Publishing in Persian Language in Iran, Afghanistan, Tajikistan, Uzbekistan, Europe and the United States*. International Alliance of Independent Publishers.

Moshiri, Farnoosh. 2005. *Against Gravity*. New York: Penguin Books.

Mottahedeh, Negar. 2008. *Displaced Allegories: Post-Revolutionary Iranian Cinema*. London: Duke University Press.

Mueller, A. Ulrike. 2011. "Far Away so Close: Race, Whiteness, and German Identity." *Identities: Global Studies in Culture and Power* 18(6): 620–645.

Musavi, Najmah. 2013. *Éclats de vie: histoires persanes*. Paris: L'Harmattan Museum of Victoria.

———. 2011. "Liberalism and the Racial State," In *State of White Supremacy: Racism, Governance, and the United States*, ed. M. Jung, J. Costa Vargas, and E. Bonilla-Silva, 27–41. Redwood City, CA. Stanford University Press.

Nadjmabadi, Shanaz R. 2010. "Cross-Border Networks Labour Migration from Iran to the Arab Countries of the Persian Gulf." *Anthropology of the Middle East* 5: 18–33.

Naficy, Hamid. 1993. *The Making of Exile Cultures: Iranian Television in Los Angeles*. Minneapolis: University of Minnesota Press.

———. 2001. *An Accented Cinema: Exilic and Diasporic Filmmaking*. Princeton: Princeton University Press.

Nafisi, Azar. 2003. *Reading Lolita in Tehran: A Memoir in Books*. New York: Random House.

Nagel, Joan. 1994. "Constructing Ethnicity: Creating and Recreating Ethnic Identity and Culture." *Social Problems* 41: 152–176.

Nahai, Gina Barkhordar. 1999. *Moonlight on the Avenue of Faith*: London: Scribner.

Nahapétian, Naïri. 2009. *Qui a tué l'ayatollah Kanuni?* Paris: Liana Levi.

———. 2012. *Dernier refrain à Ispahan*. Paris: Liana Levi.

———. 2015. *Un agent nommé Parviz roman*. La Tour-d'Aigues, FRA: Éditions de l'Aube.

———. 2016. *Le mage de l'hôtel royal*. La Tour-d'Aigues, FRA: Éditions de l'Aube.

Nanquette, Laetitia. 2011. "The Persian Novel in French: A Hybrid Genre." *Comparative Studies of South Asia, Africa and the Middle East* 31(2): 498–505.

———. 2013. *Orientalism versus Occidentalism: Literary and Cultural Imaging Between France and Iran since the Islamic Revolution*. London: I. B. Tauris.

———. 2014. "Refugee Life Writing in Australia: Testimonies by Iranians." *Postcolonial Text* 9(2) (online).

———. 2015. "Cultural and Translation Exchanges between Iran and the West (France, Germany, Great Britain, the United States)." In *Publishing in Persian Language in Iran, Afghanistan, Tajikistan, Uzbekistan, Europe and the United States*, ed. Farid Moradi, 111-130. International Alliance of Independent Publishers.

Nasr, Seyyed Hussein. 1991. *Islamic Spirituality: Manifestations*, vol. 2. New York: Crossroad Publishing.

———. 1999. "Persian Sufi Literature: Its Spiritual and Cultural Significance," *Heritage of Sufism*, vol. 2, ed. L. Lewishon. London: OneWorld.

Nassehy-Behnam, Vida. 2000. "Persian Community in France." In *Encyclopedia Iranica*, ed. Ehsan Yarshater. www.iranicaonline.org/articles/france-xviiinfo.

———. 2010. "Iranians in Britain." In *Muslim Diaspora in the West: Negotiating Gender, Home and Belonging*, ed. H. Moghissi and H. Ghorashi, 73–90. Aldershot, UK: Ashgate.

Nateq, Homa. 1994. *Karnameh-ye farhangi-e Farangi dar Iran. 1837–1914*. Paris: Khavaran.

Nazmjou, Tinouche. February 2016. "Être un éditeur iranien en France." *Bibliodiversity: Édition et engagement. D'autres façons d'être éditeur?* 4. www.alliance-editeurs.org/IMG/pdf/editeur_engage_en_france-iran_t._nazmjou-2.pdf.

Nekuee, Shervin, and Maykel Verkuyten. 1999. "Emotionele distantie en integratie: Iraanse politieke vluchtelingen in Nederland." *Mens en Maatschappij* 74: 218–234.

Oliver, Kelly. 2001. *Witnessing: Beyond Recognition.* London: University of Minnesota Press.

Omlo, Jurriaan. 2011. *Integratie En Uit de Gratie? Perspectieven van Marokkaans-Nederlandse Jongvolwassenen.* Delft, NED: Eburon.

Organisation for Economic Co-operation and Development. n.d. *Stocks of Foreign Born Populations in OECD Countries, 2000–2015.* data.oecd.org/migration/stocks-of-foreign-born-population-in-oecd-countries.htm.

Park, Robert, and Ernest Burgess. 1969 [1921]. "Assimilation." In *Introduction to the Science of Sociology.* Chicago: University of Chicago Press.

Pattie, S. 2013. "Bringing the Old into the New: Armenians and the Arts." In Middle Eastern Religious Minorities, special issue of *The Middle East in London Magazine*, ed. Kathryn Spellman-Poots and Sami Zubaida, 9(3): 10–11. School for the Oriental and African Studies in London.

Portes, Alejandro, and Jozsef Borocz. 1989. "Contemporary Immigration: Theoretical Perspectives on Its Determinants and Modes of Incorporation." *International Migration Review* 23: 606–630.

Portes, Alejandro, and Robert Manning. 1986. "The Immigrant Enclave: Theory and Empirical Examples." In *Comparative Ethnic Relations*, ed. Susan Olzak and Joane Nagel, 47–68. Orlando, FL: Academic Press.

Portes, Alejandro, and Ruben Rumbaut. 2001a. "The Forging of a New America: Lessons for Theory and Policy." In *Ethnicities: Children of Immigrants in America*, ed. Ruben Rumbaut and Alejandro Portes, 301–317. Berkeley: University of California Press.

———. 2001b. *Legacies: The Story of the Immigrant Second Generation.* Berkeley: University of California Press.

———. 2014. *Immigrant America: A Portrait*, 4th ed. Berkeley: University of California Press.

Portes, Alejandro, and Min Zhou. 1993. "The New Second Generation: Segmented Assimilation Theory and Its Variants." *Annals of the American Academy of Political and Social Science* 530: 74–96.

Prasad, Anshuman, and Pushkala Prasad. 2002. "Otherness at Large: Identity and Difference in the New Globalized Organizational Landscape." In *Gender, Identity and the Culture of Organizations*, ed. Iiris Aaltio and Albert J. Mills, 57–71. London: Routledge.

Prins, Baukje. 1997. "The Standpoint in Question: Situated Knowledge and the Dutch Minorities Discourse." Utrecht: University of Utrecht.

Rahbar, Sunny. 2015. "On the Scene, in Dubai." *Tirgan* 4: 56–59.

Rahimieh, Nasrin. 1993. "'How to Be Persian Abroad?': An Old Question in the Postmodern Age." *Iranian Studies* 26(1–2): 165–168.

Rahman, Saifur. 2005. "Iranian Investors Pump Dh730b into UAE Ventures." *Gulf News*, August 20.

Ramezanpour, Ali A. 2009. "The Dilemma of Iranian Investors in Dubai." *BBC Persian*, December 8.

Ramos, Stephen. 2012. *Dubai Amplified: The Engineering of a Port City*. Burlington, VT: Ashgate.

Rashidian, Jahanshah. 2010. "Our Iranian Identity." jahanshahrashidianrashidianblog.blogspot.com/2010/10/our-iranian-identity.html.

Räthzel, Nora 1995. "Nationalism and Gender in West Europe: The German Case." In *Crossfires: Nationalism, Racism and Gender in Europe*, ed. H. Lutz et al., 161–190. London: Pluto Press.

Rawls, John. 1971. *A Theory of Justice*. Cambridge, MA: Harvard University Press/ Belknap.

———. 1980. "Kantian Constructivism in Moral Theory." *Journal of Philosophy* 77(9): 515–577.

Reed-Danahay Debora, and Caroline Brettell. 2008. "Introduction." In *Citizenship, Political Engagement, and Belonging: Immigrants in Europe and the United States*, ed. Reed-Danahay and Caroline Brettell, 1–17. New Brunswick, NJ: Rutgers University Press.

Reis, Michele. 2004. "Theorizing Diaspora: Perspectives on 'Classical' and 'Contemporary' Diaspora." *International Migration Review* 42: 41–60.

Rogers, Amanda. 2014. *Performing Asian Transnationalism*. London: Routledge.

Roy, O. 2004. *Globalized Islam: The Search for a New Ummah*. New York: Columbia University Press.

Sabagh, Georges, and Mehdi Bozorgmehr. 1986. "Are the Characteristics of Exiles Different from Immigrants? The Case of Iranians in Los Angeles." *Institute for Social Science Research Working Papers* 2(5): 1–14. [Reprint 1987: *Sociology and Social Research* 71(2): 77–84.]

———. 1988. "High Status Immigrants: A Statistical Profile of Iranians in the United States." *Iranian Studies* 21(3–4): 3–36.

———. 1989. "Survey Research among Middle Eastern Immigrant Groups in the United States: Iranians in Los Angeles." *Mesa Bulletin* 23(1): 23–34.

Sadeghi, Sahar. 2014. "National Narratives and Global Politics: Iranian Immigrants and Their Adult Children in the United States and Germany." PhD diss., Department of Sociology, Temple University, Philadelphia.

Sadjapour, Karim. 2011. *The Battle of Dubai: The United Arab Emirates and the US-Iran Cold War*. New York: Carnegie Press.

Sadr, Hamid Reza. 2006. *Iranian Cinema: A Political History*. London: I. B. Tauris.

Safi, Mirna. 2010. "Immigrants' Life Satisfaction in Europe: Between Assimilation and Discrimination." *European Sociological Review* 2: 159–176.

Safran, William. 1991. "Diasporas in Modern Societies: Myths of Homeland and Return." *Diaspora* 1(1): 83–99.

Said, Edward. 1993. *Culture and Imperialism*. London: Vintage Books.

———. 1994. *Manifestaties van de Intellectueel*. Amsterdam/Antwerpen: Atlas.

Saint-Blancat, Chantal. 1988. *Nazione e religione fra gli Iraniani in Italia*. Padova: C.S.S.R.

———. 1989. "L'immigrazione iraniana in Italia: vera o falsa parentesi?" In *Stranieri in Italia. Caratteri e tendenze dell'immigrazione dai paesi extracomunitari*, ed. Giovanni Cocchi, 109–125. Bologna: Istituto di studi e ricerche Carlo Cattaneo.

————. 1990. "La presenza iraniana in Italia." *Inchiesta* 90(20): 59–67.

Sakumoto, Arthur, and Yu Xie. 2006. "The Socioeconomic Attainments of Asian Americans." In *Asian Americans: Contemporary Trends and Issues*, ed. Pyong Gap Min, 54–77. Thousand Oaks, CA: SAGE.

Salama, Samir. 2008. "Federal National Council Slams Visit-Visas Policy in the UAE." *Gulf News*, March 25.

Sarmadi, Behzad. 2013. "Bachelor in the City:. Urban Transformation and Matter Out of Place in Dubai." *Journal of Arabian Studies* 3(2): 196–214.

Satrapi, Marjane. 2000–2003. *Persépolis*. Paris: L'Association.

Schinkel, W., and van Houdt, F. 2010. "The Double Helix of Cultural Assimilationism and Neo-Liberalism." *British Journal of Sociology* 61(4): 696–715.

SCP (The Netherlands Institute for Social Research). 2011. Report titled *Vluchtelingengroepen in Nederland: Over de integratie van Afghaanse, Iraakse, Iraanse en Somalische migranten*, ed. Edith Dourleijn and Jaco Dagevos. The Hague: SCP.

Schuster, John. 1999. *Poortwachters over immigranten: Het debat over immigratie in het naoorlogse groot-Brittannië en Nederland*. Amsterdam: Het Spinhuis.

Sepehri, Abazar. 1988. "Contemporary Non-serial Persian Publishing in Exile." *MELA notes* 45. 6–22.

Shaheen, Kareem. 2010. "Dubai's Iranian Traders Feel Heat of Sanctions." *The National*, September 24.

Share-Pour, Mahmoud. 1999. "Self-Categorization and In-Group among Iranian children in Australia: A Replication and Extension," *Journal of Social Psychology* 139(2): 180–190.

Shavarini, Mitra. 2004. *Educating Immigrants: Experiences of Second-Generation Iranians*. New York: LFB Scholarly Publications.

Shayegan, Dariush. 2004. *Terre de mirages*. La Tour-d'Aigues, FRA: Editions de l'Aube.

Sheffer, Gabriel. 2003. *Diaspora Politics: At Home Abroad*. Cambridge, UK: Cambridge University Press.

Siino, Grazia Alessandra, and Nadia Levantino. 2016. "Islamophobia in Italy: National Report 2015." *European Islamophobia Report 2015*: 267–292. Istanbul: SETA.

Simon, Patrick. 2003."France and the Unknown Second Generation: Preliminary Results on Social Mobility." *International Migration Review* 37(4): 1091–1119.

Singer, Audrey. 2008. "Twenty-first Century Gateways: An Introduction." In *Twenty-First Century Gateways: Immigrants Incorporation in Suburban America*, ed. Audrey Singer, Susan W. Hardwick, and Caroline B. Brettell. Washginton, DC: Brookings Institution Press.

Smith, David. 2016. "Iranian Americans Dismayed by Discrimination in New Visa Regulations." *The Guardian*, January 16.

Snoj, Jure. 2015. "UAE's Population—By Nationality." *BQ*, April 12.

Spellman, Kathryn. 2001. "The Persian Community in Britain." In *Encyclopaedia Iranica*, vol. 11, fasc. 3, 273–275. New York: Columbia University Press.

————. 2004a. *Religion and Nation: Iranian Local and Transnational Networks in Britain*. Oxford, UK: Berghahn Books.

————. 2004b. "A National Sufi Order with Transnational Dimensions: The *Maktab Tarighat Oveyssi Shahmaghsoudi* Sufi Order in London." *Journal of Ethnic and Migration Studies* 30(5): 945–960.

Spellman-Poots, Kathryn. 2012. "Manifestations of Ashura among Young British

Shi'is." In *Ethnographies of Islam*, ed. Baudouin Dupret et al., 40–49. Edinburgh: Edinburgh University Press.

Spellman-Poots, Kathryn, and S. Zubaida, eds. 2013. Middle Eastern Religious Minorities, special issue of *The Middle East in London Magazine* 9(3). School for the Oriental and African Studies in London.

Sreberny, Annabelle. 2000. "Media and Diasporic Consciousness: An Exploration among Iranians in London." In *Ethnic Minorities and the Media*, ed. Simon Cottle, 179–196. Buckingham, UK: Open University Press.

———. 2002. "Collectivity and Connectivity: Diaspora and Mediated Identities." In *Global Encounters: Media and Cultural Transformation*, ed. G. Stald and T. Tufte. Luton, UK: University of Luton Press.

Sreberny, A., and R. Gholami. 2016. *Iranian Communities in Britain: A Research Report*. London: London Middle-East Institute.

Sreberny-Mohammadi, Annabelle, and Ali Mohammadi. 1987. "Post-Revolutionary Iranian Exiles: A Study in Impotence." *Third World Quarterly* 9(1): 108–129.

Stratton, Jon, and Ien Ang. 1998 "Multicultural Imagined Communities: Cultural Difference and National Identity in the USA and Australia." In *Multicultural States: Rethinking Difference and Identity*, ed. D. Bennett, 135–163. London and New York: Routledge.

Tajadod, Nahal. 2007. *Passeport à l'iranienne*. Paris: JC Lattès.

Tapper, Richard. 2002. *New Iranian Cinema: Politics, Representation and Identity*. London: I. B. Tauris.

Tehranian, John. 2008. *Whitewashed: America's Invisible Middle Eastern Minority*. New York: NYU Press.

Tenty, Tiffany Amber, and Christopher Housten. 2013. "The Iranian Diaspora in Sydney: Migration Experience of Recent Iranian Immigrants." *Iranian Studies* 46(4): 625–640.

Tololyan, K. 2007. "The Contemporary Discourse of Diaspora Studies." *Comparative Studies of South Asia, Africa and the Middle East* 27(3): 647–655.

Tsolidis, Georgina. 2014. "Introduction: Does Diaspora Matter When Living Cultural Differences." In *Migration, Diaspora and Identity: Cross-National Experiences*, ed. Tsolidis Georgina, 1–15. Switzerland: Springer International Publishing.

United Nations High Commissioner for Refugees. 2011 and 2015. *UNHCR Statistical Yearbook, Country Data Sheets*. www.unhcr.org/516282cf5.html.

United States Department of Justice, Immigration and Naturalization Service, *Annual Reports, 1970–1977* and *Statistical Yearbooks, 1978–1986* (Washington, DC).

United States Department of Homeland Security, *Statistical Yearbooks, 1986–2004* (Washington, DC).

United States Department of Homeland Security, *2007 Yearbook of Immigration Statistics* (Washington, DC), www.dhs.gov/xlibrary/assets/statistics/yearbook/2007/ois_2007_yearbook.pdf.

United States Department of Homeland Security. January 21, 2016. "United States Begins Implementation of Changes to the Visa Waiver Program." www.dhs.gov/news/2016/01/21/united-states-begins-implementation-changes-visa-waiver-program.

Vahabi, Nader. 2015. "La diaspora iranienne en France: profil démographique et socioéconomique." *Migrations Société* 27(158): 19–39.

Van der Raad, S. 2013. *Othering and Inclusion of Ethnic Minority Professionals: A*

Study on Ethnic Diversity Discourses, Practices, and Narratives in the Dutch Legal Workplace. Amsterdam: VU University Press.

Vartanian, Vahed Massihi. 2013. La Comunità Iraniana di Roma nella storia e negli ultimi 50 anni. www.zatik.com/files/La%20Comunit%C3%A0%20Iraniana%20di %20Roma%20nella%20storia%20e%20negli%20ultimi.pdf.

Varzi, Roxanne. 2006. *Warring Souls: Youth, Media, and Martyrdom in Post-Revolution Iran.* Durham, NC, and London: Duke University Press.

Vasta, E. 2007. "From Ethnic Minorities to Ethnic Majority Policy: Multiculturalism and the Shift to Assimilationism in The Netherlands." *Ethnic and Racial Studies* 30(5): 713–740.

Verkuyten, M., W. de Jong, and C. N. Masson. 1995. "The Construction of Ethnic Categories: Discourses of Ethnicity in The Netherlands." *Ethnic and Racial Studies* 18(2): 251–276.

Vertovec, Steven. 2002. "Migrant Transnationalism and Modes of Transformation." *International Migration Review* 38: 970–1001.

———. 2009. *Transnationalism.* New York: Routledge.

Vertovec, S., and S. Wessendorf. 2009. *Assessing the backlash against multiculturalism in Europe* (MMG Working Paper 09-04). Göttingen: MPIMMG.

Visconti, Luca Massimiliano, et al. 2007. "I figli delle migrazioni: G2 marketing." In *Stili migranti*, ed. Carla Fiorio et al., 107–153. Biella: Litocopyvercelli.

Vora, Neha. 2013. *Impossible Citizens: Dubai's Indian Diaspora.* Durham, NC: Duke University Press.

Wagenknecht, Maria D. 2015. *Constructing Identity in Iranian-American Self-Narrative.* New York: Palgrave.

Wekker, Gloria. 1988. "Gender, identiteitsvorming en multiculturalisme: Noties over de Nederlandse multiculturele samenleving." In *Multiculturalisme*, ed. C. H. M. Geuijen, 39–55. Utrecht: Lemma.

———. 1995. "'After the Last Sky, Where Do the Birds Fly?' What Can European Women Learn from Anti-Racist Struggles in the United States?" In *Crossfires: Nationalism, Racism and Gender in Europe*, ed. H. Lutz et al., 65–88. London: Pluto Press.

———. 2016. *White Innocence: Paradoxes of Colonialism and Race.* Durham, NC: Duke University Press.

Werbner, P. 2002. "The Place Which is Diaspora: Citizenship, Religion and Gender in the Making of Chaordic Transnationalism." *Journal of Ethnic and Migration Studies* 28(1): 119–133.

Wetenschappelijke Raad voor het Regeringsbeleid (WRR—Scientific Council for Government Policy). 2007. *Identificatie met Nederland. Report to the Government.* Amsterdam: Amsterdam University Press.

Wilterdink, Nico. 1998. "Mondialisering, migratie en multiculturaliteit." In *Multiculturalisme*, ed. C. H. M. Geuijen, 55–67. Utrecht: Lemma.

Wong, Cindy Hing-Yuk. 2011. *Film Festivals: Culture, People, and Power on the Global Screen.* New York: Rutgers University Press.

Worbs, Susanne. 2003. "The Second Generation in Germany: Between School and the Labor Market." *International Migration Review* 37: 4.

Yalda, Sara. 2007. *Regard persan.* Paris: Grasset.

Yanow, D., and M. van der Haar. 2013. "People out of Place: Allochtony and Autochtony in The Netherlands' Identity Discourse—Metaphors and Categories in Action." *Journal of International Relations and Development* 16: 227–261.

Zarmandili, Bijan. 2011. "Il mestiere dello scrittore. L'esilio e il mondo." *Bollettino di italianistica. Rivista di critica, storia letteraria, filologia, linguistica* 8(2): 425–429.

Zarrinkoub, Abdol-Hossein. 1970. "Persian Sufism and Its Historical Perspective." In *Iranian Studies* 3(3–4): 139–220.

Zhou, Min. 2004. "Revisiting Ethnic Entrepreneurship: Convergencies, Controversies, and Conceptual Advancements." *International Migration Review* 38: 1040–1074.

Zia-Ebrahimi, R. 2011. "Self-Orientalization and Dislocation: The Uses and Abuses of the 'Aryan' Discourse in Iran." *Iranian Studies* 44(4): 445–472.

Zolberg, Aristide R., and Long Litt Woon. 1999. "Why Islam Is Like Spanish: Cultural Incorporation in Europe and the United States." *Politics & Society* 27(1): 5–38.

Contributors

NESTOR RODRIGUEZ is professor of sociology at the University of Texas at Austin. He has conducted international research in Mexico, Guatemala, and El Salvador and has traveled and lectured in China and Japan. His current research focuses on Guatemalan migration, US deportations to Mexico and Central America, the unauthorized migration of unaccompanied minors, evolving relations between Latinos and African Americans/Asian Americans, and ethical and human rights issues of border enforcement. His most recent publications include *Deportation and Return in a Border-Restricted World: Experiences in Mexico, El Salvador, Guatemala, and Honduras* (New York: Springer Press, 2017), edited with Bryan Roberts and Cecilia Menjivar; *Migration in an Era of Restriction and Recession: Sending and Receiving Nations in a Changing Global Environment* (New York: Springer Press, 2016), edited with David Lea; and *Guatemala-US Migration: Transforming Regions* (Austin: University of Texas Press, 2014), coauthored with Susanne Jonas.

MOHSEN MOSTAFAVI MOBASHER is associate professor of anthropology and sociology and teaches at the University of Houston–Downtown. His areas of specialization are the Iranian diaspora, immigration, transnationalism, ethnic entrepreneurship, and globalization. He has done extensive quantitative and qualitative research on Iranian immigrants in Texas since 1993 and has published a book, a number of articles, and several book chapters on Iranian immigrant's ethnic identity, entrepreneurial activities, and integration in the United States. His most recent book, *Iranians in Texas: Migration, Politics, and Ethnic Identity*, was published in 2012 by the University of Texas Press. He has also co-edited a book titled *Migration, Globalization, and Ethnic Relations: An Interdisciplinary Approach.*

MEHDI BOZORGMEHR is professor of sociology at the Graduate Center and City College, City University of New York. He was the founding codirector of the Middle East and Middle Eastern American Center (MEMEAC) at the Graduate Center from 2001 to 2013. Bozorgmehr is one of the pioneers of scholarly work on Middle Eastern Americans, especially Iranians. He has been conducting research on Iranian Americans since the late 1980s and has published numerous articles and book chapters on the subject. He is the coauthor of *Backlash 9/11: Middle Eastern and Muslim Americans Respond* (Berkeley: University of California Press, 2009), which received an honorable mention (runner-up) for the best book award from the International Migration section of the American Sociological Association, and he is the coeditor (with Philip Kasinitz) of *Growing up Muslim in Europe and America* (Routledge, forthcoming). His most recent articles have appeared in *Ethnic and Racial Studies* and *International Journal of Sociology of Language* in 2016.

ERIC KETCHAM is a PhD candidate in sociology at the CUNY Graduate Center. He previously held a Demography Fellowship from the CUNY Institute for Demographic Research and is currently the assistant director of the Center for Integrated Language Communities.

SAHAR SADEGHI earned her doctoral degree in 2014 in the Department of Sociology at Temple University. She is an assistant professor of sociology at Muhlenberg College in Allentown, Pennsylvania. Her research is organized around several interrelated projects and themes—migration and global politics, as well as racialized and politicized belonging and social membership—which are examined through a crossnational, qualitative methods approach with a regional specialization in contemporary Europe and the United States. Sadeghi is preparing a book manuscript that examines the ways in which the national, regional, and global political context shapes experiences of racial and political stigmatization, of *being but not belonging,* and of qualified social membership among first- and second-generation Iranians in the United States and Germany. Her recent article, "The Burden of Geopolitical Stigma: Iranian Immigrants and their Adult Children in the USA," published in the *Journal of International Migration and Integration,* considers how global political dynamics stigmatize and racialize Iranians' identities and pose disruptions to mobility, belonging, and social membership.

HALLEH GHORASHI is full professor of diversity and integration in the Department of Sociology at the VU Amsterdam, the Netherlands. She is also visiting professor at the Institute for Reconciliation and Social Justice, University of the Free State, South Africa. She was born in Iran and came to the Netherlands in 1988. In 1994, she completed her MA degree (cum laude) in anthropology at the Vrije University Amsterdam. She defended her PhD dissertation *Ways to Survive, Battles to Win: Iranian Women Exiles in the Netherlands and the United States* (New York: Nova Science Publishers, 2003) in 2001 at the University of Nijmegen. Between 2005 and 2012, she held the prestigious position of PaVEM-chair in Management of Diversity and Integration at the Department of Organization Science at the VU. Ghorashi is the coeditor of several collections: *Paradoxes of Cultural Recognition: Perspectives from Northern Europe* (together with S. Alghasi and T. H. Eriksen) (Surrey, UK: Ashgate, 2009) and *Muslim Diaspora in the West: Negotiating Gender, Home and Belonging* (together with H. Moghissi (Surrey: Ashgate, 2010). Her current research focus is on the narratives of identity and belonging of migrant and refugee women along with the processes of exclusion and inclusion in the context of growing culturalism.

KATHRYN SPELLMAN POOTS is a visiting associate professor at the Middle East Institute at Columbia University and associate professor at the Aga Khan University's Institute for the Study of Muslim Civilisations. She received her MSc and PhD in politics and sociology from Birkbeck College, University of London. Her research interests include Muslims in Europe and North America, the Iranian diaspora, transnational migration networks, and gender and religious practices in the Middle East and North Africa. Her publications include the monograph *Religion and Nation: Iranian Local and Transnational Networks in Britain* (Oxford and New York: Berghahn, 2005) and two edited volumes: *The Political Aesthetics of Global Protest: The Arab Spring and Beyond* (Edinburgh: Edinburgh University Press, 2014) and *Ethnographies of Islam: Ritual Performances and Everyday Practices* (Edinburgh: Edinburgh University Press, 2012).

REZA GHOLAMI is senior lecturer in the sociology of education at the University of Birmingham, UK. He earned his PhD in the Department of Anthropology and Sociology at the School of Oriental and African Studies (SOAS), University of London, where he also conducted postdoctoral research funded by the Arts and Humanities Research Council. He is the author of *Secularism and Identity: Non-Islamiosity in the Iranian Diaspora* (London and New York: Routledge, 2015), coeditor of *Education and Extremisms: Re-Thinking Liberal Pedagogies in the Contemporary World* (Abingdon, Oxon, and New York: Routledge, 2017), and also writes about citizenship and citizenship education, Islamophobia, cosmopolitanism, and social policy.

BEHZAD SARMADI earned his doctoral degree in sociocultural anthropology from the University of Toronto in 2016. He is an applied anthropologist specializing in the financial sector. His research interests have revolved around the topics of financialization, migration, urbanism, and ethics. His dissertation research examines lived experiences of speculative urbanism in Dubai, especially among middle- and working-class Iranians. His publications appear in *Anthropology Today, Journal of Arabian Studies*, and *Ajam Media Collective.*

SANAZ FOTOUHI is an Iranian-born academic, creative writer, and filmmaker based in Australia. She holds a PhD in English literature from the University of New South Wales in literary studies. Her areas of research and interest are diaspora and migrant literatures. Her book *The Literature of the Iranian Diaspora: Meaning and Identity since the Islamic Revolution* (London: I. B. Tauris, 2015) is one of the pioneering studies of the body of diasporic Iranian writing in English. Her writing has been published in Australia and internationally in *The Griffith Review, The Southerly*, as well as the *Guardian UK* and the *Jakarta Post.* Currently, she is the director of the Asia Pacific Writers and Translators (APWT), an international literary networking organization in Australia.

LAETITIA NANQUETTE is a senior lecturer and Australian Research Council DECRA Fellow (2015–2019) at the University of New South Wales, Sydney. She holds a BA in philosophy from the Sorbonne, Paris, and a PhD in Middle Eastern studies from the School of Oriental and African Studies (SOAS), University of London (2011). Her current research project is titled "A Global Comparative Study of Contemporary Iranian Literature." Her monograph *Orientalism versus Occidentalism: Literary and Cultural Imaging Between France and Iran since the Islamic Revolution* was published by I. B. Tauris in 2013. Other recent publications include: "Persian Passages" (edited by Laetitia Nanquette and Ali Alizadeh), in *Southerly* 76(3) (2016), and "The Global Circulation of an Iranian Best-Seller," *Interventions: International Journal of Postcolonial Studies* 19(1) (2017): 56–72. She is editor for the Persian/Iranian Writing and Culture volume of *The Literary Encyclopedia*, edited Dr. Robert Clark: www.litencyc.com.

ALICE MIGGIANO obtained her PhD in Iranian studies from the University of Naples "L'Orientale" in 2015. Her areas of research include the bureaucratic Persian language and the integration of Iranian immigrants in Italy. She has conducted extensive research on sociocultural characteristics of postrevolutionary Iranians in Italy. Her most recent book publication is *Vocabolario dei termini amministrativi, commerciali e diplomatici. Italiano-persiano e persiano-italiano* [Vocabulary of Administrative, Commercial and Diplomatic Terms: Italian-Persian and Persian-Italian] (Lecce and Rovato: Pensa Multimedia, 2015). She is currently working on the volume *Venticinque anni di letteratura della diaspora iraniana in Italia. Catalogo degli autori e opere. 1992–2017* [Twenty-five Years of Literature of Iranian Diaspora in Italy: Catalogue of Authors and Works, 1992–2017]. She has been writing articles on Iranian society and culture for the online magazine *Il Caffè Geopolitico* [The Coffee Geopolitical] since 2016.

Index

Italic page numbers refer to figures.